AN INTIMATE WILDERNESS

An Intimate Wilderness

LESBIAN WRITERS ON SEXUALITY

EDITED BY JUDITH BARRINGTON

THE EIGHTH MOUNTAIN PRESS

PORTLAND ◆ OREGON ◆ 1991

Cover art and design by Marcia Barrentine
Book design by Ruth Gundle

Manufactured in the United States of America
This book is printed on acid-free paper.

10 9 8 7 6 5 4 3 2

The editor gratefully acknowledges the financial help and moral support of the Money for Women/Barbara Deming Memorial Fund, Inc. which awarded her the Gerty, Gerty, Gerty in the Arts, Arts, Arts Award for this project.

LIBRARY OF CONGRESS CATALOGING-IN-PUBLICATION DATA

An Intimate wilderness: lesbian writers on sexuality / edited by
    Judith Barrington. — 1st ed.
      p.   cm.
      ISBN 0-933377-10-X : $24.95. — ISBN 0-933377-09-6 (pbk.) : $14.95
    1. Lesbians—Literary collections. 2. Women—Sexual behavior—
    Literary collections. 3. Lesbians' writings, American. 4. Erotic
    literature, American.
    5. Sex—Literary collections.
    I. Barrington, Judith.
    PS509.L47I58 1991
    810.8'0353—dc20   91-13022

Published by The Eighth Mountain Press
624 Southeast Twenty-ninth Avenue
Portland, Oregon 97214
(503) 233-3936

Introduction

LIKE EVERYONE ELSE, I GREW UP IN A CULTURE WHICH BOMBARDED ME WITH OVERT and subtle messages about sex—heterosex, that is. These messages informed my emotional life, my fantasies, and my sense of myself. They became the norm: what "normal" humans felt and did. Like most lesbians who did not consciously identify as lesbians at a very young age (although I did act out my lesbianism), I lived in a state of perpetual confusion. I felt inadequate, knowing that the heterosexual behavior I learned to imitate was somehow not "genuine." I fell in love with women and felt guilty. I believed I was sick. I considered suicide. Even if I had somehow found a supportive lesbian community at a younger age, still I would have been living in the wider culture that failed to acknowledge my existence.

When I did eventually find lesbian books and, later, real live lesbians, I still lived inside a throbbing cauldron of heterosexuality: it inhabited magazines, yelled down from billboards, oozed from the pores of couples on the street. Movies were about it, conversations at work assumed it, jokes were based on its superiority. As a timid young lesbian just coming out, it wasn't instruction manuals that I needed (I had always managed, even before admitting my lesbianism, to translate my heart's messages into physical and sexual realities). What I needed was to see my own reality, my own feelings, and my own sexual behavior—or, even better, a less guilt-ridden, more open lesbian reality than my own—reflected in the culture around me.

Through the seventies and eighties, I participated in the flowering of women's and lesbian culture, which made a start at filling the huge void. We began to replace those male-fantasy women who had inhabited books, plays, films, ballets, operas, art galleries, and television programs, with women who were a little closer to the real thing. We also started to put into our lesbian culture—a culture we were creating primarily for other lesbians—believable dykes, instead of those tortured women, dead by the end of the book, who had so often appeared as tokens or as titillation, in mainstream culture. We tried to create real, positive women of all races and classes, who loved each other, went to work, took care of their animals, played softball, travelled the world, and had children.

Sometimes a significant movement in art or literature is created primarily on the basis of new content, which in turn influences the form in which the new content is expressed. The burgeoning of women's poetry over the past two decades has already been named such a movement by Alicia Ostriker, who described in her book, *Stealing the Language: The Emergence of Women's Poetry in America*, the recurring themes that characterized the new movement. I believe that recent lesbian writing can be seen as another important body of work, a literary movement in Ostriker's sense, with its own themes and preoccupations, and with its own emerging influences on form and language. For these two decades, lesbians have been writing in a context of feminist beliefs. We have taken giant steps in understanding ourselves, our past lives, and the diversity of our communities—steps that led to a mass of writing, a speaking out on the subject of lesbianism on an unprecedented scale. We have increasingly told the truth as we know it, first to ourselves and each other, then to the world through our writing, facilitated by the existence of an increasing number of feminist and lesbian presses. We have written about growing up as lesbians, coming out, confronting homophobia in all areas of our lives, healing from sexual abuse, and confronting the racism that profoundly affects us all. So much writing about things that were previously unspoken created the lesbian literary movement.

Some of the work we now think of as the "classics" of this movement (I think, for example, of Adrienne Rich's *Women and Honor: Some Notes on Lying*) demanded new forms of expression to fully convey the new ideas they contained. As we grappled with the complexity of creating new possibilities for our lives, our writers challenged the limitations of patriarchal and heterosexist forms and language. Our literary work, like our life work, pushed, and continues to push, at the boundaries.

So what did all this work have to say about lesbian sexuality? Many of the books I read in the eighties that had anything to do with lesbian sex might have led me to believe that most lesbians were focused on sex in one of three ways: furiously engaged in SM; furiously campaigning against SM; or heavily involved in therapy and self-help to improve their sex lives. (If I had also read lesbian romances, which I didn't, I might have concluded that all lesbians were riding off into the sunset with each other, but I doubt I would have learned much about what happened after the sun went down.)

If the social workers and therapists were busy writing books about co-dependency and how to improve your sex life by going to a hotel and pretending you don't know your lover, and if activists and scholars were duplicating papers for conferences about how feminist or unfeminist it is to tie up your lover with a silk tie or chains, what exactly were the "literary" writers saying about it all? How was *art* reflecting *life*—that is, *literary* art and *lesbian* life?

That is the question that prompted this collection. Not only did I think it would be interesting to bring together the *writers'* visions of our sexuality, I also believed that creative writing would be a rich source of information. Although we often think of nonfiction writing as the most reliable source of data, I have always believed that poetry and other imaginative writing provides truths that are often deeper, and information that is unavailable in any other form. Imaginative writing reveals states of consciousness, concrete details of daily lives, and a personal point of view which, when looked at alongside many other such personal viewpoints, paints a rich and complex picture of a subject. It made sense, then, to look at lesbian sexuality through the lens not only of our nonfiction writers but also of our poets and storytellers.

My first impression was that writings about some aspects of lesbian sexuality remain scarce. I don't, for instance, find very much about everyday, ordinary, loving, not-always-spectacular, lesbian sex: the kind that comes after the meeting, riding off into a generic sunset, and glowing for a year or two; the kind we settle into as we experience the various stages of a long, committed relationship. This happens to be the kind I know best, so I notice its scarcity quite acutely. (I'm still looking for literary reflections of my own life.) I also notice, however, the absence of writing about sexuality that endures in lives lived outside the couple model, and sexuality that happens occasionally between friends.

Yet as I looked further, I realized that despite the noticeable scarcities, there is indeed a rich supply of writing about lesbian sex. Those collected here include, from a variety of cultural perspectives: stories about our sexual awakenings as young lesbians and our sexual exploits as old lesbians; descriptions of lovemaking in a variety of relational contexts (passionate, thwarted, temporary, committed, and so on); accounts of the effects of sexual abuse on our lesbian relationships and our ongoing efforts to heal; and honest discussions of sexual lives lived through illness and dying.

This is not a collection of erotica (in spite of the Library of Congress categorization), although many such collections now exist. These pieces were chosen not for their potential to arouse but for the ideas they contain or their potential for illuminating some aspect of our sexual lives. Although good writing was a given, they were chosen as much for what they had to say as for how it was said—though some of what was said related directly to the question of how to say it. As a writer, I was curious about how other writers viewed the actual process of writing lesbian sex, and this curiosity steered me toward a whole body of work exemplified by Betsy Warland, Daphne Marlatt, Nicole Brossard, and Jeffner Allen, whose writing portrays lesbian sexuality at the same time as it articulates the inadequacies of our language to fully describe our experience. These writers are contributing to a growing body of work that examines the origins of words for their potential to convey lesbian experience. Another important challenge to the limitations of language is contained in the work of women of color like Gloria Anzaldúa, who uses words in a way that not only describes lesbian sexuality but simultaneously reflects her culture and its language.

These pieces of writing come from poets, fiction writers, and nonfiction writers. I included some theoretical essays such as Lise Weil's "Lowering the Case," Gillian Hanscombe's "In Among the Market Forces?" and the excerpt from Sarah Hoagland's *Lesbian Ethics,* and I asked some fiction writers like Barbara Wilson to write nonfiction for this occasion. All, however, are writers whose work has included in its natural course of development some portrayal of, or thoughts about, lesbian sexuality, whether in the lives of characters they created or in their own personal lives. What they have in common is that they are all serious writers with a commitment to words.

It is perhaps not surprising, then, that the problem of words themselves should emerge as one of the major preoccupations—not only from those writers mentioned above, who are directly struggling to create new language, but also from many of the others. Marilyn Frye states the problem in her essay "Lesbian 'Sex'" when she compares lesbian sexuality to gay male sex, which, she says, is *articulate*: "Lesbian 'sex' as I have known it, most of the time I have known it, is utterly *inarticulate*. Most of my lifetime, most of my experience in the realms commonly designated as 'sexual' has been prelinguistic, noncognitive. I have, in effect, no linguistic community, no language, and therefore in one important sense, no knowledge."

Frye's essay, too, makes comparisons between lesbian sexuality and heterosexual sexuality which are, she believes, two entirely different things. I had hoped that this book might shed some light on the differences and, indeed, some are suggested. One clear theme is the degree to which lesbian sexuality involves a need to be defensive or reactive in the face of homophobia. When writing about our lives, many of us continue to describe the encoded interactions of a group whose sex lives are "dangerous." There is a pervasive sense of forbidden sexuality, of a love life on the defensive against a hostile world. Although the new language we are creating may, in time, play a part in creating new sexual possibilities, our sex lives now are still under siege. For survival, like other oppressed groups, we have had to develop at least a dual vision, and an even more fragmented one if we experience multiple oppressions. Our shared understanding of this duality—*our* positive view of ourselves and *their* hostile one, and all the grey areas where the two merge—permeates these writings and goes some way toward defining our current sexuality. The poet Janice Gould, for example, describes lesbian bonds based on the shared experience of homophobia, as well as the sadness and invisibility understood by many of us to be the consequence of passionately loving a heterosexual woman.

But other differences between heterosexuality and lesbian sexuality are apparent in these writings. Not all of what distinguishes the lesbian variety is defensiveness or shared oppression; many writers aspire to a "connected" sexuality, building on the theme laid out in Audre Lorde's *Uses of the Erotic*, as they write about the search for wholeness and a sexuality grounded in everyday life. Many other differences, too, are suggested here, and there are surely even more not included.

Two of the characteristics of lesbian sexuality which speak loudly to me, though, happen to be our response to homophobia and our vision of a sexuality that is integrated into our whole lives. The writings collected here reveal not only those two themes but also the many stages of an ongoing journey out of one toward the other. For me, it is still necessary to remember that my sexuality was once a source of fear and hatred in myself and that it often still is to other people. It is, however, equally vital to me that I can read about a lesbian sexuality that transcends mere defiance: a sexuality that reveals what it might be, what it *will* be, when both language and life can unequivocally celebrate lesbian experience.

Judith Barrington

I

Marilyn Frye

Lesbian "Sex"

THE REASONS THE WORD "SEX" IS IN QUOTATION MARKS IN MY TITLE ARE TWO: ONE is that the term "sex," is an inappropriate term for what lesbians do, and the other is that whatever it is that lesbians do that (for lack of a better word) might be called "sex," we apparently do damned little of it. For a great many lesbians, the gap between the high hopes we had some time ago for lesbian sex and the way things have worked out has turned the phrase "lesbian sex" into something of a bitter joke. I don't want to exaggerate this; things aren't so bad for all lesbians, or all of the time. But in our communities as a whole there is much grumbling on the subject. It seems worthwhile to explore some of the meanings of the relative dearth of what (for lack of a better word) we call lesbian "sex."

Recent discussions of lesbian "sex" frequently cite the findings of a study on couples by Blumstein and Schwartz, which is perceived by most of those who discuss it as having been done well, with a good sample of lesbian, male homosexual, heterosexual non-married and heterosexual married couples. These people apparently found that lesbian couples "have sex" far less frequently than any other type of couple, that lesbian couples are less "sexual" as couples and as individuals than anyone else. In their sample, only about one third of lesbians in relationships of two years or longer "had sex" once a week or more; 47 percent of lesbians in long term relationships "had sex" once a month or less, while among heterosexual married couples only 15 percent had sex once a month or less. And they report that lesbians seem to be more limited in the range of "sexual" techniques than are other couples.

When this sort of information first came into my circle of lesbian friends, we tended to see it as conforming to what we know from our

1

own experience. But on reflection, looking again at what has been going on with us in our long-term relationships, the nice fit between this report and our experience seemed not so perfect after all.

It was brought to our attention during our ruminations on this that what 85 percent of long-term heterosexual married couples do more than once a month takes on the average eight minutes to do.

Although in my experience lesbians discuss their "sex" lives with each other relatively little (a point to which I will return), I know from my own experience and from the reports of a few other lesbians in long-term relationships that what we do that, on average, we do considerably less frequently, takes, on average, considerably more than eight minutes to do. It takes about thirty minutes, at the least. Sometimes maybe an hour. And it is not uncommon that among these relatively uncommon occurrences, an entire afternoon or evening is given over to activities organized around doing it. The suspicion arises that what 85 percent of heterosexual married couples are doing more than once a month and what 47 percent of lesbian couples are doing less than once a month is not the same thing.

I remember that one of my first delicious tastes of old gay/lesbian culture occurred in a bar where I was getting acquainted with some new friends. One was talking about being busted out of the Marines for being gay. She had been put under suspicion somehow and was sent off to the base psychiatrist to be questioned, her perverted tendencies to be assessed. He wanted to convince her she had only been engaged in a little youthful experimentation and wasn't really gay. To this end, he questioned her about the extent of her experience. What he asked was, "How many times have you had sex with a woman?" At this, we all laughed and giggled: What an ignorant fool. What does he think he means, "times"? What will we count? What's to count?

Another of my friends, years later, discussing the same conundrum, said that she thought maybe every time you got up to go to the bathroom, that marked a "time." The joke about "how many times" is still good for a chuckle from time to time in my life with my lover. I have no memory of any such topic providing any such merriment in my years of sexual encounters and relationships with men. It would have been very rare indeed that we would not have known how to answer the question "How many times did you do it?"

If what heterosexual married couples do that the individuals report under the rubric "sex" or "have sex" or "have sexual relations" is something that in most instances can easily be individuated into countable instances, this is more evidence that it is not what long-term lesbian couples do—or, for that matter, what short-term lesbian couples do. What violence did the lesbians do their experience by answering the same question the heterosexuals answered, as though it had the same meaning for them? How did the lesbians figure out how to answer the questions "How frequently?" or "How many times?" My guess is that different individuals figured it out differently. Some might have counted a two- or three-cycle evening as one "time" they "had sex"; some might have counted it as two or three "times." Some may have counted as "times" only the times both partners had orgasms; some may have counted as "times" occasions on which at least one had an orgasm; those who do not have orgasms or have them far more rarely than they "have sex" may not have figured orgasms into the calculations; perhaps some counted as a "time" every episode in which both touched the other's vulva more than fleetingly and not for something like a health examination. For some, to count every reciprocal touch of the vulva would have made them count as "having sex" more than most people with a job or work would dream of having time for; how do we suppose those individuals counted "times"? Is there any good reason why they should not count all those as "times"? Does it depend on how fulfilling it was? Was anybody else counting by occasions of fulfillment?

We have no idea how the individual lesbians surveyed were counting their "sexual acts." But this also raises the question of how heterosexuals counted their sexual acts. By orgasms? By whose orgasms? If the havings of sex by heterosexual married couples did take on the average eight minutes, my guess is that in a very large number of those cases the women did not experience orgasms. My guess is that neither the women's pleasure nor the women's orgasms were pertinent in most of the individuals' counting and reporting the frequency with which they "had sex."

So, do lesbian couples really "have sex" any less frequently than heterosexual couples? I'd say that lesbian couples "have sex" a great deal less frequently than heterosexual couples; by the criteria that I'm betting most of the heterosexual people used to count "times," lesbians don't have sex at all. No male orgasms, no "times." (I'm willing to draw the conclusion that heterosexual women don't have sex either, that what they report is the frequency with which their partners have sex.)

It has been said before by feminists that the concept of "having sex" is a phallic concept, that it pertains to heterosexual intercourse, in fact, primarily to heterosexist intercourse, i.e., male-dominant-female-subordinate-copulation-whose-completion-and-purpose-is-the-male's-ejaculation. I have thought this was true since the first time the idea was put to me, some twelve years ago. But I have been finding lately that I have to go back over some of the ground I covered a decade or so ago because some of what I knew then I knew too superficially. For some of us, myself included, the move from heterosexual relating to lesbian relating was occasioned or speeded up or brought to closure by our knowledge that what we had done under the heading of "having sex" was indeed male-dominant-female-subordinate-copulation-whose-completion...etc., and it was not worthy of doing. Yet now, years later, we are willing to answer questionnaires that ask us how frequently we "have sex" and are dissatisfied with ourselves and with our relationships because we don't "have sex" enough. We are so dissatisfied that we keep a small army of therapists in business trying to help us "have sex" more.

We quit having sex years ago, and for excellent reasons. What exactly is our complaint now?

In all these years I've been doing and writing feminist theory, I have not until very recently written, much less published, a word about sex. I did not write, though it was suggested to me that I do so, anything in the SM debates; I left entirely unanswered an invitation to be the keynote speaker at a feminist conference about women's sexuality (which, by all reports, turned out to be an excellent conference). I was quite unable to think of anything but vague truisms to say, and very few of those. Feminist theory is grounded in experience; I have always written feminist political and philosophical analysis from the bottom up, starting with my own encounters and adventures, frustrations, pain, anger, delight, etc. Sometimes this has, no doubt, made it a little provincial; but it has at least had the virtue of firm connection with someone's real, live experience (which is more than you can say for a lot of theory). When I put to

4

myself the task of theorizing about sex and sexuality, it was as though I had no experience, as though there were no ground on which and from which to generate theory. But (if I understand the terminology rightly) I have been what they call "sexually active" for close to a quarter of a century, about half my life, almost all of what they call one's "adult life," heterosexually, lesbianly, and autoerotically. Surely I have experience. But I seem not to have experiential knowledge of the sort I need.

Reflecting on all that history, I realize that in many of its passages this experience has been a muddle. Acting, being acted on, choosing, desiring, pleasure and displeasure all akimbo—not coherently determining and connecting with each other. Even in its greatest intensity it has for the most part been somehow rather opaque to me, not fully in my grasp. My "experience" has in general the character more of a buzzing, blooming confusion than of experience. And it has occurred in the midst of almost total silence on the part of others about their experience. The experience of others has for the most part also been opaque to me; they do not discuss or describe it in detail at all.

I recall an hours-long and heated argument among some eight or ten lesbians at a party a couple of years ago about SM, whether it is okay or not. When Carolyn and I left, we realized that in the whole time not one woman had said one concrete, explicit, physiologically specific thing about what she actually did. The one arguing in favor of bondage—did she have her hands tied gently with ribbons or scarves, or harshly with handcuffs or chains? What other parts of her body were or weren't restrained, and by what means? And what parts of her body were touched, and how, while she was bound? And what liberty did she still have to touch in return? And if she had no such liberty, was it part of her experience to want that liberty and to feel tension or frustration, or was it her experience that she felt pleased or satisfied not to have that liberty...? Who knows? She never said a single word at this level of specificity. Nor did anyone else, pro or con.

I once perused a large and extensively illustrated book on sexual activity by and for homosexual men. It was astounding to me for one thing in particular, namely, that its pages constituted a huge lexicon of words: words for acts and activities, their subacts, preludes and denouements, their stylistic variations, their sequences. Gay male sex, I realize, is articulate. It is articulate to a degree that, in my world, lesbian "sex" does not remotely approach. Lesbian "sex" as I have known it most of the time I have known it is utterly inarticulate. Most of my lifetime, most of my experience in the realms commonly designated as "sexual" has been prelinguistic, noncognitive. I have, in effect, no linguistic community, no language, and therefore in one important sense, no knowledge.

In situations of male dominance, women are for the most part excluded from the formulation and validation of meaning and thereby denied the means to express themselves. Men's meanings, and no women's meanings, are encoded in what is presumed to be the whole population's language. (In many cases, both the men and the women assume it is everyone's language.) The meanings one's life and experience might generate cannot come fully into operation if they are not woven into language; they are fleeting, or they hover, vague, not fully coalesced, not connected, and hence not useful for explaining or grounding interpretations, desires, complaints, theories. In response to our understanding that there is something going on in patriarchy that is more or less well described by saying women's meanings are not encoded in the dominant languages and that this keeps our experience from being fully formed and articulate, we have undertaken quite deliberately to discover, complete, and encode our meanings. Such simple things as naming chivalrous gestures "insulting," naming Virginia Woolf a great writer, naming ourselves women instead of girls or ladies. Coining terms such as 'sexism', 'sexual harassment', and 'incestor'. Mary Daly's new book is a whole project of "encoding" meanings, and we can all find examples of our own more local encodings.

Meanings should arise from our bodily self-knowledge, bodily play, tactile communication, the ebb and flow of intense excitement, arousal, tension, release, comfort, discomfort, pain, and pleasure (and I make no distinctions here among bodily, emotional, intellectual, aesthetic). But such potential meanings are more amorphous, less coalesced into discrete elements of a coherent pattern of meanings, of an experience, than any other dimensions of our lives. In fact, there are for many of us virtually no meanings in this realm because nothing of it is crystallized in a linguistic matrix.

What we have for generic words to cover this terrain are the words "sex," "sexual," and "sexuality." In our efforts to liberate ourselves from the stifling woman-hating Victorian denial that women even have bodily awareness, arousal, excitement, orgasms, and so on, many of us actively tried to take these words for ourselves and claimed that we do "do sex" and we are sexual and we have sexuality. This has been particularly important to lesbians because the very fact of "sex" being a phallocentric term has made it especially difficult to get across the idea that lesbians are not, for lack of a penis between us, making do with feeble and partial and pathetic half-satisfactions. But it seems to me that the attempt to encode our lustiness and lustfulness, our passion and our vigorous carnality in the words "sex," "sexual," and "sexuality" has backfired. Instead of losing their phallocentricity, these words have imported the phallocentric meanings into and onto experience which is not in any way phallocentric. A web of meanings which maps emotional intensity, excitement, arousal, bodily play, orgasm, passion, and relational adventure back onto a semantic center in male-dominant-female-subordinate-copulation-whose-completion-and-purpose-is-the-male's-ejaculation has been so utterly inadequate as to leave us speechless, meaningless, and ironically, according to the Blumstein and Schwartz report, "not as sexual," either as couples or as individuals, as any other group.

Our lives, the character of our embodiment, cannot be mapped back onto that semantic center. When we try to synthesize and articulate it by the rules of that mapping, we end up trying to mold our living and passionate carnal intercourse into explosive eight-minute events. That is not the timing and ontology of the lesbian body. When the only things that count as "doing it" are those passages of our interactions which most closely approximate a paradigm that arose from the meanings of the rising and falling penis, no wonder we discover ourselves to "do it" rather less often than do pairs with one or more penises present.

There are many cultural and social-psychological reasons why women (in white Euro-American groups, but also in many other configurations of patriarchy) would generally be somewhat less clear and less assertive about their desires and about getting their satisfactions than men would generally be. And when we pair up two women in a couple, it stands to reason that those reasons would double up and tend to make relationships in which there is a lowish frequency of clearly delineated desires and direct initiations of satisfactions. But for all the help it might be to lesbian bodies to work past the psychological and behavioral habits of femininity that inhibit our passions and pleasures, my suggestion is that what we have never taken seriously enough is the language that fore-closes our meanings.

My positive recommendation is this: Instead of starting at a point (a point in the life of a body unlike our own) and trying to make meanings along vectors from that point, we would do better to start with a wide field of our passions and bodily pleasures and make meanings that weave a web across it. To begin creating a vocabulary that elaborates and expands our meanings, we should adopt a very wide and general concept of "doing it." Let it be an open, generous, commodious concept encompassing all the acts and activities by which we generate with each other pleasures and thrills, tenderness and ecstasy, passages of passionate carnality of whatever duration or profundity. Everything from vanilla to licorice, from puce to chartreuse, from velvet to ice, from cuddles to cunts, from chortles to tears. Starting from there, we can let our experiences generate a finer-tuned descriptive vocabulary that maps and expresses the differences and distinctions among the things we do, the kinds of pleasures we get, the stages and styles of our acts and activities, the parts of our bodies centrally engaged in the different kinds of "doing it," and so on. I would not, at the outset, assume that all of "doing it" is good or wholesome, nor that everyone would like or even tolerate everything this concept includes; I would not assume that "doing it" either has or should have a particular connection with love, or that it hasn't or shouldn't have such a connection. As we explain and explore and define our pleasures and our preferences across this expansive and heterogeneous field, teaching each other what the possibilities are and how to navigate them, a vocabulary will arise among us and by our collective creativity.

The vocabulary will arise among us, of course, only if we talk with each other about what we're doing and why, and what it feels like. Language is social. So is "doing it."

I'm hoping it will be a lot easier to talk about what we do, and how and when and why, and in carnal, sensual detail, once we've learned to laugh at foolish studies that lesbians don't have sex as often as, aren't as sexual as, and use fewer sexual techniques than other folks.

Becky Birtha

Johnnieruth

SUMMERTIME. NIGHTTIME. TALK ABOUT STEAM HEAT. THIS WHOLE CITY GET LIKE the bathroom when somebody in there taking a shower with the door shut. Nights like that, can't nobody sleep. Everybody be outside, sitting on they steps or else dragging half they furniture out on the sidewalk— kitchen chairs, card tables—even bringing TVs outside.

Womenfolks, mostly. All the grown women around my way look just the same. They all big—stout. They got big bosoms and big hips and fat legs, and they always wearing runover house-shoes, and them shapeless, flowered numbers with the buttons down the front. Cept on Sunday. Sunday morning they all turn into glamour girls, in them big hats and long gloves, with they skinny high heels and they skinny selves in them tight girdles—wouldn't nobody ever know what they look like the rest of the time.

When I was a little kid I didn't wanna grow up, cause I never wanted to look like them ladies. I heard Miz Jenkins down the street one time say she don't mind being fat cause that way her husband don't get so jealous. She say it's more than one way to keep a man. Me, I don't have me no intentions of keeping no man. I never understood why they was in so much demand anyway, when it seem like all a woman can depend on em for is making sure she keep on having babies.

We got enough children in my neighborhood. In the summertime, even the little kids allowed to stay up till eleven or twelve o'clock at night—playing in the street and hollering and carrying on—don't never seem to get tired. Don't nobody care, long as they don't fight.

Me—I don't hang around no front steps no more. Hot nights like that, I get out my ten speed and I be gone.

That's what I like to do more than anything else in the whole world. Feel that wind in my face keeping me cool as a air conditioner, shooting along like a snowball. My bike light as a kite. I can really get up some speed.

All the guys around my way got ten speed bikes. Some of the girls got em too, but they don't ride em at night. They pedal around during the day, but at nighttime they just hang around out front, watching babies and running they mouth. I didn't get my Peugeot to be no conversation piece.

My mama don't like me to ride at night. I tried to point out to her that she ain't never said nothing to my brothers, and Vincent a year younger than me. (And Langston two years older, in case "old" is the problem.) She say, "That's different, Johnnieruth. You're a girl." Now I wanna know how is anybody gonna know that. I'm skinny as a knifeblade turned sideways, and all I ever wear is blue jeans and a Wrangler jacket. But if I bring that up, she liable to get started in on how come I can't be more of a young lady, and fourteen is old enough to start taking more pride in my appearance, and she gonna be ashamed to admit I'm her daughter.

I just tell her that my bike be moving so fast can't nobody hardly see me, and couldn't catch me if they did. Mama complain to her friends how I'm wild and she can't do nothing with me. She know I'm gonna do what I want no matter what she say. But she know I ain't getting in no trouble, neither.

Like some of the boys I know stole they bikes, but I didn't do nothing like that. I'd been saving my money ever since I can remember, every time I could get a nickel or a dime outta anybody.

When I was a little kid, it was hard to get money. Seem like the only time they ever give you any was on Sunday morning, and then you had to put it in the offering. I used to hate to do that. In fact, I used to hate everything about Sunday morning. I had to wear all them ruffly dresses—that shiny slippery stuff in the wintertime that got to make a noise every time you move your ass a inch on them hard old benches. And that scratchy starchy stuff in the summertime with all them scratchy crinolines. Had to carry a pocketbook and wear them shiny shoes. And the church we went to was all the way over on Summit Avenue, so the whole damn neighborhood could get a good look. At least all the other kids'd be dressed the same way. The boys think they slick cause they get to wear pants, but they still got to wear a white shirt and a tie; and them dumb hats they wear can't hide them baldheaded haircuts, cause they got to take the hats off in church.

There was one Sunday when I musta been around eight. I remember it was before my sister Corletta was born, cause right around then was when I put my foot down about the whole sanctimonious routine. Anyway, I was dragging my feet along Twenty-fifth Street in back of Mama and Vincent and them, when I spied this lady. I only seen her that one time, but I still remember just how she look. She don't look like nobody I ever seen before. I *know* she don't live around here. She real skinny. But she ain't no real young woman, neither. She could be old as my mama. She ain't nobody's mama—I'm sure. And she ain't wearing Sunday clothes. She got on blue jeans and a man's blue working shirt, with the tail hanging out. She got patches on her blue jeans, and she still got her chin stuck out like she some kinda African royalty. She ain't carrying no shiny pocketbook. It don't look like she care if she got any money or not, or who know it, if she don't. She ain't wearing no house-shoes, or stockings or high heels neither.

Mama always speak to everybody, but when she pass by this lady she make like she ain't even seen her. But I get me a real good look, and the lady stare right back at me. She got a funny look on her face, almost like she think she know me from some place. After she pass on by, I had to turn around to get another look, even though Mama say that ain't polite. And you know what? She was turning around, too, looking back at me. And she give me a great big smile.

I didn't know too much in them days, but that's when I first got to thinking about how it's got to be different ways to be, from the way people be around my way. It's got to be places where it don't matter to nobody if you all dressed up on Sunday morning or you ain't. That's how come I started saving money. So, when I got enough, I could go away to some place like that.

Afterwhile I begun to see there wasn't no point in waiting around for handouts, and I started thinking of ways to earn my own money. I used to be running errands all the time—mailing letters for old Grandma Whittaker and picking up cigarettes and newspapers up the corner for everybody. After I got bigger, I started washing cars in the summer, and shoveling people sidewalk in the wintertime. Now I got me a newspaper route. Ain't never been no girl around here with no paper route, but I guess everybody got it figured out by now that I ain't gonna be like nobody else.

The reason I got me my Peugeot was so I could start to explore. I figured I better start looking around right now, so when I'm grown, I'll know exactly where I wanna go. So I ride around every chance I get.

Last summer, I used to ride with the boys a lot. Sometimes eight or ten of us'd just go cruising around the streets together. All of a sudden my mama decide she don't want me to do that no more. She say I'm too old to be spending so much time with boys. (That's what they tell you half the time, and the other half the time they worried cause you ain't interested in spending more time with boys. Don't make much sense.) She want me to have some girl friends, but I never seem to fit in with none of the thing the girls doing. I used to think I fit in more with the boys.

But I seen how Mama might be right, for once. I didn't like the way the boys was starting to talk about girls sometimes. Talking about what some girl be like from the neck on down, and talking all up underneath somebody clothes and all. Even though I wasn't really friends with none of the girls, I still didn't like it. So now I mostly just ride around by myself. And Mama don't like that neither—you just can't please her.

This boy that live around the corner on North Street, Kenny Henderson, started asking me one time if I don't ever be lonely, cause he always see me by myself. He say don't I ever think I'd like to have me somebody special to go places with and stuff. Like I'd pick him if I did! Made me wanna laugh in his face. I do be lonely, a lotta times, but I don't tell nobody. And I ain't met nobody yet that I'd really rather be with than be by myself. But I will someday. When I find that special place where everybody different, I'm gonna find somebody there I can be friends with. And it ain't gonna be no dumb boy.

I found me one place already, that I like to go to a whole lot. It ain't even really that far away—by bike—but it's on the other side of the Avenue. So I don't tell Mama and them I go there, cause they like to think I'm right around the neighborhood someplace. But this neighborhood too dull for me. All the houses look just the same—no porches, no yards, no trees—not even no parks around here. Every block look so much like every other block it hurt your eyes to look at, afterwhile. So I ride across

Summit Avenue and go down that big steep hill there, and then make a sharp right at the bottom and cross the bridge over the train tracks. Then I head on out the boulevard—that's the nicest part, with all them big trees making a tunnel over the top, and lightning bugs shining in the bushes. At the end of the boulevard you get to this place call the Plaza.

It's something like a little park—the sidewalks is all bricks and they got flowers planted all over the place. The same kind my mama grow in that painted-up tire she got out front masquerading like a garden decoration—only seem like they smell sweeter here. It's a big high fountain right in the middle, and all the streetlights is the real old-fashion kind. That Plaza is about the prettiest place I ever been.

Sometimes something going on there. Like a orchestra playing music or some man or lady singing. One time they had a show with some girls doing some kinda foreign dances. They look like they were around my age. They all had on these fancy costumes, with different color ribbons all down they back. I wouldn't wear nothing like that, but it looked real pretty when they was dancing.

I got me a special bench in one corner where I like to sit, cause I can see just about everything, but wouldn't nobody know I was there. I like to sit still and think, and I like to watch people. A lotta people be coming there at night—to look at the shows and stuff, or just to hang out and cool off. All different kinda people.

This one night when I was sitting over in that corner where I always be at, there was this lady standing right near my bench. She mostly had her back turned to me and she didn't know I was there, but I could see her real good. She had on this shiny purple shirt and about a million silver bracelets. I kinda liked the way she look. Sorta exotic, like she maybe come from California or one of the islands. I mean she had class—standing there posing with her arms folded. She walk away a little bit. Then turn around and walk back again. Like she waiting for somebody.

Then I spotted this dude coming over. I spied him all the way cross the Plaza. Looking real fine. Got on a three-piece suit. One of them little caps sitting on a angle. Look like leather. He coming straight over to this lady I'm watching and then she seen him too and she start to smile, but she don't move till he get right up next to her. And then I'm gonna look away, cause I can't stand to watch nobody hugging and kissing on each other, but all of a sudden I see it ain't no dude at all. It's another lady.

Now I can't stop looking. They smiling at each other like they ain't seen one another in ten years. Then the one in the purple shirt look around real quick—but she don't look just behind her—and sorta pull the other one right back into the corner where I'm sitting at, and then they put they arms around each other and kiss—for a whole long time. Now I really know I oughtta turn away, but I can't. And I know they gonna see me when they finally open they eyes. And they do.

They both kinda gasp and back up, like I'm the monster that just rose up outta the deep. And then I guess they can see I'm only a girl, and they look at one another—and start to laugh! Then they just turn around and start to walk away like it wasn't nothing at all. But right before they gone, they both look around again, and see I still ain't got my eye muscles and my jaw muscles working right again yet. And the one lady wink at me. And the other one say, "Catch you later."

I can't stop staring at they backs, all the way across the Plaza. And then, all of a sudden, I feel like I got to be doing something, got to be moving.

I wheel on outta the Plaza and I'm just concentrating on getting up my speed. Cause I can't figure out what to think. Them two women kissing and then, when they get caught, just laughing about it. And here I'm laughing too, for no reason at all. I'm sailing down the boulevard laughing like a lunatic, and then I'm singing at the top of my lungs. And climbing that big old hill up to Summit Avenue is just as easy as being on a escalator.

Robin Becker

Like Breath at Your Ear

The light that stabs the blue carpet is familiar, concentrated.
You hunch at your desk writing a paper
for junior English, still wearing your school clothes.
Your mother has gone to the market, your sister is having
her lesson. It is the first warm afternoon in April
in Philadelphia, where you have spent every spring
squinting beneath your desk lamp. Outside dogs graze hedges
and catch new shoots in their wiry hair. You are still so far
from the simplest destinations; knowing this makes you slow down
and stare out the window as if you could conjure
your best friend, working on her paper across town.
You flop onto the bed and a voice comes into the room.
She tells you to take off your skirt.
With indifference, the voice instructs your hand
and you are surprised at how the words move you
up and down on the bed, and how the phrases press your stomach
into the sheets. You have never heard this timbre
in a voice before. Like breath at your ear, the air whirls
electric against your skin, chords vibrate in your arms
and you know you will grow up listening for this woman.
The voice blows syllables and you utter them now, with her, as though
there had always been two worlds, and you'd inhabited that
other one, calling and breathing across a vast and private space.

Emma Pérez

From Gulf Dreams

> There is one woman whom fate has destined for each of us. If we miss her we are saved.
>
> —Anonymous

I MET HER IN MY SUMMER OF RESTLESS DREAMS. IT WAS A TIME WHEN INFATUATION emerges erotic and pure in a young girl's dreams. She was a small girl, a young woman. Her eyes revealed secrets, mysteries I yearned to know long after that summer ended.

My eldest sister introduced us. The young woman, the sister of my sister's best friend, became my friend. At our first meeting we went to the park. We walked, then stood under a cottonwood tree for hours, exchanging glances that bordered on awkward embarrassment. I remember we avoided the clarity of the afternoon. In a few moments, after her eyes sunk tenderly into mine, she caressed a part of me that I never knew existed.

At fifteen, I hadn't known love. I don't know if I fell in love that day. I know I felt her deeply and reassuringly. Without a touch, her passion traced the outline of my face. I wanted to brush her cheek lightly with my hand, but I, too frightened, spoke in riddles, euphemistic yearnings: the sun so hot; the trees so full; the earth pressed beneath me.

Weeks passed before I saw her again. During those long nights, I dreamt but did not sleep. Lying in my bed next to an open window, the breezes aroused me. They made me feel a peculiar edginess, mixed with calm. It rained. A soft drizzle fell on my face through the netted screen. I dreamt of her fingers brushing my skin, lightly smoothing over breasts, neck, back, all that ached for her. A fifteen-year-old body ached from loneliness and desire, so unsure of the certainties that her body felt. Nights like this would bring her to me. Never sleeping, half-awake to ensure that it was she embracing me. In those dreams we touched carefully. By morning, I rose exhausted. For those few weeks, sleepless, restless dreams exhausted me.

The day I would see her again held me in fear and anticipation. Far more than these emotions, I felt relief. I felt relieved because to see her would satisfy me, if only momentarily. To see her again, my body spoke to me. To see her eyes envelop mine. I had to remember their color. I had to see the olive hands that caused so much delight. I had to know that I had not invented her for dreams.

It was morning. A hot, dusty, gravel road linked our homes. My eldest sister drove to the young girl's house to see her own best friend. I sat, the passenger, staring out at fields, rows of cotton balls, white on green, passing quickly, the motion dizzying my head and stomach. My sister, familiar with my nausea in moving vehicles, had wrapped a wet face cloth in a plastic bag. The coolness of the moist rag soothed my forehead. As an additional precaution, I had stuffed two brown paper bags, one inside the other, under the car seat.

When we arrived, she was sitting on a porch swing hanging from a worn, wooden house, the paint peeling with no memory of color. Our sisters hugged, went into the kitchen, poured coffee and prepared for gratifying gossip. We were not alone; brothers, sisters, a mother, faces and names I can't recall—the introductions necessary, trusting, unsuspecting. No one knew why I had come. To see my new friend, they thought. To link families with four sisters who would be friends longer than their lifetimes, through children who would bond them at baptismal rites. *Comadres.* We would become intimate friends, sharing coffee, gossip, and heartaches. We would endure the female life cycle—adolescence, marriage, menopause, death, and even divorce, before or after menopause.

I had not come for that. I had come for her kiss.

We walked through tall grass. Silent. A path led to the shade of a tree. I watched her waist and hips, rhythmic, broad, swaying. At sixteen, her hips and breasts were a woman's. Under the tree, we avoided eyes, avoided touch, avoided that which I hoped we both wanted. I stared at her. She grabbed handfuls of dry leaves, sifting them through her fingers, methodically repeating her exercise. For an instant, I forgot her name. I could not place her. She was foreign, a stranger. The memory loss buffered my pain. So painful to watch the distance between us. I left that day without renewal. I knew the dreams would cease. I began to repair the damage. I revived the mundane. I sought its refuge.

The dreams did not cease. I saw her with him. That day under the shaded tree, she had spoken about a young boy. She craved his delicious expert mouth, she said. She told me he had sucked her nipples. He was careful not to hurt her or impregnate her. Instead, he licked her moistness. He loved her. No other boy had ever licked her softness.

Those were my dreams. The morning I lost my memory, forgot her name, I watched her lips relive desire for him. At night, they appeared in my bedroom. Invaded my bed. Even there, she belonged to him.

I did not envy him. I despised him, his coarseness, his anxious determination. She longed for someone to arouse her soul. Each time she dared to look directly into my eyes, she quickly averted hers. She alerted the passion, then repressed it immediately, her fear, a reproach against me.

Her desire for him pierced me. Still, I wanted her. I wanted her to come alone at night just as she had those first two weeks when exhaustion fulfilled me.

We became friends. The promise of female rituals enraged me. We met weekly, then monthly, then not at all. Her boy became her cause. Often, I spotted him in the fields. His strong, brown back bending over to pick the cotton that filled the trailing sack. A perfectly beautiful back, I thought. She was in love with a beautifully strong, muscular, brown back.

As a young woman of fifteen in a nearly coastal Texas town, I didn't recognize love. In a town where humidity bred hostility, I memorized hate. Bronze in the summer, with hair and eyes so light that I could pass through doors that shut out my sisters and brother, I envied their dark color and brown eyes. I grew to resent my own because they set me apart from my family. At four, my sisters convinced me I was adopted. Eyes so green, this was not my family. At five, I took a butcher knife, sat calmly, sadly, on the pink chenille bedspread, threatening to slice away at tanned skin. I remember the scene like a dream. Always the sad child, burdened.

When I stared into cameras, I didn't smile, laugh, or clown as children do, so unfamiliar to me how my cousins giggled with each other. My mother framed photographs that captured the sadness, held it squarely like a package with a time bomb that would not explode for years. Right now the sadness only watched. There was one photograph. Not yet one year old and I laughed openly and happily. Evidence of childhood. I wondered, when did the sadness begin?

◆ ◆ ◆

I missed her. Daily, hourly, I missed her. Since that meeting under the tree, I had retrieved pride to dismiss longing. The pride surfaced. It guided me through the day. It stopped me from climbing into my sister's white Dodge. Weekly, my sister traveled that gravel road to confer with her *comadre*.

One Saturday morning I tucked away pride, answered longing and sat, the passenger, the victim. She half-expected me. Took my hand, led me to her bedroom, sat me down on her twin bed next to her. She spoke reasonably. She had missed me. Why had I stopped coming? Why had I stayed away so long? She relied on my friendship, a passionate friendship, she called it. Mute, I looked away, paralyzed, embarrassed, hurt. She played at my emotions under the guise of friendship. We had moved far beyond that first day when we refused to acknowledge clarity.

A knock on the door, the interruption was inevitable. Through the door, her mother announced his intrusion. He waited on the porch swing, waited to take her for a ride in a borrowed black Chevy, waited to drive her to deserted fields and back roads where boys tested their virility.

Her eyes sparkled. He gave them an amused sparkle. She examined my face searching for jealousy. At an early age, I learned to exhibit indifference with sad eyes. She misinterpreted the sadness and chose jealousy. I watched through the window. It framed them, froze them like a photograph. He wrapped his arm around her waist. The black Chevy rolled away, rocks crackling under the wheels, dust spreading, leaving a brown film on my sister's white Dodge.

I would not see her again for a year.

My mother's house rested behind my father's workshop. My older sisters told me there had been a house before this one where they and my brother had lived. I even lived there until my first birthday. Then, my father moved us closer to the railroad tracks, next to the cotton gin.

I memorized the routine of caring in that two-bedroom home for six people. My cousins thought we were rich to live in a house my father bought with the G.I. bill. They lived in timeworn rented houses. Ours was newer, but hidden behind an aluminium building, my father's upholstery shop, my favorite playground. It became our favorite playground. Among the stripped chairs and couches waiting for floral designs to hide the bare frames, among the velour scraps and sharp nails, my brother and I played. My father's hammering was our financial security, his love proven over and over. Sometimes he hammered for sixteen hours daily, stopping only for ice water and saltine crackers. My brother and I were messengers, carriers delivering our mother's tenderness to our father down a worn path from the house to the shop.

My brother became the necessary companion throughout childhood. *Los cuates*, the twins, our family named us. Inseparable. He, small-boned, petite, eternally naive, was younger than I in every way but years. Accustomed to his companionship, I resented how he shunned my invitations to films or parties as we grew older. Maybe he resented me. I, bigger, light-skinned, had caught up with him in school, made friends and passing grades. Maybe I reminded him too much of the white world outside our home. Maybe, in mastering the language of survival, I too became an outsider. He no longer allowed me to share his dreams. Long before, I had stopped listening to them.

At fifteen, I didn't hate boys. I even liked some of them. Between the young gigglers with hard-ons and the older cat-callers with hard-ons, the choices were few. Finally, I chose one. I chose an outsider, white-skinned, blue-eyed, so blond his hair was white. In two years together, through daily phone calls, weekly films, and obligatory kisses, I refused to let him inside. Years later, after we ended daily phone calls, when his wife was at work, I mounted him as he lay on his living-room floor. Too guilty to take me to a white woman's bed, too ashamed, his face flushed. In seconds, it was over. A beginning and an end were wrapped in one humiliating afternoon.

When I was fifteen and chose him, he released a numbness that had protected me from her. The protection gone, the numbness lifted, the dreams revived. She returned alone at night, to soothe, to nurture, to explain why we loved only in dreams. I fell deeper. She would never leave, not as long as he stayed. Now she protected me from passage into female rites.

He wore pain. His face a grimace, his voice unctuous. He loved to wear pain. A young boy of seventeen from Alabama, he mistrusted his mother's anger. He and his father colluded. They misunderstood her thick, white body, her calloused hands, her bitterness. Domestic service in Alabama was Black women's work. In Texas, Mexican women cleaned white women's homes. Her white skin had not guaranteed that privilege.

She did not marry above her family. She married a poor boy, a hard worker like herself. The man she married spotted a strong build for healthy babies and a double salary. He raised her son to despise her strength. The son took her bitterness and made it his own. How could she have known a son would deceive her?

When I met him, I inherited his contempt for a mother he neither respected nor pitied. I inherited him the moment when a boy's ambivalence turns cocksure. Arrogance takes over, tenderness cannot be public. Maleness, so convinced of its superiority to the feminine, evolves.

I became cold, withdrawn. Only she could break through. I resisted as long as I could. Her glance, a smile, a playful word would melt me. Once again, longing disrupted me.

◆ ◆ ◆

I spotted her at a local market. The clerk, an elderly Anglo from Louisiana with an emphatic Southern drawl, harassed her. She placed a loaf of white bread on the counter. He refused to add the thirty-three cents to her family's account. Their payment was late again. She argued with him, then pleaded. I enjoyed watching her argue, resented her pleading. Finally, the store manager, a middle-aged, pot-bellied man and son of the clerk, walked to the check-out stand. His eyes seduced her body. Her smile convinced him. Promptly, he added thirty-three cents to her bill. She had begun payment with a smile. It found her in his shabby, filthy office on a cot that stunk like mildew. I judged her. I would continue to judge her until I too stripped for men whose power robbed my dignity.

When I began to dream that night, I saw her on the store manager's cot, lying on her stomach, her buttocks smooth and firm. His hand moved across her back, finding her soft, heart-shaped ass. He rubbed up and down, then in circles, enjoying her muscular flesh. But it was me who kissed her eyes. And it was she who encircled my nipples with her tongue. Awakened from the dream, I quivered. I felt her go to him, her boy, the one she nurtured. I felt her loving him again. She would not leave him easily. I knew that.

Routine and books comforted me. The summer over, fall gave me hope. I studied. I sublimated. I worked at K-Mart.

Persistent patterns from my past still paint my future. I sought protection. I know now that his white skin stood like armor between me and an unjust town. I liked this boy from Alabama whose blue eyes witnessed poverty in his own home. I liked his big shoulders, his tight, freckled forearms. We became lovers who kissed on Friday nights at drive-in theaters where I avoided sex.

Fatigue overtook my strength. His demands doubled. Familiarity gave him license to give me orders. My resistance led to petty arguments, so typically the high school sweethearts' drama. He was muscular, popular, a straight-A white student; I was Mexican, but smart and somewhat pretty, therefore acceptable. After a year, his habits bored me. The kisses no longer stimulated. My eyes wandered to neighborhood boys, to *pachucos*, so coolly sexy, so dangerously off limits. My eyes wandered but at night I waited for her.

I think I realized I had always been in love the moment I saw her again. My heart sank. I fought tears. While I had busied myself with the boy from Alabama, she had grown more beautiful. Being in love, I thought, has made her more beautiful. Her hair fell around her face. She saw me. We had not spoken since that day in her bedroom. She smiled. She walked in my direction, I tried to smile but my lips deceived me. My expression puzzled her. When she hugged me, she buried her head between my neck and shoulder, resting comfortably, feeling like just yesterday we had lain in each other's arms.

The smell of her hair, I had only imagined its scent for so long. Why was she holding me? She asked how I had been. She had seen me often, she said. She had seen me at school, the park, in town, with the boy from Alabama. She questioned me, seeking answers. Was I happy? Did I love him? Her voice bubbled. Quickly, I masked my emotions. I hid behind him. I pretended that he was special. I don't think I lied when I said I loved him. I felt love for him. I had hidden behind that type of love for so long. Yet, seeing her reminded me that I had only practiced at love. I practiced kisses and language with him. The smell of her hair woke me. Realization struck. She was different.

I'm not sure how she was different, but she felt unlike before. But then, I hadn't really felt her. I carried her around inside me always, but physically, I'd never really touched her. I imagined entering her, enjoying that ration of her, but only when and if she wanted me.

I could not compete with her past, nor could she with mine. There was no competition, only commonality. Our souls touched before in a life where my love for her was not forbidden.

How can I explain that she was the core of me? I say this over and over, to you, to myself. We merged before birth, entwined in each other's souls, wrapped together like a bubble of mist, floating freely, reflecting rainbows. This was before flesh, before bones crushed each other foolishly trying to join mortal bodies, before the outline of skin shielded us from one another. We both know this, that we came from the same place, that we were joined in a place so uncommon that this world, which bound us in limitations, could not understand the bond that flesh frustrated.

We became intimate friends again, desperately engaged. This time she stared longingly after me when I walked by with the boy from Alabama. She began to love me. I had not stopped loving her, nor would I stop.

I thought that writing this years later would finally release me from her. But I feel no reprieve. Not yet. Maybe the only resolution is in the act of loving. Maybe I had to love her enough to let her go. I had to begin to love her more than I loved my selfishness. I knew what I had to do but I wasn't ready. I cried.

We became enraptured and entrapped. We were addicted to each other's eroticism. A kiss on the cheek inflamed me for hours. I witnessed her greed. Teasing reached new heights. Could I let go of my addiction to her, to her body, to her words? Would I let go? The desire to desire her—my weakness. I didn't care. I risked seeing her every day despite the moodiness she provoked. Her boyfriend grew more and more threatened each time I appeared. His hostility sharpened. Mine became silent and distant when he saw her approach. She and I, trapped in social circumstances. Propriety kept us apart.

Some women exude sex simultaneously with erotic movements. She was that woman. Her scent alone emitted sensuality. I learned how boys had damaged her. I felt her damage. She punished me when I refused to continue the pattern with which she was so familiar. When I denied her the fight she sought, she would finally look elsewhere. So accustomed to brutality, she chose to play the victim. We sensed that dynamic in each other. She knew that if the game didn't work the first time, eventually I would play anyway. I couldn't resist her when I saw her agonizing. After running to him, he would oblige by hurting her, then she would come to me. And I rescued her, then resented my duty to her. And so we played this deceitful game, angry because we didn't know how to stop. I would spit fierce words at her. I abused her in long paragraphs filled with accusations. Sometimes, without uttering a sound, I hurt her. I manipulated just as she did.

I couldn't let go. Whatever bound us went beyond friendship. And through our games I recognized when she would leave me again, each time she would be gone a little longer. She returned to him, the boy with the strong brown back. I almost faced him on the path that routinely led me to her. I watched motionless from the street. The fog, the dull sky, and the cold air warned me. He opened the door I had opened so often. I couldn't cry. I stood, the numbed observer. Long before he traced my steps to her door, I knew. I knew that it was over again. She was tired of repeating the pain, the pleasure, then more pain. I was tired of her lies. I listened when she lied to him on the telephone while I sat on her bed. Only now did I hear that the lies were for me. I wanted truth, but I believed her lies because I believed my heart.

I refused to say good-bye. It is far better not to know when something is over. It is far better not to imprint that image permanently in one's mind. I prefer to walk through the habits of the day, treating good-bye as if it were not that at all, as if tomorrow we'll meet again for coffee. I began to mourn her. I don't know when I said good-bye, but I anticipated the moment. And it happened. The image marked in a memory that I shielded from myself for years. I had to forget that predetermined second. So much more is stamped in my mind—her smile, her breath, her persistence. She wore me out. I needed rest.

Suniti Namjoshi

I Give Her the Rose

I give her the rose with unfurled petals.
She smiles
               and crosses her legs.
I give her the shell with the swollen lip.
She laughs.   I bite
               and nuzzle her breasts.
I tell her, "Feed me on flowers
               with wide open mouths,"
and slowly,
               she pulls down my head.

Not for Years but for Decades

I. Fact

WHEN I WAS TWELVE I FELL IN LOVE WITH DANNY KAYE. FOR ALMOST A QUARTER of a century I have regarded that crush as the beginning of my sexual life. But "sexual" is a dangerous word precisely because it splits one part of experience off from the rest. It was only when I began to ask, not about "sex" or my "sex life" but (more vaguely) about my "feelings" and about "emotional attachments," that I began to recall other things, some earlier, that the official classifications of "sex" censored out and made unimportant. Perhaps that's the function of official classifications. Names are given to things by the privileged and their naming is (wouldn't you think?) to their own advantage, but in the area of sexuality women are emphatically not a privileged class. So let's ask about "friends."

At eleven I played erotic games with girlfriends, acting out nominally heterosexual stories I (usually) had made up. One script (minus the kissing and touching we added to it) I showed my mother, who praised it but laughed until she cried at one stage direction, which has a lover climbing a rope ladder to his sweetheart's window, being discovered by her parents, and gloomily exiting by climbing back down the ladder. About this time I went on my First Date with a nice, plain, gentle, thoroughly dull little boy called Bill (we called him "Bill the Hill"). The necking he wanted to do bored me, but I was tremendously proud of having a First Date. At about that time, one winter's evening, one of my girlfriends seductively and skittishly insisted on kissing us all good night; that night I dreamed I was being led further and further into a dark forest by an elf who was neither a girl nor a boy, rotting oranges as big as people hung on the trees, and when a storm began, I woke in terror, knowing perfectly well that I had dreamed about my friend and that I was feeling for her what ought to go on with Bill the Hill. I told my mother about it and she "handled it very well" (as my analyst said many years later).

She said it was "a stage."

That summer I was in summer camp and all the twelve-year-old girls in the bunk necked and petted secretly (with each other) but the next summer everybody seemed to have forgotten about it. Certainly nobody mentioned it. Everybody remembered the "dirty jokes" we had told every night for hours (grotesquely heterosexual or homophobic stories I thought the other children had invented) and none of my friends had forgotten the (heterosexual) serial stories I had made up and which several other little girls continued. But that whole summer of fumbling with your best friend had become invisible. Since nobody else mentioned it, I never did either.

My best friend was Carol-Ellen. I called her my "best friend," not my "lover." I had strong and sometimes painfully profound feelings about her and would have been miserably jealous if she'd preferred anyone else to me. Yet I never thought that I "loved" Carol-Ellen or that what we did was really "sex" (although it was somehow not only sex, but a far worse kind than the boys' panty raids or girls staying out with boys after curfew). I never gave to what had happened between us the prestigious name of "love" (which might have led me to stand up for its importance) or the wicked-but-powerful name of "sex." What I had begun to learn (in "it's a stage") continued that summer, that my real experience, undefined and powerful as it was, didn't really exist. It was bad and it didn't exist. It was bad *because* it didn't exist.

Simultaneously with being mad about Carol-Ellen, I read Love Comics. I believed in them. (Everybody read them and everybody, I suspect, believed in them.) Like dating and movies and boys, they were about real love and real sex. I remember disliking them and at the same time not being able to stay away from them. They demanded things of me (looks, clothes, behavior) which I disliked, and they insisted on the superiority and importance of men in a way I detested (and couldn't connect with any of the little boys I knew at camp). But they offered a very great promise: that if only I would sacrifice my ambitions and most of my personality, I would be given a reward—they called it "love." I knew it was in some way "sexual." And yet I also knew that those hearts and flowers and flashing lights when the characters kissed didn't have anything to do with sex; they were supersex or ultrasex; they were some kind of transcendent ecstasy beyond ordinary life. They certainly didn't have anything to do with masturbation, or with what Carol-Ellen and I were secretly doing together. I think now that the most attractive reward held out by the Love Comics (and later by the movies, the books, and the psychoanalysts) was freedom from responsibility and hence freedom from the burdens of being an individual. At twelve I found that promise very attractive. I was a tall, overly bright and overly self-assertive girl, too much so to fit anybody's notions of femininity (and too bookish and odd to fit other children's ideas of an acceptable human being). If anybody needed an escape from the guilt of individuality, I certainly did. The Love Comics told me that when it came right down to it, I wasn't any different from any other woman and that once love came, I would no longer have to worry about being imprisoned in my lonely, eccentric selfhood. The hearts and flowers and the psychedelic flashing lights would sweep all that away. I would be "in love" and I would never have to think again, never agonize over being "unpopular," never follow my own judgment in the face of criticism, never find things out for myself. This is the Grand Inquisitor's promise and I think Germaine Greer is quite right to see in the cult of "romance" a kind of self-obliterating religion. I didn't know that at twelve, of course. Nor did I know enough to look at the comic books' copyright pages to see which sex owned them, published them, and even wrote them. But I believed. And if I hadn't gotten the message from comic books, I would still have gotten it (as I did later) from movies, books, and friends. Later on I would get the same message from several (not even one!) psychiatrists and psychology books. Nor did the High Culture I met at college carry a different message. The insistence on certain kinds of looks and behavior, the overwhelming importance of men, and the sacrifice of personality and individuality (as well as the promised rewards) were always the same. (The only thing college added was contempt for women—which didn't change the obligation to be "feminine.")

Ti-Grace Atkinson calls this the heterosexual institution.

Time passed. Carol-Ellen went to another camp. At fourteen I felt for a male counselor of nineteen the vulnerability, awkwardness, and liking

I've since learned to call "erotic tension." Somebody else asked him to the Sadie Hawkins Dance and I cried in the bathroom for three solid minutes. I didn't know him well and didn't feel for him with one quarter of the intensity I had for Carol-Ellen, but this time I had an official name for what I was feeling; I called it "love." I think what drew me to him was his kindness and his lack of good looks, which made him seem, to me, like a fellow refugee. He was embarrassed at the dance (about me, I suspect) and roared about, clowning, which disillusioned me. I don't believe Carol-Ellen could have disillusioned me; I knew her too well and she was too important to me. I don't remember his face or his name, although I remember Carol-Ellen's perfectly (possibly because I took good care to get a snapshot of her). And Carol-Ellen, though of course a fellow creature, was not a fellow refugee; she always seemed to me far too good looking and personally successful for that, so much so that I wondered why nobody else noticed her beauty. I always felt graced by Carol-Ellen's picking me for her best friend; after all, she could've been friends with anybody. But somewhere in my feelings about Bernie (Sidney? Joe? Scottie?) was the disheartening feeling I came to recognize later in my dealings with men: *He'll do.*

The year before that, in junior high, an older boy of fifteen (a popular person whose acquaintance I coveted) complimented me on a scarf I was wearing and I responded as we always did in my family: "Thanks, I got it at...." He laughed, partly amused, partly critical. "I didn't ask you where you got it! After all, *I'm* not going to get one." I knew that I had made a social mistake, and yet my embarrassment and shame were mixed with violent resentment. I knew then that the manners I had been taught (they seemed to me perfectly good ones) were now wrong, and that I would have to learn a whole new set for "boys." It was unfair. It was just like the Love Comics. I knew also that somewhere deep down I didn't believe in the absolute duality of male and female behavior (in terms of which he'd criticized me) and that somewhere in the back of my mind, in a reserve of boundless arrogance, I was preparing revolutionary solutions for such people: *That's false and I know it. And just you wait.*

Yet all of this: revolution, Lesbianism, what have you, took place in profound mental darkness. I wrote moody Lesbian poems about Carol-Ellen, played with the idea of being a Lesbian, a tremendously attractive idea but strictly a literary one (I told myself). I wrote a Lesbian short story, which worried my high school teacher into asking me if I had any "problems you want to talk about." I knew the story had bothered him and felt wickedly pleased and very daring. The story itself was about a tall, strong, masculine, dark-haired girl (me) who falls in love with a short, slender, light-haired girl (?) and then kills herself by throwing herself off a bridge because the light-haired girl (although a Lesbian) will have nothing to do with her. I couldn't imagine anything else for the two of them to do. A few months later I began a novel (without connecting it with the story): here the dark-haired girl has become a dark-haired young man and the two lovers do get together (here I *could* image something for them to do) although light-hair eventually breaks the love affair off. On what grounds? That she's a Lesbian! The young man, by the way, does not kill himself.

At the same time I began to wonder what pregnancy felt like and to write poems about Being Female, which I thought meant having no mind and being immersed in some overwhelming, not necessarily pleasant experience that was much bigger than you were (no, I didn't yet even know that D. H. Lawrence existed; it was Love Comics again). I fell in love with a male gay friend and went with him and his sister to the Village, where they adjured me to pretend I was eighteen ("For God's sake, Joanna, put your hair up and wear earrings!") so that we could drink real liquor in a real bar. I had disturbing dreams about him in which he came to the door of my family's house in a dress and a babushka. (At the time I interpreted the dream as worry about his effeminate mannerisms. Now I'm not so sure.) Later, in my first year of college, he came to visit and I teased him into kissing me; it felt so good that the next day I insisted on going farther. The only place we could use was the dormitory lounge, and possibly because of the publicity of the location, things turned out badly; he got scared, I got nauseated, and after he left I spent a wretched hour surrounded by friends, who cheerfully told me that the first time was always rotten. The housemother, a youngish psychologist, told me the same thing, and when I told her about my feelings for women (I must've had them, although I can only remember telling her about them) she said I was "going through a stage."

Somehow, in a vague and confused way, I didn't believe that. I found *Mademoiselle de Maupin*, a nineteenth-century novel in which a woman disguises herself as a man and has a love affair with a woman and a man

(I thought the man was a creep and was really only interested in the woman). I wore slacks and felt defiant and ashamed. I tried to find out about Lesbianism on campus and annoyed my friends ("This school is awful. Do you know there are Lesbians here?" "Where! Where!" "Oh, Joanna, *really*."). I acquired a best friend for whom I had painful, protective, profound feelings, etc., without ever recognizing, etc. I found another "elf" and followed her around campus at a distance, feeling embarrassed. I went out on dates, which were even more crucial than they had been in high school, and got kissed by various men, which mildly excited and not so mildly disgusted me. My best friend told me stories about Lesbianism in her high school, in which everyone was a Lesbian except her, but when I wanted to go with her to a Lesbian bar in New York (over vacation) she wouldn't, and when I desperately asked her to pretend we were lovers in front of a third person, whom I said I wanted to shock (I didn't know myself at that point exactly what I was doing) she got very angry and upset.

So I gave up. It wasn't real. It didn't count, except in my own inner world in which I could not only love women but also fly, ride the lightning, be Alexander the Great, live forever, etc., all of which occurred in my poetry. I regarded this inner life as both crucially important and totally trivial, the source of all my vitality and yet something completely sealed off from "reality." By now I had learned to define the whole cluster of feelings as "wanting to be a man" (something I had not thought of before college), and saw it simultaneously as a shameful neurotic symptom and an indication of how much more talented and energetic I was than other women. Women with "penis envy" (another collegiate enlightenment) were inferior to men but were somehow superior to other women although they were also wickeder than other women. My best friend thought so. The psychology books my mother read thought so. The movies seemed to think so. Two years later the second "elf" turned up one summer (we had become distant friends) and the whole business started all over again. I now recognized it as a recurrent thing. I laughed at it and called it "penis envy." It was about at that time that I began the first of a long series of one-way infatuations with very macho men (these lasted into my thirties), agonizing experiences in which I suffered horribly but had the feeling that my life had become real and intense, even super-real, the feeling that I was being propelled into an experience bigger and more overwhelming than my own dreary life, a life I was beginning to detest. The first man I picked for this was my best friend's fiance. I kept the infatuation going, totally unreciprocated, for almost a year. He left school, they split up. I managed to go out with him once (we necked) and felt, in immense erotic excitement, that if only he would love me I could submerge my individuality in his, that he was a "real man," and that if I could only marry him I could give up "penis envy" and be a "real woman."

It sounds just like Love Comics.

In high school I believed (along with my few friends) that college would see an end to the dating game, to the belief that women were inferior to men and that intellectual women were freaks. But it was in college that I first got lectures about "being a woman" from boys I knew, and heard other women getting them, heard that so-and-so knew "how to be a woman," and was surrounded by the new and ghastly paraphernalia of dress rules and curfews. (My parents had been extremely permissive about where I went and with whom.)

After my twelfth summer I had gone (very early) into a high school where I knew nobody; I became depressed. In college I became more depressed. I went to the school psychiatrist, who told me I had "penis envy" and was in love with my father. I was willing to agree but did not know what to do about it (he said, "Enjoy life. Go out on dates.") and became even more depressed. By the end of graduate school I no longer had problems with "feelings about women"; I felt nothing about anybody. Occasionally I slept with a short, gentle, retiring man for whom I felt affection but no desire; puzzlingly, the sex didn't work. Later, when I got into my twenties and into psychoanalysis, and began to feel again, I "fell in love with" handsome macho men who didn't know I existed; I hated and envied them. The more intense and unreal these one-way "love affairs" were, the more dead and flat my life became in between. (When the man was not inaccessible, I made sure I was.) I got married to a short, gentle, retiring pleasant man (*He'll do*) and worked very hard at sex, which I loathed. I fell in love with a male homosexual friend because he was so beautiful and his life was beautiful and I wanted to be part of his life. I certainly didn't want to be part of my own life. I acquired a series of office jobs, none of which I could bear to keep ("Isn't there anything you like about your job?" "Yes, lunch hour.") I went into analysis because I was extremely depressed and very angry, and when my analyst asked (once) if I had homosexual feelings, I said "Oh, no, of course not," without even thinking. Even if it hadn't been nonsense, everybody knew that the real problem was men, so I thought endlessly about men, worried about men, worried (with the active help of my analyst) about the orgasms I wasn't having with men, worried about my childhood, worried about my parents, all in the service of worrying about my relation to men. Nothing else mattered. When my analyst asked me if I enjoyed sex, apart from orgasm, I remember wondering mildly what on earth he meant. It's quite possible that analysis did help me with my "dependency problems," although for a man who urged me to be independent he was remarkably little concerned at my being economically dependent on my husband; he thought that was okay; I didn't; for one thing my husband hated his job as much as I hated mine. He told me that my relationship with my mother was bad (I agreed) but when I talked about my father I would get so enraged (about all men, not just about that one) that he would become tolerantly silent and then tell me I was showing resistance. He once said that if I'd been born a boy, I could've turned out much worse: "You might have been homosexual." He said that what had saved me from going really crazy in my childhood was my father's love. He once remarked that I had intense friendships, and I said, "Yeah, I guess," not at all interested. But apart from the two remarks I've noted we never talked about my homosexuality. We talked about my "frigidity."

I remember someone in the group (I was in group therapy for years) asking me if my husband was a good lover, and my absolute, blank helplessness before that question. I remember analytic remarks that enraged and baffled me: that getting married showed "ego strength"—I had done it partly because I was running out of money and couldn't stand working, a motive of which I was bitterly ashamed and which I never told anybody; that it was surprising that my husband could "function sexually"—I had an impulse of absolute rage, which I suppressed; that I was afraid I would be physically hurt in the sex act—"No, I'm afraid I'll turn into a 'real woman,'" "But you are a real woman"; that I could be "active" by telling my husband what to do to me; and that men and women had different social functions but the same dignity—"Yeah, separate but equal," and that one I actually said out loud.

If analysis did any good, it certainly did not do it in the area of sex. Perhaps having some stories published helped. Being invited to writers' conferences and, for the first time in my life, meeting people like myself helped. (Question: Why is it so hard making friends in group therapy and so easy making friends at writers' conferences? Answer: Because writers are crazy.) Years later when I heard the phrase "the iron has entered your soul" I entirely misunderstood it. I thought that when you passed a certain point in misery you could really take the misery into you and turn it into strength. Perhaps I did that somehow. I made the first genuine decision of my adult life and left my husband—I was panic-stricken, clearly a matter of "dependency problems" but also a matter of getting out of the heterosexual institution. I got a job I liked, partly by accident ("You mean they'll pay me for *that*?"). I learned to drive. I got a job in another city and left analysis. I was desperately lonely. I kept "falling in love" with inaccessible men until it occurred to me that I wanted to be them, not love them, but by then feminism had burst over all of us. I stopped loving men ("It's just too difficult!") and in a burst of inspiration, dreamed up the absolutely novel idea of loving women. I thought at the time that my previous history had nothing to do with it.

Just before I left my husband I had a dream, which I still remember. (I had begun to have nightmares every night after we made love.)[1] I was alone in a city at night, walking round and round a deserted and abandoned schoolhouse, and I couldn't tell if I was frightened because I was alone or frightened because I wasn't alone. This dark schoolhouse was surrounded by uncut grass, and grass was growing in the cracks of the sidewalk. I sat down on the front steps, in a world unutterably desolate and deserted, wishing very hard for someone to take me away from there. Then a car, containing the shadowy figures of a man and a woman in the front seat, pulled up, and I got inside, in the back seat. The car began to move and somehow I strained to keep it moving, for I suspected it wasn't going anywhere; and then I looked down and there, through the floorboards, grew the grass.

There was no car. I was back on the steps, alone. And I was terrified.

It was years before the phrase "grass growing in the streets" connected itself to the dream. (I knew from the first that it was about being alone.) I think now that the deserted schoolhouse is psychoanalysis (where I am to be "taught" what to be), and that the shadowy man and woman are what psychoanalysis is teaching me; that is, the heterosexual institution. But the schoolhouse is dark and deserted, grass grows in the streets (as was supposed to happen in the 1930s here if that radical, Roosevelt, won), the man and woman are only shadows, and I'm totally alone in a solitary world. Marriage is an illusion. My "teacher" is nonexistent.

It seems to me now the only dream I've ever had, aside from (a possible) one in childhood, that's genuinely schizophrenic, with the changelessness of madness, the absolute desolation, and the complete lack of hope.

But it didn't happen. Instead I got out.

II. Fantasy

But now we reach problems. Am I a "real" Lesbian?

There is immense social pressure in our culture to imagine a Lesbian as someone who never under any circumstances feels any attraction to any man, in fantasy or otherwise. The popular model of homosexuality is simply the heterosexual institution reversed; since heterosexuality is (supposedly) exclusive, so must homosexuality be. It is this assumption, I think, that lies behind arguments about what a "real Lesbian" is or accusations that so-and-so isn't "really" a Lesbian. I have been attracted to men, therefore I'm not a Lesbian. I have few (or no) fantasies about women and do have fantasies about men; therefore I'm not a Lesbian.[2] This idea of what a Lesbian is is a wonderful way of preventing anyone from ever becoming one; and when we adopt it, we're simply doing the culture's dirty work for it. *There are no "real" Lesbians*—which is exactly what I heard for years, there are only neurotics, impostors, crazy virgins, and repressed heterosexuals. You aren't a Lesbian. You can't be a Lesbian. There aren't any Lesbians. Real Lesbians have horns.

Since we are outside the culture's definitions to begin with, most of us are not going to fit the culture's models of "sex," not even backwards. There is the Romantic Submission model for women. There is the Consumption Performance model for men. A few years ago *Playboy* came out with a cover made up of many small squares, each of which contained a picture of part of a naked woman: a single breast, a belly, a leg, two buttocks, etc. There were no faces. I had just come out at this time, and was very upset and confused because I couldn't respond to this model. Not only wasn't I relating to women that way; I hated the model itself because I had spent so much time on the other end of it and I knew what that detachable-parts business does to a woman's sense of self. Did this mean that I was not a Lesbian? Not by *Playboy*'s standards, certainly. Mind you, I was not therefore a healthy or good woman. I was merely sick, criminal, or crazy. Oddly enough, I don't think I've ever felt guilty about sleeping with women per se; I always felt that my real crime was *not sleeping with men*. After the first euphoria of discovery ("Joanna, for Heaven's sake will you lower your voice; do you want the whole restaurant to know?") what plagued me—and still does—is the nagging feeling that in not sleeping with men I am neglecting a terribly important obligation. I'm sometimes attracted to men I humanly like; when this happens I feel tremendously pressured to do something about it (whether I want to or not). When I don't act on it, I feel cowardly and selfish, just as I used to feel when I didn't have orgasms with my husband. Women, after all, *don't count*. What happens between women *isn't real*. That is, you can't be beaten up on for more than twenty-five years and not carry scar tissue.

Unfortunately there is something we all do that perpetuates the whole business, and that is treating fantasy as a direct guide to action. Suppression doesn't only affect behavior; it also affects the meaning and valuation we give behavior. And it affects fantasy. The popular view is that daydreams or other fantasies are fairly simple substitutes for behavior and that the two are related to each other in a simple one-to-one way, i.e. what you can't act out, you daydream. I don't believe this. For years I did, and was sure that my heterosexual fantasies indicated I was a heterosexual. (My Lesbian fantasies, however, could be dismissed as "wanting to be a man.") I think now that fantasy, like any other language, must be interpreted, that it does not "translate" simply into behavior, and that what is most important about it is the compromise it shows and the underlying subject matter at work in it. For example, fantasies about "sex" may not be about sex at all, although the energy that feeds them is certainly sexual. I know that in growing up I had fantasies about rescuing Danny Kaye from pirates at the same time that I loved Carol-Ellen. I couldn't find my fantasy of a gentle, beautiful, nonmasculine, rescuable man in any of the little boys I knew; there was only dull Bill (*He'll do*) and the creeps I hated and feared who grabbed me at parties or came up to me in assembly and said, "Baby, your pants are showing." By the age of fifteen I was having two kinds of fantasies: either I was an effeminate, beautiful, passive man being made love to by another man or I was a strong, independent, able, active, handsome woman disguised as a man (sometimes a knight in armor) who rescued another woman from misery or danger in a medieval world I could not picture very well. The first kind of daydream was full of explicit sex and secret contempt; the second was full of emotion and baffled yearning. Whenever it came time to go beyond the first kiss, I was stopped by my own ignorance. There was a third daydream, rarer than the other two, in which I was an independent, able, strong woman disguised as a man and traveling with my lover, an able, strong man who alone knew the secret of my identity. This kind was not satisfying, either emotionally or sexually, and I think I tried it out of a sense of duty; the one virtue it had was a sort of hearty palship that I liked.

In a sexual situation there are at least two factors operating: who you want the other person to be and who you want to be yourself. If I try to analyze my own past fantasies, I come up with one theme over and over, and that is not who the Other is, but what kind of identity I can have within the confines of the heterosexual institution. What I'll call the Danny Kaye fantasy is William Steig's *Dreams of Glory* with the sexes changed: little boy saves beautiful adult woman from fate worse than something or other. (If you look at the early Kaye films, you find that something of the sort is indeed happening, although not nearly to the extent I thought when I was twelve.) I still think that if I had emerged at puberty into a female-dominant culture in which little girls could reasonably dream of rescuing handsome, gentle, sexually responsive (but noninitiating) men from peril, I could have made an uneasy peace with it. I would probably have ended up the way a good many men do within the heterosexual institution: homosexuality for them remains an area of profound uneasiness, although their outward behavior and what they allow themselves to feel matches the norm.[3] However, even the cultural artifacts that turned me on in my youth all took it back in the end, just as Mae West's wooing of Cary Grant in *She Done Him Wrong* is shown up as a fake in the end of the film; he's really a tough cop. In fact, though this model of sexuality is not totally inconceivable and unspeakable, it turns up rarely and is explicitly disallowed. The sixties produced it in grotesque form in Tiny Tim; it took the seventies to produce David Bowie. But the heterosexual institution is wary of this model; it's politically very dangerous. And heterosexual men are trained to avoid it like the plague. Even as a fantasy it disappeared early in my adolescence.

Fantasy Number Two was cued off at age fifteen or thereabouts by something I read, and later on there were movies about Oscar Wilde and so on. (I have never ceased to be amazed at the fact that works about male homosexuality can exist in libraries, quite respectably bound, some even minor classics. They're few enough, but Lesbian works are far fewer.) The one film I hoped would be about Lesbianism (*Maedchen in Uniform*) wasn't and disappointed me very much. This fantasy got more and more important as I got older, more depressed, *and more outwardly conforming to the heterosexual institution.* There were years in my twenties when this was the only way I could daydream about sex at all. I had, by that time, put into this fantasy all the explicit fucking that never got into the others; I'll give you all the passivity and charm you want—if only I'm not a woman.

Number Three (woman/woman) began early; it was modeled on a (totally sexless) parodic little story by Mark Twain about a woman disguised as a man entitled "A Medieval Romance." At fifteen I added material from *Mademoiselle de Maupin.* For close to a decade my knowledge of Lesbianism was limited to these two fictions, one of them a parody (I was too naive to spot this at twelve), and although the emotional tenacity of this fantasy has been awesome, I never put much "sex" into it. I did not, after all, know what women did with each other.[4] And since the only way I could get near a woman was to disguise myself as a man, I had to protect my disguise (otherwise she wouldn't want me). So it was all impossible. Also, I was uneasy about wanting anybody else to "be the girl," since I knew what a rotten deal that was; I couldn't imagine anybody choosing it voluntarily. And how dull she was! But because I was a sort-of-a-man I couldn't very well love anybody else. Lesbianism modeled on the heterosexual institution didn't work and I had not the dimmest social clue that any other form of it could exist. And in my heart I think I would infinitely have preferred the reality of loving a woman to any fantasy; the very fact that it was a fantasy used to make me cry (in the fantasy). So this daydream also dies eventually.

The woman-disguised-as-a-man with a man was a pale one; it was too close to the reality of the heterosexual institution. Male attire is flimsy protection for the culturally harassed female ego. I used this one rarely.

A fantasy that appeared sporadically through my teens and (like the male homosexual fantasy) got heavy in my twenties was explicit hetero-sexual masochism.[5] It was physically exciting, erotically dependable, and very upsetting emotionally. I never connected this one to Love Comics and never imagined that it might have social sources; I thought I had invented it, that it meant I was a "real woman" and "really passive," and also that I wanted to be hurt and that I was crazy.

There were two situations I never used in any of my fantasies: a woman loving a man and a man loving a woman. That is, I could never imagine myself in either role of the heterosexual institution. I think now that the heterosexual-masochistic fantasy was a way of sexualizing the situation I was in fact in, and that one of the things it "means" (in trans-lation) is that I was being hurt and I knew that I was being hurt *because* I was a woman, that it was not sexual at all (as I had been promised) but that I wished to goodness it would be; then at least I would get some-thing out of it. I also suspect that sadomasochism is a way of preventing genuine involvement; either he wasn't emotionally there and present or I wasn't, and anyhow *the only thing* I can get from all of this is an orgasm.

The one cultural cue I had in abundance was the Dominance/Submis-sion model of the heterosexual institution. The one cultural cue I barely had at all was Lesbianism (there is no cultural vocabulary of words, im-ages, or expectations in this area). Oddly enough, for someone who thought she "wanted to be a man," I never imagined myself a man at all; by what sheer cussedness I managed to resist that cue, I'll never know.

What do people do with their sexuality? Whatever they can, I think. I think fucking can "work" within a wide variety of physical conditions. And the head trips may not be connected to what one responds to in real life at all. In a fine essay on female sexuality, Linda Phelps says that fe-male sexuality is "schizophrenic, relating not to ourselves as self-directed persons, not to our partners as sexual objects of our desire, but to a false world of symbols and fantasy.... It is a world whose eroticism is defined in terms of female powerlessness, dependency, and submission.... In a male world, female sexuality is from the beginning unable to get a clear picture of itself." She says also that many women "have no sexual fantasies at all" and those who do "often have the same sadomasochistic fantasies that men do."[6]

Yeah.

Looking back, I think my fantasies were desperate strategies to salvage something of my identity, even at the expense of any realistically possible sexuality. There was, of course, this behavior with women that I wanted, but I couldn't talk about that; it was the most taboo of all. (My first incredulous words at thirty-three: "You mean that's *real*?" Yes, I knew it happened, but....) I recognized my Lesbian feelings at age eleven; less than a year later I could no longer even recognize *what I was actually doing*, let alone what I later wanted to do. The only remotely positive encouragement I got, as well as the only analysis or naming, was the "stage" business. So partly I hung on in a muddled way and partly I gave up; after sixteen I gave up completely. The nonverbal messages were too strong. I think that anyone trying to maintain behavior important to them in the face of massive social pressure can only do so in a crippled and compromised way (especially in isolation), whatever form the crippling takes. Whether it's guilt or an inability to fantasize or an inability to act. Or perhaps a constant reshuffling of the roles prescribed by the heterosexual institution. As I got older things got worse; in my twenties I began to have occasional night dreams in which I was physically a man. I dreamed that a bunch of men was running after a bunch of women with felonious intent. I dreamed that I was being unmasked as "not really a man" and that everyone was laughing at me. As I had progressed from college to the less sheltered graduate school and from there to the not-at-all-sheltered job market, my situation became worse and worse. I wasn't a man (let alone a homosexual man). I certainly couldn't love women, I was a *woman* and *women* loved *men*, and dull, gentle men weren't "really" men and if I liked them I wasn't "really" a woman (and anyhow I didn't like them except as friends; sex with them was no good). I was out of college now, I had to earn my own living, I had to get married, I had to shape up and have orgasms, this was the *real world*, dammit.

So I read Genet and Gide (I scorned *The Well of Loneliness*, which I came to much too late anyway) and believed that art and life were totally separate. By then I really did want to be a man (for one thing, men didn't have such horrible lives, or so the heterosexual institution informed me).

I was married. I was frigid. I couldn't earn my own living. I wasn't sure I was a writer. Psychoanalysis seemed only to prove more and more that the impossibility of my ever being a "real" woman was my own fault. I was hopelessly crazy and a failure at everything. My analyst, in the kindest possible way, pointed out to me that my endless infatuations with inaccessible men were not realistic; I tried to tell him that for me nothing was realistic. My maneuvers for retaining some shred of autonomy within the iron-and-concrete prison of the heterosexual institution were getting desperate; they now involved wholesale transformations of identity or the direct translation of my real situation into "masochism," which terrified and disgusted me. (I only brought myself to write about these fantasies many years later, by which time they had lost much of their glamour.) I knew that I did not really want to sleep with men. But that was sick. I did want to sleep with men—but only in my head and only under very specialized circumstances. *That* was sick. In short I had—for close to twenty-five years—no clear sexual identity at all, no confidence in my own bodily experience, and no pleasure in lovemaking with any real person. I had to step out of the heterosexual institution before I could put myself back together and begin to recover my own bodily and emotional experience. When I did, it was only because the women's movement had thoroughly discredited the very idea of "real" women, thus enabling me to become a whole person who could then pay some attention to the gay liberation movement. (My most vivid feeling after my first Lesbian experience: that my body was well put together, graceful, healthy, fine feeling, and, above all, *female*—a thought that made me laugh until I cried.) Whenever people talk about the difference between politics and personal life, I'm dumbfounded. Not only were these "political" movements intensely "personal" in their effect on me; I can't imagine a "political" stance that doesn't grow out of "personal" experience. On my own I would never have made it. I can still remember—and the institutional cruelty behind the incident still staggers me—telling my woman-disguised-as-man-with-man fantasy to my psychoanalyst, and this dreary piece of compromise (which did not, in fact, work erotically at all) met with his entire approval; he thought it was a real step forward that I should imagine myself to be a "real" woman being made love *to* by a "real" man. Then he said, smiling:

"But why do you have to be disguised as a man?"

There's a lot I haven't put into this story. For example, the years of limbo that followed my first Lesbian affair ("What do I do now?"), the overwhelming doubts that it had happened, which attacked me when I had to live an isolated life again in a world in which there exists absolutely no public sign that such things happen, or the self-hatred and persisting taboos ("Women are ugly"; "Vaginas are slimy and strong and have horrible little teeth") or the terror of telling anyone.

As I said, by the time I read *The Well of Loneliness* I had learned that the whole business was absurd and impossible. (The book's gender roles also put me off.) I never dared buy one of those sleazy paperbacks I saw in drugstores, although I wanted them desperately. I was terrified to let the cashier see them. (Mind you, this didn't mean I was a Lesbian. It only meant that if I read all of the arousing scenes I glimpsed in them, I might become so aroused that I might go to a bar and do something Lesbian, which would be awful, because I wasn't one.) I suppose not reading about all those car crashes and suicides was a mild sort of plus, but I don't think it's a good idea to reach one's thirties without any cultural imagery for one of the most important parts of one's identity and one's life. So I've made some up. I hope that in filling the fantasy gap for myself, I've helped fill it for others, too.

I would like to thank various literary women for existing. Some of them know me and some do not. This is not an exhaustive list. Among them are: June Arnold, Sally Gearhart, Barbara Grier, Susan Griffin, Marilyn Hacker, Joan Larkin, Audre Lorde, Jill Johnston, Marge Piercy, Adrienne Rich, and too many more to put down here.

Postscribbles

1. Overheard at a gay conference, Lesbian to gay man, nearby a woman minister in "minister suit" trying not to smile: "We're *all* in drag."

2. A common way to cloak one's hatred of and dismissal of an issue is to snot it, i.e., the outraged ignorance of the reviews of Marge Piercy's *Woman on the Edge of Time* and the more sophisticated (and more hateful) reviews of Adrienne Rich's *Of Woman Born*.

3. The paralysis of the "open secret," everyone reassured about their generosity and your safety—*except you*. Or the (even worse) open secret

which everybody knows *except you,* a closet so vanishingly small that it's collapsed into a one-dimensional point and extruded itself (possibly) into some other universe, where it may be of use, but not in this one. A well-meaning woman friend, upon learning that I was a Lesbian, "That's all right. It's nobody's business but yours."

4. Some white male reviewer in the *New York Times* speaking slightingly of the *irredentism*[7] of minority groups in our time. The Boys never cease to amaze me.

5. That isn't an issue.

That isn't an issue *any more.*

That isn't *really* an issue any more.

Therefore why do you keep *bringing it up?*

You keep *bringing it up* because you are crazy.

You keep *bringing it up* because you are destructive.

You keep *bringing it up* because you want to be annoying.

You keep *bringing it up* because you are greedy and selfish.

You keep *bringing it up* because you are full of hate.

You keep *bringing it up* because you want to flaunt yourself.

You keep *bringing it up* because you deliberately want to separate yourself from the rest of the community.

How do you expect me to support a person as crazy/destructive/annoying/selfish/hateful/flaunting/separatist as you are?

I really cannot support someone as *bad* as that.

Especially since there is no really important issue involved.

6. Vaginas do *not* have sharp little teeth! Pass it on.

Notes

1. And only *if* we had made love.

2. Up to about a year ago.

3. I don't mean that such men are "really" homosexual. That's going back to the model of the heterosexual institution again. They've suppressed a good deal of themselves, although what is allowed to exist isn't necessarily false.

4. I have only recently become aware of the extent of my own woman-hating and my own valuing of male bodies as more important, valuable, strong and hence "beautiful" than

female bodies. Even a Lesbian wouldn't want an (ugh) *woman!* Even if she loved her. Feelings of inferiority climb into bed with you.

5. I'm talking of "masochism" as most women I know understand it: i.e. humiliation, shame, embarrassment, impersonality, *emotional misery.* Physical pain was not part of it; oddly enough, physical pain is what most men I know assume to be "masochism."

6. "Female Sexual Alienation" by Linda Phelps, reprinted in *The Lavender Herring: Lesbian Essays from* The Ladder, eds. Grier and Reid, (Baltimore, Md.: Diana Press, 1976) pp. 161-170. Ms. Phelps does not address herself exclusively to gay women. I think in this area she's probably right not to, as I suspect the mechanisms are the same for both, though one would suffer more symbolic distortion and the other more total obliteration.

7. Italian radicalism of the late 19th century calling for a unification of all the Italian-speaking peoples, i.e. nationalism: by extension, fighting for the rights of a group which perceives itself to have common interests. How wicked.

Gale Jackson

From the precision of the embrace:
clove and challdice

rise sally rise.

how body becomes home; becomes firm as floors and foundations to
build from. sunlight wakes her. the loud silence overcomes
her dreams. city dreams. in a cab. she sits
up. locusts thump. the old mule brays. a rooster
crows. chickens, sweeping the dirt yard with their fitful
wings, scatter. the sea repeats and repeats its
monotone. the mysterious thing that lives between the ceiling
and roof scurries back and forth over her head. she looks at
the clock and rises, hesitant, to close the shutters the other
woman had opened to the night. challdice, she thought to
herself, was afraid of the dark.

body. home. floor. shutters. she stands looking back
at sleep's knotted arms. then she goes to the kitchen to warm
black bread and to make tea; one sweet, one without, both dark and
strong and pungent.

outside the window locusts are devouring the petunia tree by
covering it with their bodies and eating and eating until one,
its belly full, might drop to the earth and another take its
place. hand suspended on the shutters she watches them,
remembering how they came flying in like a dark cloud on july's
tail. from habit she looks towards the eastern sky,
anticipating the next sounds. the roar of engines fills her

waiting and from the shadow of the sun reconnaissance planes drone
into sight. morning maneuvers. like one large angry bird,
three planes chart a steep ascent and then, whipping at the
western clouds, turn quickly and in unison back towards the
base. she draws back the shutters. the dogs whimper behind
her and, to let challdice sleep, she hurries to fill their
pan. steps out into a wet morning. the sunlight
brilliant. she spits. the dogs are eating a rabbit between
them and their mouths are bloody and thick with fur. challdice
gives them water, the house gives them porch shade. the other
americans have named them lady and fred but they are wild
dogs. they run in brambles. they hunt their prey for food.

"nayah, dio, thria, thresera, pendi, exey, epti, octo…"
"baby!" she calls back "baby!" she laughs a little nervous,
concerned, coming barefoot quiet through the hallway so as not to
startle the sleeptalking awake.

"ndecka, thodecka, deckathria…"

"baby" she says finally, softly, gently reaching to wake
challdice who is nested in the blankets, the wool, the *fokati*,
even in this summer's heat. "wake up chad…" she paused, in
her eyes   the twisted mouth   "wake up chad you talkin' in
your sleep."

she jumps up bright-eyed and wild. hair standin' up. "i was
counting it back"
"it's okay chad it's really okay." she gathers her up in her arms, all
of it; the girl, the pillows, the blankets, the dreams, the
books, the pencils, the masses of hair. "hush. hush. no wonder
you have bad dreams with all this shit in the bed with you."
"i was counting it back. there was too many people
killed. we couldn't get out…"
"hush."
"we couldn't get out. it was all on fire. i was looking for
you. we was trapped on the wrong side and i was looking for

you and i was counting it back like dorothy going back to kansas
after oz."
"baby" she laughed now, a teasing laugh "baby come on"
"ain't no after oz wife"
"hhhush!"
"i'm losing it.   these dreams" she shakes her head.
she tightens her arms around her. "it's okay chad it's okay just hold
me, just hold on."

how body becomes home how hand becomes direction how tired limbs
embrace.   roosters crow.   chickens scatter.   mule
brays.   sheep bleat.   locust thump.   corn
whispers.   locusts feed.   planes dot the sky.   the women
embrace.

Minnie Bruce Pratt

#70 *Lower Matecumbe Beach*

I was telling Janis about the midnight you and I
played the is-she? game outside the 7-11, eyed
the women, hair-cut, nail-length, shoe-style,
was the walk like a sailor on ground always
moving? someone who walks on water every day,
and the look telescopic? far to near, an embrace
bold, unnoticed in the line for eggs and cigarettes:
like the two who almost fooled us, sweater twinsets,
tinted blondes, no touching, heads up, straight
except through plate glass we watched them bend
to a trivial decision, poking at bread, what kind,
their bodies rocking together, a rush, hot wind
shaking the waves, as we hooted and shook the car,
made them with our looks, waiting for the Sunday paper,
late Saturday night. Janis said: *Sounds like a far-
out movie.* Yes, that's what we've said of us. So why

isn't someone filming? They've already missed wild
scenes, like when we were miserable and arrived
at Matecumbe Beach. Traffic back-up on the Keys,
locked on the room-wide island by accident. Speed
out of the car, slam both doors, down to white clay
and aquamarine. We begin to forgive in the water, wade
out the deep edge. Behind, cars rim the horizon, chrome
north to south. Hundreds of tourists ramble and groan
past the silver snack truck, the man selling UFO

kites, a rescue squad, a young man grinning with suntan
oil, a heterosexual pair holding a beer, legs fanned
limp on a towel. All stare out to sea except one woman
who seems asleep, straw hat flat on her face.

We are the only swimmers in the water. It could be
a helicopter zoom-in, first scene in the movie,
us up to our thighs in transparent water, sidling
deeper, up to our hips, arched feet gliding
on slick bottom, a tease of waves, idling,
fondling through murk our feet make, toes nipped
by unseen faint pain. Facing, you unzip,
your breasts bob, naked pearl, shocking. I grip
you, and you slip fingers up my sagging pants,
up my cunt, twist, gritty thrust. The sea demands,
cross-purpose. You push me up, off-balance,
and who will get me? Open to terror, the waves,
but you are rocking me on your hand, take me, take
me, and I begin to come in the white glare of waves,
a roaring I think is me, but keeps going, and you
shake me, jelly, say, *Don't worry*. It's a big blue
motorboat showing off deeper, sputter, zoom,
might as well have been helicopter with camera,
the way you had me in front of the seven-mile jam.

We'd been fighting days about sex, the cool sham
of not touching, pretence, the jealous friend, shame,
our hands clenched, anger and us so hot, in flames,
the ocean likely boiled around us, steamed,
all the tourists with mouths open, but who knows?
No one was filming, and we were focused on up close.

So that got missed, and the next scene, where I tore
up this, first version, like my own flesh. We'd fought
about what it meant, to touch, not touch, how we'd sought
lovely lust, and how to talk it, show it, how we'd fucked,
made love, what words shall I use? How we'd fought

to have each other out in the open, more than a game.

I wish you could have me now instead of this long same
scene: distance, me at the typewriter, you in the darkroom,
necessary but monotonous.

                         Not like Matecumbe Beach,
or my fantasies of how we could both drive maniac and meet
halfway. What's on the map? West Hazleton, or Frackville,
or MacAdo, a drive through lumpy snow to some chill
slushy parking lot, jump out and rush you, what a thrill,
your tongue pushed hot in my mouth. You have me on your hip,
right there, another scene, one of a lifetime, and why isn't
someone with a movie camera getting this all down on film?

2/27/88
for Joan

Minnie Bruce Pratt

#65 *Parked Down by the Potomac*

We don't say we're too old for this.
Instead I pick you up at your house, slide
over to passenger, and you're driving
me around at midnight, straight scotch,
bourbon and water in glasses engraved
B, from no wedding of ours.
                                    Parked
down by the Potomac, we drink and talk
about football and politics by the grey-
green cold molten luminescent water.
Your tongue probes my mouth, hot, hotter.
Making out down by the river, like back home,
no truck, but you in your baseball cap, tough
and dykey like no one else who ever drove
me anywhere. Your wide small hands cover
my side, hot.
                        Covering me: was the beginning
then? We disagree on how to count the years,
but here we are by one of our calendars,
end of the summer, September, starting up again.
The crickets complain, somewhat pitiful,
and we don't care.
                              We drive off, windows
down, you with bare forearms, sleeves rolled up,
seductive with hidden soft inner elbows.

Your hands turn and glimmer on the wheel.
We talk and I watch, wanting your hands on me,
wanting you to turn me over, over, turn me.

10/5/87
for Joan

Anna Livia

Lust and the Other Half

THE BEGINNING OF THE DROUGHT IN JEAN AND ROWENA'S SEXUAL RELATIONS HAD coincided with Melanctha Adam's visit to London on a lecture tour promoting her new book, *My Life as a Sex Radical*. Rowena, assiduously practising to be young and impressionable, had got caught up in Melanctha adulation. Jean suspected Rowena's new interest had arisen in order to fill the gap which sex usually occupied. Jean had recently taken to supporting Stella Maris, Melanctha's opposite number, as it were, in the faint hope that a good argument might stimulate a good time in bed. If Rowena's dalliance with the New Orthodoxy gave her no more than an expanded vocabulary with which to discuss what she and Jean did in bed, or rather, had done in bed before Rowena took her body away, that would be better than Jean's misgivings allowed her to hope for. In the back of her mind lurked the nagging anxiety that all this "sexual articulation," as Rowena put it, was an elaborate mask to hide what was really wrong between them. The words, the concepts had been in common lesbian parlance for at least the millennium; the trouble was that Rowena could not bring herself to use them. She'd had only one woman lover before Jean, who, Jean was convinced, was part of the problem.

Jean yearned to open her loving arms once again to sweet, succulent Rowena for a long night of mouths and skin and flesh and sweet, old-fashioned lesbian sex, the naked, woman-to-woman kind with all the fingers, tongues, and tenderness God had given them and without extraneous items like dildos, leather straps, sex manuals, sex therapists, and kitchen sinks. All the paraphernalia which served only to take their precious attention away from each other at a moment when "paying attention" was the only possible point of the encounter.

"Melanctha Adam's such a goddamn liberal, you'd have your work cut out to make her sound even half-assed. Picked her name out of Gertrude Stein and never bothered to read the story it came from," sneered Jean. Anger always made her scornful.

"Melanctha is warm, friendly, and charming," Rowena pouted. "You only call her liberal because she doesn't try to censor anybody."

"What's charm got to do with it?" snapped Jean. "She was speaking at a conference, not a dinner party." Jean did not want to have this argument. She did not want to argue on these terms. And here she was, right in the middle, as usual.

"Talking of dinner, did you hear about the time Stella Maris got invited to Gloria's? They say she was worse than an obstreperous parrot, biting teeth and shitting on silk shirt sleeves."

"Melanctha on a public platform is like Donald Duck trying to tap dance. Whereas Stella has a brain the size of a satellite dish. And she has the strength of her convictions."

"So has Melanctha."

"There is no strength in Melanctha's politics. She's pro-SM, pro-public sex, pro-paedophilia..."

"At least Melanctha's in favour of something. Stella's just anti-sex. Probably never had an orgasm."

"Neither have I," muttered Jean. "Not for so long I'm surprised I remember what it means. Must be a race memory."

Studiously, Rowena ignored her lover's mutter.

"Stella is pro-lesbian," declared Jean. If they weren't going to have sex, at least she could win the argument.

"Melanctha is pro-lesbian," Rowena returned, giving not an inch.

"Must be thinking of different lesbians," Jean sighed. While Rowena was busy regarding lesbian sexuality as a delicious secret only recently unearthed by the bravery of the sex radicals, there was very little Jean could say. No hint of judgement (and certainly no physical practice) was to interfere with the delicate unveiling process. If in doubt you consulted a manual, not the woman at the launderette, your neighbour, your lover, or your own body.

"Rowena," Jean said, patiently, "that woman thinks sadism's just one of life's adventures."

"Oh I know," chirruped sweet Rowena. "But I've met some of those

SM women. When I went to hear Melanctha. They're very young, you know. They were nice, held the door for me."

"They were, doubtless, polite."

"And I saw this punk girl, about sixteen, very frightening to look at, in Piccadilly Circus…"

"Punks aren't, necessarily, into SM."

"They wear the same clothes," asserted Rowena. "This tramp had a fit or something, right there on the pavement, and no one did anything except the punk. She stepped right in and stuck her fingers down his throat."

"Oh good," said Jean. What could she say when this innocence Rowena was so determined to safeguard was exactly what had attracted her in the first place?

"Rowena, I'm not talking about kind-hearted sixteen-year-olds. In California, Pam Fornica carved a swastika on her lover's shoulder. There are women who have had to have hysterectomies, women who are permanently incontinent and will need to wear nappies for the rest of their lives because of SM encounters. Can you imagine…?"

"Yes!" Rowena shouted. "You always do this. Every time. You…you…you tell me things! Like that awful book, *Gyn/Ecology*. Full of horrors. You do it to up the ante, don't you Jean? Talk about an SM relationship, what do you think we've got?"

Jean could think of absolutely nothing to say. She might as well be throwing bottles into the sea, there was as much chance of a rational reply.

Rowena stormed off to work, for which she was already late. Every time. Every bloody time. She and Jean had what seemed to Rowena a perfectly equal exchange of opinions, and then Jean would lift the whole discussion from under her and throw down something so hideous that all she could do was beg, "Don't tell me about it." Rowena was tired of having the wind knocked out of her. It was not fair. There was Jean's experience of SM, taken from books, Rowena suspected, since Jean had never been to California, and there was Rowena's experience of SM, taken from real live women she had actually met. Two subjective accounts, each equally possible, though Rowena's was always nicer. And every bloody time Jean's version won. How could you have a relationship with a woman on the basis that she win every argument? And if Jean really felt as contemptuous of Rowena's reasoning as she appeared, then what the hell was she doing in a relationship with Rowena? Was it Rowena's inferiority which attracted her? Huh. Rowena wished, as always, that she had put this to Jean while they were arguing but, as always, she had chickened out. Jean had more experience of everything than Rowena, who had had only one lesbian relationship before, and even then she had never dared tell Jean the truth about it.

Rowena was cycling along the tow path of the Kensal canal, past the new Sainsbury's and the lone fishermen, the trees and tombstones of the two graveyards casting thick shadows on the filthy water, when something caught her eye. Only a very persistent, and very flamboyant, something had a hope in hell of catching Rowena's eye. She was not so much upset as shaken, shocked, though New Orthodoxy people declared themselves unshockable. This something was so persistent that it followed Rowena's bicycle, sitting doggedly in her peripheral vision. It was as flamboyant as a champagne magnum bobbing about in an urban canal. Exactly as flamboyant, for a champagne magnum is what it turned out to be. Rowena fished it out with distracted fury. Inside was a slip of paper. She found a lolly stick by a clump of balding grass, stuck it through the neck of the bottle and scrabbled for the piece of paper.

"Every orgasm a wanted orgasm," it said.

Rowena, unused to being apostrophised in this manner by subaqueous anima, was a little nonplussed. Nonplussed is a thoroughly English state and Rowena spent a lot of her time in it. It is peculiarly suited to situations where emotion is required, but one is not quite sure which. Eventually, alas, one has to settle for one. Surprise would have been perfectly appropriate. Like a young doe, a lady may be gracefully startled on almost any occasion. Unfortunately, Rowena was not surprised; she expected communication from strangers. She had the sort of sweet, round face and small, chubby figure which inspire confidence and make of their owner a perfect best friend. Only the vehicle of this communication was unusual. Messages in bottles come from foreign shores and require painstaking translation from the classical Aramaic before the heroine can be rescued. Rowena had fished the champagne magnum out of a swell of old tyres, bits of wood, used durex and a bent syringe. The Kensal canal is not the most romantic glade.

"Who are you?" Rowena wrote back on a torn piece of shopping list. Questions are a useful fielding tactic. She placed her message in an inkpot newly emptied for the occasion. One might sacrifice two fluid ounces of blue black for the pleasure of a new thought. Rowena giggled. How could you have an orgasm against your will? "That's like saying you can't have sex against your will," Jean's voice answered implacably. Rowena flung the inkpot into the canal and flounced back onto her bike, but Jean's voice continued, "Incest survivors have had orgasms when they were raped. It's just a physiological reaction." Rowena sped off again, riding straight over a fishing line in her anxiety to get away from Jean and her horror stories.

That afternoon another bottle awaited her.

"I am the lesbian who turns the page and makes a cup of tea when the sex scene begins. Why can't we leave our heroines to attend each other in private?"

"I think we should be grateful to the lesbians who have opened up our sexuality as an area of contemplation," Rowena replied primly in a mixed-herbs jar. The New Orthodoxy dictated that in the bad old days lesbians had not talked about sex, thereby creating sadomasochism, but that all this had changed now that a few brave women were saying loudly and clearly that they liked to fuck and, what's more, so had their mothers. Quite why adult women had to call upon the shades of their ancestors, Rowena did not know. Evidently there were subtleties as yet beyond her. She hoped in time to sophisticate even those remote out-posts of naïveté still maculating her psyche. Meanwhile she was relieved to have an opinion and be able to trot it out as firmly as though she had coined it herself.

"Since when have lesbians not talked about sex, written about sex, dreamed about sex?" demanded the next message.

Maybe the message writer was unaware of the New Orthodoxy. Rowena decided to start small. It was nice to be able to talk about these things without anyone yelling at her.

"Have you heard of political lesbianism?"

The answer came back so fast, the bottle might have been waiting in the water before Rowena even threw hers in.

"You're going to tell me it's a theory that a lesbian is a woman who, for political reasons, does not fuck men. You're going to tell me it leaves out the main point: sex with women, lust, desire, craving, salivation. You're going to tell me all about compulsory heterosexuality and the lesbian continuum. Then you're going to say that the continuum belittles sex. You have decided to bore my pants off, which, I suppose, is one way to do it." Rowena was nonplussed again. Well, to be honest, she was somewhat minussed. It is hard to have the strength of your convictions when they are on loan from someone else.

"What do you want?" she wrote.

"Debate, discussion, the clash of cymbalic minds."

"Fancy yourself, don't you?"

"Now you're talking. How about a little verbal sparring. Or even a lot. Just don't give me any more clichés."

But Rowena had, at last, decided on an attitude. She was going to be affronted.

"I am tired of these damp diatribes under glass," she wrote. "I am a dyke of the eighties. I eat fast food and drive at 120 mph. I'm excited by the work of the sex radicals because it puts lust back on the map. I read lesbian detective stories and have no dependents; not that I'm undependable, I'm just good at stating my needs. I never asked to be a lesbian activist. I want to be a word processor and rule the world like the others."

"Yeah?" came the reply in a fiery Tabasco sauce bottle. "Bet you call prostitutes 'sex workers' 'n' all."

But Rowena did not stoop to fish it out. She by-passed the canal and rode to work by Meanwhile Gardens. She wore tight fawn trousers, the kind which look like tights which straight women approaching forty imagine will allow them to pass for twenty. The dyke of the eighties is passing for a straight woman passing for twenty.

Rowena had misgivings. New Orthodoxy lesbians were, liberatedly, butch or femme and while it was quite clear to her who was which in her relationship with Jean, she had become a lesbian because she was looking for someone like herself. What's more, she had found one, and it wasn't Jean. That was the relationship she had had with Edith, the one she did not want Jean looking too closely at. But it was irrelevant now; Rowena hadn't seen Edith for five years. There was more to it than that; there was always more to everything. Things were complicated enough already without going into Edith. There were some ideas Rowena found it difficult to reconcile; sexual attraction was meant to be based on differ-ence and yet what Rowena yearned for was the balm of like minds. Oth-erwise you'd sleep with men, wouldn't you. You couldn't have sex with a woman just because heterosexuals don't want you to. Surely the les-bian had to want to.

"Labia labia labia cunt clitoris vagina," Rowena chanted aloud quickly, and swivelled her chair three times to exorcise her blasphemy. Maud, her co-worker, glanced up, gave her a considering glance and went back to her database.

Rowena imagined a series of New Orthodoxy penances: three labia and a vulva for suggesting that lesbian sex can be boring; a vulva and an anus for saying it in print; six hot wet throbbing cunts for not putting your hand up your partner's dress while dancing in a crowded bar. How many did you get if neither you nor your partner owned a dress? Rowena had always known she went about sex all wrong. Now New Or-thodoxy had provided her with standards: lots and often; you can never be too loud or too public. Rowena began to write a message, not on the screen where Maud could intercept it, but on the back of an envelope.

"Can you be a lesbian and not like sex?"

Rowena gazed round for a bottle. There was a nearly empty atomizer on Maud's desk. Rowena took it and put the note inside. She dropped it in the canal by Sainsbury's that night while filling her shopping trolley.

The morning brought two responses, one from Maud, the other from the message writer.

"Have you seen my atomizer?" said Maud's.

"Elucidate your own paradox," said the other.

Rowena tried to settle to work, but Maud would fuss.

"Have you seen my atomizer? I'm sure I left it right here on the win-dow sill. I always leave it there, next to the plants. Well? Have you?"

"What?"

"Seen it?"

"I threw it away."

"You threw it away? What do you mean, threw it away? Where?"

"In the canal. What does it matter? Don't make such a fuss."

"You threw my atomizer away? In the canal? Why? Just tell me that—why?"

"It was empty. It was practically empty. What's the big deal?"

"You don't throw things away because they're empty, Rowena. You fill them up. What am I to spray the air plants with now?"

"I'll buy you a new one."

"I don't understand you. You shout sex words to yourself, you've been late every day this week and you throw other people's atomizers in the canal. What's the matter? You in love?"

"Probably."

"Well, do something. Consummate it. My plants aren't safe with you in this state."

Rowena nodded. This was recognizable New Orthodoxy advice. When in doubt: have sex; no doubt: have sex. Rowena wrote a note.

"You said you were the lesbian who makes a cup of tea when the sex scene starts, and picks the book up again once they've finished and had time to arrange themselves? Well, I sit through those films: *Cunts I Have Creamed, Rise and Rise of Hermione's Clitoris,* you know the ones, with the glorious parade of wet red, or purple, vulvas, and I fall asleep. I wake myself up snoring sometimes and have to pretend I just came like all the others. Reminds me of those movies by Chantal Akerman where the heroine washes up plate after plate after plate."

As soon as this was written, and before she could have second thoughts, Rowena told Maud she would take the post out, jumped on her bicycle and pedaled furiously down to the canal. She felt excited, as though she had just understood, or was just about to understand, something important. That sex without emotion didn't turn her on? No. She was immeasurably emotional about Jean, only miserably inferior. She sat on the bank and gazed sightless as a pair of black rubber flippers floated past. There was a damp paper sticking out of the foothold.

"Explicit sex amounts to no more than naked genitals and multiple orgasm. We are led so far up the garden path we are lost in the potting shed." Their messages must have crossed on the crest of a wave. Rowena felt despondent. The correspondence was exciting, and certainly romantic, but it had begun to feel like an elaborate game. Rowena wanted a person as well as a thought. She sat for a while on the tow path, opposite the tombstones, and remembered what had made her a lesbian. She was not tempted to write it down. It probably would not have made sense if you hadn't lived through it.

◆ ◆ ◆

Rowena had slept with a lot of people, men and women. But what made her a lesbian was her best friend, Edith, and Edith she had never slept with. Edith wouldn't, but for Rowena it hadn't mattered. Rowena would have agreed never to have sex again if only she and Edith could live together forever and be devoted to each other. Edith was the first person she had met for whom she was prepared to give up sex. It was contrary to all New Orthodoxy precepts, but it was the unadorned truth. Rowena, in common with many basically untruthful people, had great respect for the truth when it suddenly thrust itself upon her. She did not know what to do with this new treasure except to gaze at it, turn it around, poke it. What had been so glorious about Edith was the way she and Rowena matched each other. They had it down to a fine art: intonation, clothes, mannerisms. One could take the phone receiver out of the other's hand and continue her conversation, having not only the same voice, but the same opinions. It was too late, and too enormous, to mourn Edith, and Jean was so different from Rowena. Was it possible for lesbians to be "different but equal"? Rowena remembered Jean's expression when asked her opinion of Rowena's new slimfit fawn trousers. It was not for this Rowena had become a lesbian; but if lust is off limits to soul-mates, how could she be a lesbian at all?

Rowena imagined a series of soft touches and delicate gestures, appreciative laughter. If they could not be the same, surely they could savour their differences? As she trailed her hand in the water, breaking the perfect, perpetually changing rainbow of an oil spot, Rowena remembered the slow blossoming of lust, one sweet afternoon when she had surprised Jean by turning on *The Marriage of Figaro* and dancing, dancing, dancing. Alone at first. Clothed, at first. And all the time kissing, and all the time, to the beat. Rowena's finger was slithering over Jean's devoted clitoris, hand drenched with one last orgasm, then Jean's hand inside her, four thighs parted, knees and heels bending, tapping, and Cherubino was crooning that she finds no peace and can't honestly say that she minds, when a woman with a shopping bag grimaced,

"Blimey. They tell you not to litter Britain, but they don't provide any litter bins."

"In Britain," said Rowena, "They expect you to take your litter home with you."

Rowena was tempted to chuck one last message into the canal, but it would be better to tackle Jean face to face. As she rode back along the tow path she noticed an unlikely-looking blue medicine phial dipping up and down in the water but did not stop to fish it out. The phial bobbed on, propelled by a slight wash from a slow gliding barge, to be pulled in and unscrewed by another mysterious stranger who would read, with perplexity and pleasure,

"You are not my other half, nor has my soul a mate. But stretch out your hand and I will take it, show me your step and I will pace it, give me the favour of your faith."

Chrystos

Your Tongue Sparkles

sun on water now in my mouth memory rich as real
kisses I understand to my root   to bone ancestors where red
& so new   you speak without calluses despite our scars
Woman down my throat you stir my heart nectar where bitterness
has fought to seed
O you rainy tongue   you amaryllis tongue   you early spring
tongue   you smooth black leather tongue   you firemoon tongue
you goosebumps tongue   you soft bites tongue   you feather
tongue   you take me all in tongue   you fill me up tongue
you butter tongue   you maple syrup tongue   you rising
wind tongue   you creamy silky tongue
you fine fine tongue
you knows the way
tongue

I Could Carve

these words in stones to leave on the moon or farther
Dark black smooth ones   Pink gray dappled beach granite
Green ones with white feather smoke lines   I could weave
your name through every muscle of my body black with longing to be
in
you   Have your mouth & fingers take me farther than the moon
dappled with colors I've seen only in my sleep while your body
prays beside mine through smooth nights   No more bones cocks
horses drag me in terror   These answers in your feather green
eyes   whose questions were dark until near a fire
at the beach you sat on a driftwood log   our eyes were one light
while the sun considered farther shores   You walked with me
as I carried buckets of salt water to douse forgotten flames
whose smoke I smell in my hair now as your hands
collect me carefully   sorting colors for smooth cloth
tied with feathers   My heart hears your voice   gallops
like black silk   You brush me   my muscles ripple dreams
Our smoky thighs dapple stars
I put my questions under stones   Lap you
in
Shores of desire drink me with new horses whose feet of smoke dance
on the moon weaving answers through every moment
Suns in our bellies as we dream of sleeping beside each other
until through a fire of years

we are no more than dust rolling itself into stones
Our fingers traced with granite where we've carved our bodies Our
in

for BJ Collins

Robin Becker

The Subject of Our Lives

The storm has started and they say it won't stop.
Not for you, hanging on in the office after everyone has left.
Not for the ponies in my friend's paddock, huddled and still
and turning white. I know from your voice that you like
this moment—a Friday afternoon, the city between us, a few hours
of paperwork before you can think of dinner or a movie

or sex. I have been thinking about the snowstorm, and about a woman
from Chicago who put me on skis and ordered me to follow her
into the woods. That was years ago, and I've stopped thinking
about her, except during blizzards, everybody powerless and stuck
without milk or cream. Now I see that love is really
the subject of our lives: the authority with which you opened

your jacket and placed my hand, rigid, near frostbite,
against your breast, waiting for the heat to make its miraculous
leap; the gentle rabbi leading my parents from my sister's grave.
The ponies stir at the sound of grain hitting a metal bucket,
carried by a woman who regulates their hungers. How many times
have I confused hunger and love, love and power? My head ached

for years, it seemed, following someone's beautiful back.
My sister wouldn't sleep or wake beside one person long enough to
learn something. *Trust me,* you say, and I'm struck by the force
of your voice, the imperative form of any verb spoken in bed.

Come home.

No, stay where you are. Longing will serve us while snow thickens the sidewalks, delays the subways, tightens every street in town.

Then

I was due home at seven, and you were
staying downtown. We shared a premature
glass of white wine.
                    "I'll walk you downstairs."
                                            "Sure."
Out on the dim landing, you pushed the door
shut behind us, one hand on the small
of my back, then, pushed me back against the wall
hung with winter coats. I almost slipped
in the half-dark; half-gasped as you unzipped
my pants and tugged them down, silencing my
exclamation with your tongue, your thigh
opening mine. I grabbed your ass with one
hand, hair with the other. You began
stroking my belly, but I pulled you close
against me, covering what you'd exposed.
You whispered, "Should I get down on my knees
and lick you?"
              "No, with your hand, like that, there, please!"
Mouth on your mouth, I rode you, barely stand-
ing up, or standing it. You moved your hand
past where I put it, through the parting, wet
for you already, spread me, and I let
you deep in, while your lips went soft beneath
my mouth, and I tasted salt behind your teeth.
Your fingers brought the juices down around

what swelled into your palm, until you found
where it would come from. Inches of my bare
skin burned against your jeans. Into your hair
I pleaded, "Let me," but you wouldn't; pulled
a centimeter back, instead. The chill
air on my skin pulsed through me like a smack,
and, for a breath, I let my head fall back
against the linen sleeves and woolen folds,
then drew you onto me, so I could hold
myself up to your kisses, while you took
me, out and in, with your whole hand. I shook,
off balance, needed it, you, just there. I
thrust up against you. Then my inner thigh
muscles convulsed, and I bore down on you,
wrenching out "Now!" as heat arrowed into
the place you had me, till I couldn't stop
it coming, crushed against you, half on top
of you, or you on me, breathed through your lips
a huge, collapsing sigh. Arms around my hips,
holding my ass, you kissed me as I hung
on your shoulders, prodded my hair back with your tongue.
You covered me till I recovered my
balance, and my butt, to say, "Good-bye."
"Call you later."
                    "Ummm." Buttoned, I pushed
away, blinking, stepped back. "I've got to rush!"
and watched my footing down three rickety
flights toward twilight traffic in Chelsea.

Pat Parker

aftermath

for Marty

Did you know I watch you
as you cuddle with sleep?
Propped on my elbow,
close, your breath brushes
back silence
like a swimmer parting water.
Your lips are tight
now.
If I close my eyes
they become a cool drink
full and wet
house an active tongue
that travels my body
like an explorer
retracing familiar ground.

If I close my eyes
I can feel your tongue
dart
from my ear
to my neck
to the crevice
a prospector
pause to take samples
inspect the ore
then move on.

If I close my eyes
I can feel your tongue
wrap around my nipples
tuck them
deep
in the corner
of your mouth
and suck them
suck them
parched flowers.

If I close my eyes
oh love
if I close my eyes
I become once again
your hopeless captive
ready to submit.

I think of the
straight person who
asks what do you
do in bed?
Oh
how many times
have I
asked the same thing.

Dorothea Smartt

The Passion of Remembrance

Well!
I've always wondered
how those Nigerian sistahs
did move in those tight-ass skirts!
My skirt
flares out
from below my knees—so I could still
twis' an' shout
flash my leg through the slit
split on my lef' side

But y'know which part of me feels confined?
Well!
In this skirt I will not be slow-dancing
with some nice-looking sistah
We willnot sit face-to-face
her knee my knee
between each other's legs
fingers tracing patterns on the inside of my thigh
making me hold my breath
and count to ten

We willnot dance
legs entwined sending the pulse of the music
holding each other with legs and arms
bodies tightly together

I willnot
open your legs wide with mine
caan mek she hip-bone grine wid mine
I willnot wear the bruises of such passion

I willnot be lying back
vunerable in surrender in anticipation
of your mouth leaning
on me in me

Nun'na dat!
I'm bound from my wais' down
my bum an' thighs held tightly together
for no woman (or man for that matter)
So how do I get my serious pleasure?
In spite of padded bra slip an' tight blouse?
will my nipples still feel
extra-sensory-perception
when they brush your full breasts?

"Nice-girls" doan sit wid d'legs open
and let the sun stream into them
warming them outside in
doan keep d'hands pressed between their legs
hanging onto a memory—
I can still feel your tongue in me
Dancing?!
We making love
wid our close on
a sistah t'sistah art

Beth Brant

Her Name Is Helen

Her name is Helen.
She came from Washington State twenty years ago through
broken routes
of Hollywood, California,
Gallup, New Mexico,
Las Vegas, Nevada,
ended up in Detroit, Michigan where she lives in #413
in the gut of the city.
She worked in a factory for ten years, six months, making
carburetors for Cadillacs.
She loved factory work.
She made good money, took vacations to New Orleans.
"A real party town."

She wears a cowboy hat with pretty feathers.
Can't wear cowboy boots because of the arthritis
that twists her feet.
She wears beige vinyl wedgies. In the winter she pulls on
heavy socks to protect her bent toes from the slush and rain.

Helen takes pictures of herself.

Every time she passes those Polaroid booths,
one picture for a dollar,
she closes the curtain and the camera flashes.

When she was laid off from the factory
she got a job in a bar, serving up shots and beer.
Instead of tips, she gets presents from her customers.
Little wooden statues of Indians in headdress.
Naked pictures of squaws with braided hair.
Feather roach clips in fuchsia and chartreuse.
Everybody loves Helen.
She's such a good guy. An honest-to-god Indian.

Helen doesn't kiss.
She allows her body to be held when she's had enough
vodkas and Lite beer.
She's had lots of girlfriends.
White women who wanted to take care of her,
who liked Indians,
who think she's a tragedy.

Helen takes pictures of herself.
She has a picture on a keychain, along with a baby's shoe
and a feathered roach clip.
She wears her keys on a leather belt.
Helen sounds like a chime, moving behind the bar.

Her girlfriends took care of her.
Told her what to wear
what to say
how to act more like an Indian.
"You should be proud of your Indian heritage.
Wear more jewelry.
Go to the Indian Center."

Helen doesn't talk much.
Except when she's had enough
vodkas and Lite beer.
Then she talks about home,
about her mom,
about the boarding schools,

the foster homes,
about wanting to go back to see her people
before she dies.
Helen says she's going to die when she's fifty.

She's forty-two now.
Eight years to go.

Helen doesn't kiss.
Doesn't talk much.
Takes pictures of herself.
She touches women who are white.
She is touched by their hands.

Helen can't imagine that she is beautiful.
That her skin is warm
like redwood and fire.
That her thick black hair moves like a current.
That her large body speaks in languages stolen from her.
That her mouth is wide and full and when she smiles
people catch their breath.

"I'm a gay Indian girl.
A dumb Indian.
A fat, ugly squaw."
This is what Helen says.

She wears a t-shirt with the legend
Detroit
splashed in glitter across her large breasts.
Her breasts that white women have sucked
and molded to fit their mouths.

Helen can't imagine that there are women
who see her.
That there are women
who want to taste her breath and salt.

Who want a speech to be created between their tongues.
Who want to go deep inside her
touch places that are dark, wet,
muscle and spirit.
Who want to swell, expand two bodies into a word
of our own making.

Helen can't imagine that she is beautiful.
She doesn't kiss.
Doesn't talk much.
Takes pictures of herself so she will know she is there.

Takes pictures of herself to prove she is alive.

Helen takes pictures of herself.

Cherríe Moraga

La Ofrenda

STRANGE AS IT MAY SEEM, THERE IS NO OTHER WAY TO BE SURE. COMPLETELY SURE. Well you can never be completely sure but you can try and hold fast to some things. Smell is very important. Your eyes can fool you. You can see things that aren't there. But not smell. Smell remembers and tells the future. No lying about that.

Smell can make your heart crack open no matter how many locks you have wrapped 'round it. You can't see smell coming so it takes you off guard, unaware. Like love. That's why it can be your best friend or worst enemy depending on the state of your heart at the time.

Smell is home or loneliness.

Confidence or betrayal.

Smell remembers.

Tiny never went with women because she decided to. She'd always just say, "I follow my nose." And she did and it got her ass nearly burned plenty of times, too, when the scent happened to take her to the wrong side of town or into the bed of the wife of someone she'd wish it hadn't in the morning.

She hated to fight. That was the other problem. She never stuck around for a fight. "The only blood I like," she'd say, "is what my hand digs out of a satisfied woman." We'd all tell Tiny to shut her arrogant mouth up and get her another drink.

Christina Morena stood in front of me in the First Holy Communion line. Then by Confirmation, Tiny'd left most of us girls in the dust. Shot up and out like nobody's business. So, Christina, who everyone called Tina, turned to Tiny overnight and that's the name she took with her into "the life." Given her size, it was a better name to use than Christina and certainly better than mine, Dolores. Dottie, they used to call me years later in some circles, but it never stuck cuz I was the farthest thing from a freckled-faced bony-kneed gabacha. Still, for a while, I tried it. Now, I'm back to who I was before. Just Lolita. Stripped down. Not so different from those Holy Communion days, really.

When we were kids, teenagers, we came *this* close to making it with each other. *This* close. I don't know what would've happened if we had, but I couldn't even've dreamed of doing it then. Yeah, I loved Tiny probably more than I loved any human being on the face of the earth. I mean I loved her like the way you love familia like they could do anything— steal, cheat, lie, murder, and you'd still love them because they're your blood. Sangre. Tiny was my blood. My blood sister. Maybe that's why we didn't do it back then. It'd be like doing it with your mother. No, your sister. Tiny was my sister like no sister I've ever had and she wanted me and I left her because she'd rather pretend she didn't and I was too stupid to smell out the situation for what it really was. I kept watching what was coming outta her damn mouth and there wasn't nothing there to hear. No words of love, commitment, tenderness. You know, luna de miel stuff. There was just her damn solid square body like a tank in the middle of my face with tears running down her cheeks and her knees squeezed together like they were nailed shut on that toilet, her pants like a rubber band wrapped down around her ankles and I ran from her as fast as my cola could take me.

"Fuck fuck chinga'o, man, fuck!"

"Tina…," I can barely hear myself.

"Tiny. The name's Tiny."

"What're you doin' in here?"

"I'm crying, you faggot. That's what you want, isn't it? To see the big bad bitch cry? Well, go get your rocks off somewhere else."

"I don't have rocks."

"In your head!"

But I never loved anyone like I loved Tiny. No body. Not one of those lean white or sleek black ladies that spread their legs for me and my smooth talking. There was blood on my hands and not from reaching into those women but from Tiny's hide. From my barrio's hide. From

Cha Cha's Place where you only saw my ass when the sophisticated college girls had fucked with my mind one too many times. That's something Tiny would have said. We weren't meant to be lovers, only sisters. But being a sister ain't no part-time occupation.

"Lolita Lebrón," that's what they used to call me at Cha Cha's. Of course, they didn't even know who Lolita was until I came in with the story of her with the guys and the guns taking on the whole pinche U.S. Congress. They'd say, "Hey, Lolita, how goes the revolution?" And then they'd all start busting up and I'd take it cuz I knew they loved me, even respected what I was doing. Or maybe it was only Tiny who respected me and all the others had to treat me right cuz of her. Tiny used to say her contribution to La Causa was to keep the girlfriends of the machos happy while they were being too revolutionary to screw.

But it was me she wanted. And I needed my original home girl more than I needed any other human being alive to this day. Growing up is learning to go without. Tiny and me—we grew up too fast.

"Do you think Angie could want me?"

So there we are, fifteen years later, me sitting on the edge of her bed, playing with the little raised parts of the chenille bedspread while my sister there is taking off all her damn clothes, tossing them on the bed, until she's standing bare-ass naked in front of me.

"Look at me." I can't look up. "Lola."

I'm still playing with the balls on the bedspread.

"Look at me. C'mon, I gotta know."

"Tiny, give me a break, man, this is too cold. It's fuckin' scientific, no one looks at people this way."

"You do."

She was right. So, I check her out. There I am staring at her with my two good eyes, the blue one and the brown one, and I knew she wanted my one hundred percent true and honest opinion that she could count on me for that since we were little...so I sat there looking at her for a long time.

"C'mon, man, does it hafta take so long? Jus' answer me."

The blue and the brown eye were working at this one, working hard. I try to isolate each eye, see if I come up with different conclusions depending on which eye and which color I'm working with. Figure one is the European view, the other the Indian.

Tiny goes for her pants. "Fuck you."

And then I smell her, just as she reaches over me.

Her breast falling onto my shoulder, something softening.

A warm bruised stone.

I inhale. Grab her arm.

"No, wait. Let me look at you."

She pulls back against the dresser, holds the pants against her belly, then lets them drop. She's absolutely beautiful. Not magazine beautiful, but thirty-three years old and Mexican beautiful. The dresser with the mirror is behind her. I know that dresser. For years now. It didn't change, but Tiny...she did. The dresser is blonde. "Blonde furniture," very popular among mexicanos in the fifties. We are the children of the fifties. But the fifties have gone and went and in the meantime my Christina Morena went and changed herself into a woman. And in front of this blonde dresser is brown Christina. Christina Morena desnuda sin a stitch on her body and she looks like her mother and my mother with legs like tree trunks and a panza that rolls round into her ombligo como pura meil. And breasts...breasts I want to give back to her, compartir con ella que nos llenan a las dos.

"Well...?" she asks.

And it had never occurred to me that we had grown up. The hair below her belly is the same color as her head. A deep black.

Denso.

Oculto como un nido escondido.

Un hogar distante,

aguardándome.

It didn't stop there. She needed me to touch her, that's all. Is that so much to ask of a person? Angie and her wouldn't last long. Tiny didn't let her touch her. She never let any of 'em touch her.

"Never?"

"Never."

"I don't get it. What do you do then?"

"I do it *to* them."

"But I mean do you...you know?"

"Get off? Yeah. Sure."

"How?"

"Rubbing. Thinking."

"Thinking. Thinking about what?"

"Her. How she's feeling."

"You ever think about yourself?"

"No one's home."

"What?"

"I don't gotta picture, you know what I mean? There's nobody to be. No me to be...not in the bed, anyway."

So, I put my hands inside her. I did. I put them all the way inside her and like a fuckin' shaman I am working magic on her, giving her someone to be.

"Fuck fuck chinga'o man, fuck."

"Shut up," I say.

"What?"

"Don't say shit."

"But...."

"Shhhh." I press my fingers against her lips.

"Don't say nothing, Tiny." Open your mouth and tell me something else....

She smells like copal between the legs. Tiny, Tina who stood in front of me in the First Holy Communion line, smells like

fucking copal

sweet earth sap

oozing outta every pore

that dark bark tree

flesh kissed

I couldn't kiss her, only between the legs

where the mouth there never cussed

where the lips there never curled

into snarls, smoked cigarettes, spit

phlegm into passing pale stubbled faces

mouthing dagger

dyke

jota

mal

flor

I kissed her where she had never spoken

where she had never sang
where...
And then we are supposed to forget. Forget the women we discover
there between the sheets, between the thighs, lies, cries.
 But some things you don't forget
smell.

I close my eyes
and I am rubbing and thinking
rubbing and thinking
rubbing and remembering
what this feels like, to find
my body, una vega
anhelosa, endless
llano
de deseo
Dónde 'stá ella
que me regaló mi cuerpo
como una ofrenda a mí misma?
Ella
Lejana.
Una vez,....mía.
I open my eyes
...Desaparecida.
I would've married Tiny myself if she would've let me. I would've. I
swear to it. But, I was relieved when she put on her pants and told me to
get out. I was relieved because I wouldn't have to work for the rest of my
life loving someone. Tiny.

But I *was* willing to stay. This time I wasn't going nowhere. I mean,
where was there to go, really? The girl was family and I knew her. I
knew her and *still* loved her, so where was there to go? You spend your
whole life looking for something that's just a simple matter of saying,
"Okay, so I throw my lot in with this one." This one woman y ya!

Tiny knew she wouldn't last that long.
She was already telling me in her thirties how tired she was, fighting.
And then I read it, right there in the *LA Times*. All these women, lesbians

who never had babies, getting cancer. They never mention Tiny's name, but Tiny was there, among the childless women, among the dead.

I thought, what's *this* shit? Women don't use their breasts like biology mandates, and their breasts betray them? Is this the lesbian castigo? AIDS for our brothers, cancer for us? Hate thinking like this, hate thinking it's all a conspiracy to make us join the fucking human race.

I burn copal.
Her name rising up with the smoke,
dissolving into the ash morning sky.
Her flesh, softening like the sap
turned rock, returning liquid
to the earth. Her scent inciting…
memory.

I inscribe my name, too.
Tattooed ink in the odorless
flesh of this page.

I, who have only given my breast
to the hungry and grown,
the female and starved,
the women.

I, who have only given my breast to the women.

Joan Nestle

Esther's Story

I HAD HEARD OF ESTHER. SHE WAS TOUGH, A PASSING* WOMAN WHOSE LOVER WAS A prostitute. Sea Colony talk. We all knew stories about each other, but like huge ice floes, we could occupy the same ocean without touching. This night we touched. She was sitting at the bar speaking a soft Spanish to Maria, the bartender from Barcelona. Amidst the noise and smoke, Esther sat straight and still, a small slim woman who dressed butch. Her profile was severe, grey hair rising from her forehead and waving back in the classic DA style. A small mole broke the tautness of her face. I do not remember how our contact began, but at some point I was standing between her legs as she sat with the lights of the bar at her back. Her knees jutted out around me like a sharp cove on a rocky shore. She joked with me, and I worried that I could not hold her attention. I was not sure I wanted to. We were wary of each other, but an erotic need had flashed between us, and neither of us would let it go.

Later that night she offered to take me home. We agreed to go for a drive first. The night was dark, and Esther drove with ease, one hand on the wheel, the other holding her endless cigarette. She told me how she had left Ponce, Puerto Rico, her grown sons, and her merchant-sailor husband, to come to America to live like she wanted. Her family had cursed her, and she had built a new family here in New York. Her life was hard. Her girlfriend gave her a lot of trouble; they both had struggled with drugs, but life was getting better now. She enjoyed driv-

---

*The word *passing* is used here to represent a Lesbian who looked like a man to the straight world. She wore men's clothes and worked at what was considered a man's job, such as driving a taxi or clerking in a stockroom. Language here is inadequate, however. Neither *passing* nor *transvestism* explains the experience of the passing woman. Only she can.

ing the taxi, and because her customers thought she was a man, they never bothered her. I looked at her, at the woman in a neat white shirt and grey pants, and wondered how her passengers could be so deceived. It was our womanness that rode with us in the car, that filled the night with tense possibilities.

Our ride ended in a vast parking lot at Jones Beach. Spotted around the lot were other cars, far enough away from each other so that lovers could have privacy. We sat in silence for a while, with Esther's cigarette a sharp red circle moving in the car's darkness. She put out the light and turned toward me. I leaned into her, fearing her knowledge, her toughness—and then I realized her hands were trembling. Through my blouse, I could feel her hands like butterflies shaking with respect and need. Younger lovers had been harder, more toughened to the joy of touch, but my passing woman trembled with her gentleness. I opened to her, wanting to wrap my fuller body around her leanness. She was pared down for battle, but in the privacy of our passion she was soft and careful. We kissed for a long time. I pressed my breasts hard into her, wanting her to know that even though I was young, I knew the strength of our need, that I was swollen with it. Finally she pulled away, and we started the long drive home. She asked me if she could spend the night. I said no, because I had to get up to go to work in a couple of hours and because I could no longer balance my need for Esther and the fear that I was beginning something I could not control. She said she would call. She told me later that I was the first woman who had said no to her. She said it with admiration, and I felt dishonest. It was not femme purity that kept me from her that night.

A few weeks passed, and I was sitting in the back room of the Sea Colony waiting for Vicki to return from cruising in the front room. A Seven-and-Seven appeared on the table. "Compliments of her," the waitress said, gesturing to the corner. I turned to see Esther smile, constrained but amused. Later in the night, when all things were foggier, I heard a whisper in my ear, "You will be mine." I just saw the shadow of her face before she disappeared.

She called not long after, and I invited her to dinner. I knew I was testing my boundaries, and I think she was too. I was a young femme seeking the response of women I adored, needing their desire deep inside of me. I had brought several women home to my railroad apartment on

East Ninth Street, but usually I was in control: I was sexually more expressive and on my own territory. From the first with Esther, I knew it would be different. I was twenty, and she was forty-five. I was out only two years, and she had already lived lifetimes as a freak. Her sexuality was a world of developed caring, and she had paid a dear price for daring to be as clearly defined as she was.

The day of our dinner dragged at work. I knew I would not have time to change from work clothes and cook dinner before she arrived. At least that was my excuse for staying in my heels, nylons, and dress. But the deeper reason was that I wanted her to see my competent femme self, self-supporting and sturdy, and then I wanted her to reach under my dress, to penetrate the disguise I wore in a world that saw me as having no sexuality because I had neither boyfriend nor husband.

I bought a steak and mushrooms on the way home, prepared a big salad, and set the oval table in the third room, the combined living and bedroom. This was a scene I had prepared many times before, my foreplay of giving. Each time I had felt fear and pride that two women could dare each other so. At seven-thirty she knocked. I opened the door breathlessly, as if I had run a long way. She walked past me and stood in the center of the living room, looking around, while I explained that I had not had time to change. She was wearing a white-on-white shirt with ruffles down the front, sharply creased black pants, and loafers. Her slimness shone clean and sharp. All of a sudden I felt everything in the apartment was too big: I was too big, the table was too full, my need was too big. Esther stood quietly, looking at the set table filled with my offerings.

"Can't I do something for you please," she said. She examined the old apartment until she found a chair that needed fixing. "I'll fix that for you."

"No, no please, you don't have to."

"I want to."

She left and returned in a few minutes with some tools. She turned the chair upside down and repaired it. Only then would she allow herself to sit at my table. "So much food." We both ate very little, weighed down by the erotic tension in the room.

After dinner I asked if she would mind if I took a bath. Since I had started working at age thirteen, I had a need to break the work day from my own time by taking a bath. The hot water marked the border between my world and theirs. Tonight there was another reason as well. I knew we were going to make love and I wanted to be clean for her. Since my tub was in the kitchen and there were no doors between the rooms, it meant she could watch as I bathed. She did not. When I finished, I put on a robe and went to sit next to her. Joan Baez played on the phonograph, and we spoke half in English, half in Spanish about our lives. She asked me about my job, school; I asked her about her girlfriend, driving the taxi.

The room was dark. We always met in darkness it seemed. I knew that soon she would touch me and I was already wet with wanting her. Here, now, on the bed, all the offering would be tested. We both had power in our hands. She could turn from me and leave me with my wetness, my need—a vulnerability and a burden. I could close up, turn away from her caring and her expertise. But neither happened. With extreme tenderness she laid me down. We kissed for a few minutes, and soon her hands knew I was not afraid. She smiled above me, "I know why you took that bath, to be clean for me." We began caring but demanding lovemaking. As I rose to her, she said, "*Dámelo, Juanita, dámelo.*" I strained to take and give to her, to pour my wetness in gratitude upon her hands and lips. But another part of me was not moving. I was trying so hard to be good for her, to respond equally to her fullness of giving, that I could not come. She reached for pillows and put them under my hips. My legs opened wider. I held Esther's head in my hands as her tongue and fingers took my wetness and my need. I had never felt so beautiful. She reached deep into me, past the place of coming, into the center of my womanness. But I could do no more. I put my hand over her lips and drew her up along my body.

"Please, no more. It feels wonderful, and you have given me deep, deep pleasure."

"Come home with me, I have things that will help."

I knew she meant a dildo, and I wanted her to know it was not a lack of skill or excitement that was stopping me. It was her forty years of wisdom, her seriousness, her commitment to herself, and now her promising of it to me, that scared me. She lay still beside me; only her slenderness made lying on that small bed possible. I turned to touch her, but she took my hand away from her breast. "Be a good girl," she said. I knew I would have to work many months before Esther would allow me to find her wetness as she had found mine. The words, the language of my people, floated through my head—*untouchable, stone butch.* Yet it was Esther who lay beside me, a woman who trembled when she held me. Before she left she told me if I ever needed to reach her in the afternoons, she was next door sitting with an old woman, *una vieja,* a woman she had known for years who was now alone. She gave me the woman's number.

The next day was Saturday, and I spent the morning worrying about what I had done, my failure to perform. One-night stands are not simple events: sometimes in that risk-taking a world is born. I was washing my hair in the sink when I heard a knock at the door. Expecting a friend, I draped the towel around my naked shoulders and opened the door to an astonished delivery man. He thrust a long white box toward me as he turned his head. I took the box and closed the door. I had never had a messenger bring me a gift before. Twelve red roses lay elegantly wrapped in white tissue paper, a small square card snuggled between the stems:

> *Gracia, por todo anoche,*
> De quien te puede amor profundamente
> *Y con Sinceridad*—Esther

For one moment the lower East Side was transformed for me: unheard-of elegance, a touch of silk had entered my life. Esther's final gift. We never shared another night together. Sometimes I would be walking to work and would hear the beeping of a horn. There would be Esther rounding the corner in her cab with her passenger who thought she was a man.

Irena Klepfisz

dinosaurs and larger issues

for rachel

i

1. & 2.   the first two nights
she lay   diagonally across
the bed   clutching at the blankets
she refused me   room & warmth

3.   the third night
she told me   i can't handle
this   i can't handle   it
i slept   in the living room

4.   the fourth night
she said   this has to be
the last night   & moved
close to me

5.   the fifth night
she did not speak   about
it.

ii

they're never as big as i imagine
rachel informs me   whenever i enter

the reptile house   expecting cobras
to be jammed   wedged   bursting out of
into   every corner of the cage   muscles
tensing   i am always disappointed
with their slenderness   their comfort
and ease   as they relax   draping casually
over plastic trees

whales   she is earnest   should
be as big as ocean liners   instead
they swim content   in aquariums
trained to jump and leap   and it's true
they're large   but not like
they're supposed to be

rachel's eyes   narrow and widen
i do not reveal   some dinosaurs
full grown   were no bigger
than hens   that she could have
roasted   and served them
for dinner   with no fear of
leftovers

iii

in the dark   her features
are distinct   her skin white
translucent.   i see outlines
of bones.   she is crystal
my fingers   feel the thinness
of the flesh.   her mouth
is hard   demanding.   she
keeps her head turned away.
she does not look   directly
at me   except to brush away
the hair from my face   before

her tongue penetrates my mouth.
then her eyes close quickly.
i study the hand's gesture
try to give it meaning.

in the dark   her features
are strong.   she lies relaxed
ready to accept   the touch
of my tongue   ready to be cupped
sucked into me   later she says
i cannot reciprocate.

iv

no i don't enjoy this
she says   biting my hand.
her mouth   which holds
endless kisses   will never
say yes to me   just the hand
across my back   like a heavy hammer
or a quick furtive kiss
on the back of my neck
tell me   perhaps   yes.

i just don't like cunts
she says   i don't like
them   she says to me.

v

i am sorry if i've made
you unhappy   i told her
sitting   at the furthest end
of the couch
                don't make

yourself so important
she answered   with confidence
there are larger issues
at stake.

vi

it's not the kind of person
you are   i try to explain to her
you have the power   to lift
your hand   to touch me as i pass
or to walk towards me   and hold
my face   so it's not the kind
of person   you are

vii

at night   the vestiges
of other ages   influence
us.   there are
the sucking sounds   of your mouth
with mine   the moans of an ancient language
i easily recognize   my tongue
urging you on   slowly   deep
beneath the sea   or in some secret
cave   our nails: clawed   we hold
each other   you and i
released from an unexpected
danger.   exhausted we lick
each other's wounds   inflict
new ones   sharply.   our voices
echo   through the cave
return   and clash   on hard rock.
we know our bodies   and do not mind
them/ourselves   losing all sense

of proportions   limits.   we are equal
here   you and i.
afterwards   in the fire's flames
we see   cumbersome dinosaurs
rubbing their necks   against
each other   making small   sweet noises
tame and huge   so much larger than we dared imagine.

Olga Broumas

Field

I had a lover. Let us say we were married, owned
a house, shared a car. The trees were larch, white birch,
maple, poplar and pine, the mountains granite,
and three months of the year verdantly lush. We met

cows, sheep and horses on our walks up or downhill
a fine dirt road. In time, my lover came to take
another lover, of whom I also became enamored.
There is a seagull floating backward in a rare

snowstorm on an Atlantic Ocean bay as I remember this,
its head at an angle that suggests amusement.
This younger lover flew home to a far southern state
and returned in a large car with several rare instruments

and a Great Dane, a very spirited animal who had to
be returned to a family estate in the Midwest soon thereafter,
having discovered and devoured a neighboring farmer's chickens.
The seagull flies laboriously into the wind

the length of my windows, then settles to be floated back.
It is a young bird, wings black-tipped and grey.
We added a room to the cabin that summer, the work done
by a young sculptor from the college, one who seemed

to be continuously counting, a devotional attitude
that appealed to me. One evening we returned to find
a note pinned to our door, Call Ted abt a possible free piano.
That it did not materialize did not affect my feelings

toward him and in September I moved my area into this room.
Fifteen by seventeen, it had a long wall of salvaged windows,
a door with a sturdy ladder to the forest floor,
a wall of the enormous cedar logs of the main cabin

and, to it, a soundproof door with a double window
Ted had devised. Our younger lover took over my old area,
and my lover continued working upstairs
where the rising heat of the Franklin caused her

to take off her clothes frequently, as well as open a window.
We bought a large futon for my room, and next to it
laid a smaller futon, what is called a yoga mat, turned
the quilts sideways and slept facing the luminous birches

in differing night lights. Enormous fireflies
when the temperature hovers at thirty near midnight,
early September, late June. Daylight was often a wrathful time,
and it is a tribute to the height of our spirits

that we barely noticed, gliding over it as we did
over friends and professions. The phenomenon of three hearts
dilating as if in unison, eyes diverging toward
each one, rare, blasted our systems with tremendous energy

and within the year we packed each a bag, compromised
on five instruments, of which two collapsible, and a small amp,
and flew to a continent where one of us knew one country's
language. We traveled, fought, separated and reunited

for six months, then were joined by an old friend, traveling
with whom we thought a lover, who turned out

a companion instead, a tall, stately model with the gait,
approaching us on the beach, of a sulky seven-year-old.

Our younger lover's age, they played music together,
and together got stranded in an inflatable boat
whose outboard motor they'd flooded. *I sacrifice
myself to the sea*, chants our lover, unforgettable

in this scene if unwitnessed, as the model struggles
with the four flimsy oars and *Row, damn it!*
They made it to shore half a mile east of our house,
and were towed by a small speedboat belonging to a man

who had tried to fix their motor, he standing in
his fiberglass, they trailing behind, past the entire
village on their wooden chairs outside the grocery,
the eating house, the front garden doors. The model

was extremely cheerful at dinner, having hauled the canvas
tub to the yard, our lover wounded in pride and spiteful.
We lived in that house on the edge of the water
for two months, until our money ran out and we returned

to our wooded hill, our friend and companion to their town
by the eastern tip of a Finger Lake, seven hours by car
further inland. My lover and I found our jobs
during our leave had been embittered by our firm's

acquisition by a larger establishment affiliated with
the military. We resigned, or rather, refused the new
firm's offer, and shortly thereafter moved to my friend's
town where I accepted a federally funded position for

my skills in music and massage, a divergence
that delighted me. We rented a farm out of town, partly
on work exchange, feeding and caring for two horses,
two dogs, one of them slightly mad, six cats and a senile

bunny. This our lover agreed to do, as well as stacking
most of nine cords in a fit of jealousy every morning
of the week my lover was in California. There were actually
face cords, the pile would have measured four and a half

in our old county. They made a terrific racket,
hurled across the yard into the barn, where the dogs
from their pen greeted them. The farm was on a straight
north-south road, they couldn't be trusted loose

in the four-wheel-drive traffic, they were barn animals
and couldn't be kept in the house, but their barking
from their large, humane, indoor-out pen with running brook
and bales of hay had an ungrateful sound that made us

ignore the fence when they broke it, to the chagrin
and later vituperation of the owner who kept our deposit.
My lover returned from California with three bottles
of fine red, one of them a Petite Sirah; purple velour

tops for us, and the seedling of a new self profoundly
and coincidentally engendered by a brief affair with
the lover I'd left to move East to our cabin. Our younger
lover didn't recognize the smell under the fingernails

as I did, with pleasure. It is impossible to disengage
from jealousy someone told me in graduate school.
It challenged me to find a course that wouldn't feed it,
and have put my mind to it since, profiting only

from a general graciousness, nonchalance, fatality. The snowfall
that winter was heavy and the winds tore savagely to one side
of our four-mile road. By what should have been midspring
our lover had contrived to be collected to the faraway

southern state and we did not care to pursue the deposit.
Though we were broke, a sensation like shutters beating

bodily in the stillness that followed the April storms
preoccupied us exclusively, though I did see the lilacs

crashing it seemed through the old barn walls,
and the hill go green on the stain of the belly shot doe
before the snow. We moved, with my friend, to California
for a summer job arranged by my old lover, and we four

spent the season specifically amiably, in fairly rigid
pair formation, I and my friend—who had first become
my lover under my younger lover's hand while abroad by the sea,
a gesture delicate and precise, savored by all and regretted

bitterly and immediately by the youngest—my old lover and
my lover. We lived and worked, teaching nutrition, healing
and survival skills to young adults, in what had been a Navy
compound on a Pacific coast beach and had long hours

of simple sitting, and staring. I brought my guitar
and practiced hearing in detail my picking against foghorns
and gulls. My lover sang. My friend was a little insecure
far from home, and clung, peacefully, to my middle.

In the fall we moved to be half the staff at the halfway
house here. The pay was low but secure and we each rented
a studio facing the bay for the off season. We did not travel
together. Rather, my lover flew directly, my old lover

via the Midwest to visit family, and my friend and I
drove the car. *Snow Creek, Lake Crescent, Ruby Beach,*
Humptulips, Tokeland, Palix, Parpala, Hug Point, Arch
Cape, Perpetua, Darlingtonia, Bliss 14, Pacific Fruit

Express, Grace, Power County, Sweetwater, Harmony,
Adora, Amana, Homewood, Vermillion, Presque Isle.
We've lived here four months, a full holiday season,
friends from inland and the West. My lover and I

bicycle the dune roads to the ocean. The winter is mild,
and the bay home to seven varieties of duck that I've
sighted, and seagulls and pipers and pigeons that sit
on the railing to hear the guitar and are annoyed

and shift and scold if I should lose my concentration
for their flattery. My friend and I cook meals for our
festivities, and make love for exquisite hours when I may
scream and contort myself but on leaving the house

remember nothing, no, not nothing exactly, I remember
if put to it, but not ordinarily. My old lover and I
are affectionate, my lover and I are cheery, and our
younger lover recovered and moved to a large city nearby

and infrequently visits my lover and lately, lightly, me.

Janice Gould

My Crush on the Yakima Woman

It was raining along the Columbia River
that November I lived on the farm.
One morning at 6:00 a.m. the Yakima woman
drove the gravel road to my place.
She had come to pick me up.

She was sure pretty, that woman,
with her wide face, obsidian eyes,
and hair the color of blackbird wings.
She had slim long legs, and every guy
at the cannery where we worked
was sick for her.
But it was me she took home
to meet her kids.

Her husband was out hunting that weekend.
I saw him only once
when he came home, changed clothes,
and went off with a beer in his hand.

She waved good-bye,
not bothering to get up.
I strummed my guitar.
She listened and smoked.
Then she said, "Sing some more."
So I threw back my head

and sang "Your Cheatin' Heart"
in a way Patsy Cline would have understood.
And the Yakima woman thought about it,
smiled, and said, "That was real good."

So I played and drank,
sang and cried. Finally
she asked, "Do you want to go to bed?"
She did not mean with her.

I slept on the sofa,
she slept in her thin chemise.
The kids slept scattered all over the floor.
About four in the morning I got up
and looked at the sky. It angered me
to see it cold and full of stars
above the black fir forest.

Janice Gould

A Married Woman

One day you agreed to meet me
in my cold house on the hill.
You came early.
It was Saturday, raining.
I'd waited for you for days, weeks.
The evening before your visit
I'd set the table with a white cloth
and placed two purple iris
in a glass vase.
You came with your photographs and stories—
and then we made love
in my wide bed.

Outside, redwood trees scratched at the window
and rain came down
from thick rolling clouds.
We drank wine and ate bread,
we kissed and lay sleeping,
our mouths nearly touching.
Hours later, our lovemaking over,
I was restless, hungry.
I kissed the back of your neck,
stroked your thighs.
The rain was still falling.

Let's go, I said, where there are horses.
I was trembling with desire,
not sure how to bridge the distance.
Off we drove, slightly drunk,
with our bag of apples.
The horses were in an open field,
out in the green hills:
bay, chestnut, pinto, gray.
Come feed them, I said.
I'll show you how.

But you laughed
and wouldn't stand with me by the fence
where the horses stamped
and tossed their heads,
smelling the apples,
baring their teeth at one another
ready to nip and bite.
You were dismayed by their size,
their slobbering muzzles
and jealous natures,
the hot curious energy which brought them
to the fence and my outstretched hand.

Later you confided your fear of animals
as you lay in my arms
in the front seat of my car.
It was late and we were down
by the brown churning river.
The clouds had descended.
I thought about a fear of animals,
and then my mind went quiet.
I watched the rain batter the windshield.

Janice Gould

Foster Family

In October rain blew in from the ocean
and came down hard in the Willamette Valley.
One night it rained till midnight,
then in the morning
fog rose from the river.
The clouds lifted. We took the horses—
you on the gelding,
me on your bay mare—
and rode out to the apple orchards.

Gold light flecked the trees, the fruit,
the water in ditches.
We each rode silent
in separate hungers.

When we turned home
it was late afternoon.
"Let's race," you said.
We'd reached the far pasture.
You dug your bootheels deep
in the gelding's flanks
and shot away. I had to follow.
Crouched low, I heard
the bay's hard breathing,
felt her sweat fly to my eyes
like the hot tears of panic

I sometimes shed.
I could see the farm lights
gleaming like faint emeralds
in the gauzy dusk.

We came in the kitchen, mud-spattered,
breathless, to steam and your family
breaking thick biscuits into their stew.
No one spoke but your old grandma
who muttered her low nonsense
till your mother's hand slapped
flat on the table.
She tore into you like a badger,
snarled the words love
and lesbians.
It was all so familiar.

I escaped to the narrow bed
your family provided, tucked
beneath a shelf of *Reader's Digest*s.
I saw that night we had things in common
besides the way your face fought humiliation.

Lesléa Newman

August Night

My lover reaches her hand up into me
drawing out a perfect melody
and I who never raise my voice
in anger or in song
moan and sigh, scream and shriek
from dusk 'til early dawn

Picture this:
a strong woman with lavender overalls,
short dark hair that stands up straight
and a labrys swinging from one ear
walks home from a dance;
her hands in her pockets
her steps light and firm
her body still keeping time
to the music she just heard.
Watch her undress and climb into bed
naked, the soft summer air
a caress against her sweaty skin.
See her smile as she falls
into a dream
of holding a warm girl in her arms,
their hips swaying together
their bellies whispering secrets to each other
all across the floor.

Now picture this:
some boys, maybe three or four
stand in silhouettes against the darkness
outside the woman's house.
Watch the tall one pour a can of gasoline
over a mattress,
down the front, up the back, over the sides.
See them all heave it against the front door
while the woman sleeps,
her cat at the foot of the bed,
her old dog's paws twitching through a dream.
Stand back as the short one lights a blue-tipped match.
Run as the mattress bursts into flames.

…and I who never raise my voice
in anger or in song
moan and sigh, scream and shriek…

Now the woman wakes in terror
at the screech of her smoke alarm
against her ear. She leaps
out of bed, runs to the front door
only to be driven back by the heat
on her skin, the smoke
in her throat and eyes.
Something inside her
guides her to the back door
which opens easily
onto a calm night full of stars.
Something inside her
guides her back to the bedroom
to pull on a t-shirt
call for the cat
lead the old arthritic dog

down the three steps into the yard.
Now she stands there
wrapped in a neighbor's robe,
her arms around her dog
her house up in flames
the fire scorching
her heart.

> ...from dusk 'til early dawn...
>
> My lover reaches her hand up into me
> drawing out a perfect melody
> and I who never raise my voice
> in anger or in song
> moan and sigh, scream and shriek
> from dusk 'til early dawn

Judith McDaniel

She Had Not Expected This Sudden

She had not expected this sudden
thaw   the wet mouth of spring
on her cheek   her thigh   lusty
and raw   at an hour when she
had been sure of the snow
sure the quiet time would linger
before the torrential spring.

Stay   she warned the plants
and deep-rooted bulbs   stay
she felt danger in the quickening
light and in the sap-starting
warmth   don't move
against the season   stay.

And yet she opened   wet
like summer rain   she opened like
a windblown jonquil   nodding
serenely at the edge of a crusted
snow melting from the rim
of a hill   joyfully   she opened.

From Sister Gin

WITH A LATE SEPTEMBER SUNSET OF LAVENDER-GOLD BEHIND HER AND THE SMELL of fish and seawater making her hungry all over, Su stepped into the inside of her love's house for the first time. The flat straw rug made the soles of her feet ache through sandals and long to be kissed. Mamie Carter kissed her on the cheek after the custom. Seizing that proximate cheek's smell with her nostrils, Su inhaled her reward and knew better than to kiss back.

They sat on the back porch and watched the sun set over Wrightsville Sound, on that old weathered porch of an old two-story beach house where Mamie Carter had spent her summers as a child (and subsequently her children and then her grandchildren), one of the few houses to withstand all the hurricanes—sat listening to the leftover summer sounds of children's water games and deploring the increasing number of motored boats each season replacing the elegant sails. The martini threw a skin over Su's brain wiping out the city as they sat in the gentle decay of the day, the house softly decaying behind them, the summer itself mature and used and gracefully marked, letting out its last few days with the dignity of a menopausal woman releasing her last few eggs, knowing that they were for form only, that the season was over but there was no hurry about slipping over into the next, it will come in its season and here, these my last are as worthy as my first.

Su felt ashamed that she had been afraid...of Mamie Carter who was as legal in all her tentacles as old Wilmington itself; of her own passion which, here on this clan-protected porch, could be sublimated into charm as if she were a real member of that impeccable clan.

Shaking her olive free from its gregarious ice, Su heard Mamie Carter's voice off her left ear asking her to fetch them each a refill, because Captain wasn't here, because she was alone, expecting no one but Su this evening. Su took each glass in a grip firm enough to break them—someone could still drop in, would come visit, seeing the lights, her car, could drop by for hours yet, this being the tradition of the beach, the gregariousness of ice and an island.

They talked of the town's recent rapes and the bizarre circumstance of the two rapists' being laid out, tied to a board, one on the steps of the old folks' home, one in the front yard of the councilman who pulled the largest vote and was therefore mayor. Both rapists were white, short-haired, in their middle thirties, and were found nether-naked and tied outstretched to a piece of plywood in the shape of an x. Since the first rape had been of a sixty-five-year-old woman of color, it was thought that the first man's punishment was the work of a Black Klan group. The rapist had hysterically insisted that the old woman sent five old women spirits after him but no one paid him any mind. The second rape victim had been a junior high school girl, forced at stranglehold to suck off her attacker; since she was white and since in this case too the rapist had babbled of five grannies who, though masked, had white hands, some of the townspeople wondered if there were witches still afoot.

"Posh," Mamie Carter said. "What kind of talk is that? Black Klans and witches. Next thing they'll say the free-booters are back haunting the Cape Fear."

"What do you think?" Su asked.

"I think the rapists are getting a big fuss made over them. They're not the victims."

"Do you think it was really...women who did it?"

"*Old* women?" Mamie Carter's black eyes glinted with laughter. She stood up. "You know, I can't wear flat-heel shoes any more," she said, looking at her medium-heeled sandals below white sharkskin slacks. "I wore high heels so long my Achilles' tendon is permanently shortened."

"Do you?"

Su followed her strong slightly-humped back into the house. "These slacks are from before the war. Would you feel bad if a real shark had given his skin for them?"

The inside of the house was dark after the bright twilight reflections of the porch. Mamie Carter led Su to the kitchen and flicked on the light.

"You've painted it yellow!" Su remembered to speak loud. "Yellow is my favorite color."

"Mine too." Mamie Carter's smile was a caress. "Have you ever thought of wearing a bright yellow wig? Now don't try to talk to me while I'm fixing dinner. You know I can't hear you when my back is turned."

"Now that streak there," Mamie Carter said, nodding at a white swath across the middle of the dining room table, "was made by the yankees. They came to my grandmother's house and took everything they could. Since they didn't have any way to carry off the table, the yankee officer sent to the kitchen for some vinegar and poured it across there. It won't come off. Have some more shrimp, Su." Mamie Carter wiped her mouth delicately and smiled. "Old tables tell old tales."

"Mamie Carter," Su said, her fingers holding the ancient heavy lace of her napkin, her other fingers resting on the heavy stem of the goldleaf wine glass, her eyes staring at that bright elfin face leaning toward her through the candlelight. "I've never eaten such delicious shrimp."

"It wasn't too hot, was it?" Mamie Carter had cooked the tiny North Carolina shrimp with sour cream, wine, onions, mushrooms, and a lot of cayenne. "I don't taste anything without cayenne any more. Besides, it's the only way I can keep my grandchildren from eating every meal with me."

"It made all other shrimp seem bland, diluted, incomplete, wan, and colorless. Unworthy of notice." All unmarked tables, unlined faces, modern clothes, new napkins, streamlined wine glasses, all young or middle-aged things were thrown into a heap of inconsequentiality which, like herself, Su felt to be unfinished, unseasoned, green and smooth and callow. "I think I am in love with you, Mamie Carter."

The bright elfin face smiled broadly and did not answer.

Had she heard? In this pocket of the past, within dark wood and the dark saltiness of a September tide coming in and the faint rust smell of old screens and occasional sound of wind flapping the awnings, Su felt herself suddenly dead. She doubted that she had spoken. She had been switched into afterlife where words did not need to be spoken. She had left her amorphous dully-young fifty-year-old body behind and drifted through the definite world of the dead, the epitomized grave, the capsule of self which carried in its concentrate all the love she had ever sought. Mamie Carter did not need to hear; she would know.

A spare hand marbled with a bulging network of veins reached for Su's. "I know."

"Of course you do," Su said, laughing, unable to move her own hand caught in a cave beneath that perfect antique one.

"I've known for a while."

"Of course you have!" Su's smile was as stiff as her body balanced off the touch of that hand. "I should have known you'd know."

"Mamie Carter?" She held that final face taut on a thread of sight. Her hand closed across the silk bones that were Mamie Carter's hand, curled up-reaching on a free patch of sheet in the middle of a Queen Anne bed. Memory was already claiming the sight of her dimpled flesh, infinite dimples winking in their softness, skin so old it had lost all abrasives, rid itself of everything that can shield the body against the world; skin vulnerable, nonresilient, soft forever—Su's fingers had to resist the longing to take some of that flesh and mold it.

"Yes, perfect?"

Su sunk her face into the ageless curve of her love's shoulder and smothered a giggle. "There is one extraordinary thing about us that I have to say, even here on these romantic rainswept sheets, even at the risk of hearing your 'posh'...your silk is matched only by our exquisite ability to prolong swallowing, our mutual toothlessness allowing for such a long balance on the tip of flavor: I just never imagined that the delights of age would include the fact of endlessly drawnout orgasms. Did you always know?"

"You like it, too?"

"Without leaving us with a mouthful of cotton wadding. Without wearing down flavor. Without diminishment. With the loss of nothing at all, in fact, except fear."

"I always thought, if old age could be beautiful, life would hold no more terrors. Now if you'll stop talking a minute, Su, I want to get up and put on my negligee."

Mamie Carter swung her legs out of sight, turned her beautiful back, and slipped into a charcoal-red robe—really slipped, but then she had

had sixty years' practice. Su saw in her mind her coveted breasts, bound flat to her chest when she was in her twenties to produce a flapper fashion, hanging now from the base of the breastbone like soft toys, too small to rest a head upon, fit for a hand to cuddle very gently like the floppy ears of a puppy.

Memory moved her hand to Mamie Carter's belly—skin white as milk, finely pucked like sugar-sprinkled clabber; memory dropped her hand to Mamie Carter's sparse hair curling like steel—there was strength between her legs and no dough there where the flesh was fluid enough to slip away from the bone and leave that tensed grain hard as granite and her upright violent part like an animal nose against Su's palm. The impact of memory bruised. Su said, to the back that could not hear, "Don't you dare die, Mamie Carter Wilkerson."

Now, as Su was feeling wicked lying in bed while Mamie Carter sat up in her little armchair with the rose-colored skirt, a flash began in a tiny prickling over her upper skin. Last night, just as she had reached to kiss Mamie Carter the second time, reached toward those lips as to a dandelion, she had felt this same beginning prickle and a tear had dropped down each cheek, prewetting the flash with despair.

"You're flashing, Su," Mamie Carter had said.

Tears streamed as if they would flood out the flash and Su had said helplessly, "Why now? Why why why *now?*"

"Why not now?" Mamie Carter had said gently, laying Su back down on the bed, circling her shoulder, stroking her cheek and neck and breasts. "Why not now?" she had said, kissing the shame from Su's flushed lips, sliding her cheek over the sweat of Su's doubly-wet cheek and slippery forehead. Her arm had reached through Su's legs and she had held her in an infant curve, whispering again, "Why not now?" as Su slipped down into the abandon of hotly wetting herself and the flash had raged, burst, and slowly subsided.

Now, lying wickedly in bed, Su ducked under the prickles and welcomed the flash which centered her whole extraordinary body in a fever of change.

"What about Bettina?" Mamie Carter said and Bettina's voice echoed in the room, her blue quilted robe accusing.

I'll always love you, Bettina had said twenty years ago, when always had been forever. Now, with always cut in half, it seemed she had exchanged her mobility for a foundation of quicksand which would suck the house in after it. But still Bettina said it, and even now the words made her feel safe inside their sucking sound.

"*I'll* always love you, Su," Mamie Carter said with a small dry laugh like a kick. "Now Bettina's old enough to know better than to compare her 'always' with mine...certainly old enough to know better than that and I naturally know exactly how old she is since her mother and I had our daughters the same month." Mamie Carter held Su's flailing head. "When I say always, perfect, it's an underbid."

"Mamie," Su said to feel the impertinence of using that bare name. "Did you really fall in love with me?"

"No. I just wanted to get you in bed where I could hear you."

Maureen Seaton

The Bed

We build a bed
of plywood and carriage bolts,
hoist ourselves
high above earth, laughing
at the clarity of our dreams.

"Stop at any playground,"
they say, "single out
one little girl at hopscotch
or running down a slide, and think:
you were that young once,
that vulnerable."

We admire our bed,
its four corners fit together
in peace, the strength
of its wide platform. We inhale
the perfume of fresh-cut wood, dive
naked into grandma's quilt.

"Forgive yourself
your lack of vigilance in the night,
flesh that violated yours.
See how small you were,
how your white socks
dribbled into red shoes."

Nothing breaks when we love.
We fling ourselves
into mornings as if crazed,
confront the tired faces of night.
In our new bed,
we are miraculous.

Louise Wisechild

Mine

I. 1954–1973

"Don't touch yourself there." My mother steals my hand from my crotch.
  "But he...." I am tiny.
  "Keep your legs together— girls make men do bad things."
  "But he...." I am seven.
  "Be careful of strange women in the locker rooms of P.E."
  "But he...he...here...." I am twelve, holding a razor blade to my wrist.
  "Don't talk like that, young lady. It isn't...nice."

He is the men who can't control themselves. He is saying grace over my dinner. He is the soldiers in foreign cities, the strangers with candy, the author fucking with his pen, the men dining on porno. He is taking care of me when my mother is gone, finding shadows to hide in.

My vulva is a mouth closed over a long stuffy tunnel of secrets backed up to my womb. The secrets are a wasting disease. I am being turned from my body by the authority in his hands.

I put my heart in my girlfriend's locker.

He pulls me away from her, imprinting his penis in a tunnel I have no names for. In my family, sex is unspoken. Sex is not nice.

I am torn from my body, flung through his sticky web toward the ceiling. He has taken my clit captive and my elbows, my legs. He has gagged the lower mouth and rubbed himself so hard into my brain that I forget.

What is mine cannot be seen.

II. 1979–1985

I have gone to find my heart in my girlfriend's locker. I have a passionate affair with her in my mind. But as her touch moves from my imagination to her bedroom, my mouths split away from each other; my face turning toward her, my pelvis turning away. Her hands move lower, her fingers tangle in the forgotten gag. The lower mouth opens—but not to admit her. The lower mouth speaks a brutal past made present in aftershocks that bend me double in pain. I see him. I don't know who she is.

"Stop." The magic word, the word that has never worked before. She stops. I repeat it as if I could gag myself again with it. I cannot get enough of saying it. "Stop. Stop."
She holds me in her arms but I watch from an untouchable place on the ceiling. I can read her face, just on the other side of his. She is frightened. Then guilty for her own hands, her own desire. Then mad at me. "When?" she asks. "When?"

I don't ever want to, I think, but can't say. Ashamed of what I see and can't see, my words come out sideways.

III. 1979–1985

My therapist is the woman who wants nothing from me. We sit in a closed box. I stare at the carpet. The words of my vagina track the walls. I yell back at the lower mouth. "I hate sex. I hate my body for the moments I want to have it. I hate that she keeps wanting it from me."
"But your lover is she. She has no penis like he."

"It is not just his penis. This vulva is his too, the lower mouth telling

120

his dirty stories. His story, history. I didn't, couldn't, can't stop him. What I don't own I can't give to her."

"The stories are yours," the woman who takes nothing away from me says.

I give the lower mouth a bed where my feet can stretch from end to end and meet no one. I listen to the stories, finding them with my hands. I begin trying to love this loud lower mouth. To find a place for her in me.

IV. 1982–1985

The lower mouth will not stop talking now that she has started. A panoply of horror spread weekly on the floor like crayon drawings. Because this woman wants nothing from me, I am safe to take the floor, to feel the freedom around my body. I kick at him with my legs. I defend my mouths with my arms. I say to him, "You had no right!" She who wants nothing from me listens as I find my story, watches as I take it into my muscles.

Finally a word comes up from my belly. "Mine."
I hear my mother's voice: "Don't be selfish."
I say, determined, "Mine."
I hear his voice: "Whore."
I say, losing energy, "mine?"
The woman watching says, "Say it until you believe it."
"Mine. Mine. Mine. Mine."

My mouths are a chorus.

V. 1986

My lower mouth yawns, reaching for comfort toward the light of my clitoris. My vagina mends with the passing of my blood. I paint my face with my blood; a large red holy healing mouth of a warrior, a goddess, a clown. My mouths create me.

I lean against a cedar tree and journey down the full spring river, high in the canyon below me. I lie face down in pine needles and move with my hands, joining the light of my clit with the red spacious folds of my vagina. I am full of myself and then the light spills. I bring my scented fingers to my nose and touch my throat with my blood.

VI. 1987

My lower mouth is wet, a new embarrassing hunger, like adolescence but without sin. My lower mouth pulls me toward her. We have sex at all hours of the day and evening and afterwards eat Ethiopian food with our fingers, licking them and flirting with our eyes. My skin is busy tasting. In orgasms, I have visions of sacred ancient rooms where the lower mouths of women are joined on silk and sand.

My lower mouth does not want to admit it, but I am not completely nude with this lover. Our upper mouths are always in battle. I wear a shield around my heart. I have pulled the lower half of my body away from him. But I am a lesbian, I want it all. Heart and hand and desire.

I sleep alone again, waiting for my heart to meet my hand.

VII. 1988 –

Now, this is now, really, not memory, but life going forward.

In this room, I am without fear. I unlace my boots and remove my shields. The air is tender with words, the room peach with candlelight. I am held between our lips. My low mouth stirs, bringing moans and passionate gladness that vibrate my toes and hands. I smile and notice the fine blond hair of her eyelashes. Her heart slides into my open mouths. We are making a story. In this body. Mine.

Lesléa Newman

How It Isn't and Is

I want it light, playful
like the almost accidental brush
of the back of my hand against your nipple
one evening as we lie on the bed

I want it natural, unthinking:
the hardening of your nipple
against my hand

I want it automatic, spontaneous:
the way your nipple rises
to meet my mouth

I want it urgent, strong:
your hands groping and tearing
at my jeans

I want it smooth, yielding:
my wetness against your fingers

I want it uncontrolled, wild
like your moans against my ear

But this is not how it is

One of us remembers what he did to us

when we were two or five or seven
One of us remembers what she did to us
when we were twelve or twenty

And one of us has to stop

Or one of us is afraid
she won't come
or she'll come too soon
or she'll come too much
or she'll take too long
or one of us has to get up in the morning
or one of us is expecting a call

So neither of us asks, offers, looks, touches
without a long complicated discussion
about how, how much, where, where not to,
when, when not to, how fast, how slow,
how hard, how soft
until half the night is over
and we wonder if it's worth it

And then I get sad that it's not easy
or at least easier
And then I get mad
that there's so much tension in our lives
and here too

And sometimes I want to kill your mother
for teaching you that passion only leads to pain

And sometimes I want to kill my father
for teaching me that love equals sex equals shame

But most of the time I kill
this desire in me
for your sweet breasts under my tongue

your warm cunt against my thigh
your hot breath in my ear
your voice rising joyous and free
from your beautiful throat
when you come to me full
of my love and your own
song

Gloria Anzaldúa

Nightvoice

When we met I fell
into her eyes like falling
into warm rock
blurting out everything how my cousins
took turns at night when I was five eight ten
her eyes asked for nothing
but I turned myself inside
out plucked my heart
and offered it to her.
She looked away
I hated the coaxing in my voice
that bitch whine
and then she said *bueno*
just this once.

It rained hard that day and afterwards
she sat up and stretched
arms and bare back glistening.
The sounds of the *ranas*
entered the room with the night
both were deafening.

I stood at the door
of the heaven I thought out of reach.
When I touched her I could barely
breathe and the smell of her:

toasted almonds and yeast.
I could never get near it enough
the wanting making my arms weak
the taste of her—even now if I bring
my fingers up to my nose
I get a whiff of her.

     Lightning scored the windowpanes
     a brutal light hit my eyes
     filling the room   surprising
     the shun in her face
     she slid it back behind her eyes
     but I'd seen it
     and by the time thunder
     shook the mirror
     something else had entered the room
     and I knew she would leave me
     parts of her were walking out
     into the *llovisna*
     toward the lightning piercing the horizon.

She lay   beached
on the white sand
and before the sweat dried on her body
I knew she needn't
have done anything
one stroke
of her hand on my belly
and I would have gone off again
but I lay on the white sheet
mouth full of sand
my face shut like a door.

     Somehow the thunder had gotten inside me
     and I wanted to say I'm not your *perra*
     a cheap shot but it would have
     softened her mouth

by then I wanted nothing from her
had turned away and lay listening
to the rain and the frogs.
The birds had stopped singing.

When her hand touched me
I almost screamed.
I pulled back into my
self, made myself numb
but the cat her hand found me
and I the mouse had no more
holes to hide in.
I came to lose myself
and for that I never
forgave her.

Bueno: all right
Ranas: frogs
Llovisna: rain
Perra: bitch, as in female dog

Judith Barrington

Body Language

The thing that makes me crazy is
how much I wanted her—
the simple act of longing
year after year, till finally
she took my hand and held it
pressed to her small right breast.
That kind of longing
turns your whole torso into a cavern
where despair echoes wall to wall
and hope leaps like a fœtus.
My complicity confuses the issue.
How to say the word: *abuse*
when my body tells another story—
not a tale of clenched self-protection
but an epic, my young arm
reaching out for her breast,
my back spreading wide to her touch?

The thing I go back to is
the rain on the window—
water washing all over the pane
as hand moves to breast
and someone seduces someone else.
My complicity clouds the definitions
like that misted window,

one side of its thin old glass
steaming with the heat of breath and skin
while the other
leans into the storm, weeping.

Melanie Kaye/Kantrowitz

eyes

for ML

after the hysterectomy you won't take estrogen
you say you've had enough of cancer
you watch your lines deepen
you feel your cunt go dry   you say
it's all shriveled

I say *it's pretty*
you are pretty   you
won't believe me

◆ ◆ ◆

under the sheet your legs spread
feet cold in the stirrups

the RN chats *at my age   49   I learned to ski   just started   this*
time something for myself   sticks her hand up into you   *oh yes*
she says   *atrophied   the tissue thins out & looks sort of shiny red*
what we call little old lady's vagina: welcome

at the table's head I pet your hair
I'm grateful you're not embarrassed
you're grateful I don't pretend

◆ ◆ ◆

later you say
See   I told you

want to look?   (I'm placing the mirror near the lamp
on the floor)   *come look*
I want you to see   how pretty

you're afraid

come on

you squat over the mirror
I'm in the bathroom peeing & I hear
oh
it IS pretty

see
I told you   racing towards you slightly
dripping   *see*   you
laughing over the mirror

Barbara Rosenblum

From Cancer in Two Voices:
Living in an Unstable Body

MY DOCTOR PUT IT TO ME VERY CLEARLY: I HAD TO HAVE CHEMOTHERAPY, SURGERY, and radiation, in that order. I had to have chemotherapy for three months before surgery because the tumor in my breast was too large to remove surgically. It had grown too quickly and was now virtually inoperable. Chemotherapy would shrink the tumor, permitting surgery without skin graft. There was another reason for chemotherapy first: the cancer had spread to my lymph nodes, including a supraclavicular node near my collarbone. That was an indicator that metastatic processes were already occurring throughout my body. It was a serious, aggressive cancer and I would require the most aggressive treatment available.

Before the first treatment, my doctor prepared me for the various side effects I might experience. My hair would fall out, I'd have mouth sores, I'd vomit, and I'd lose my period. So, after the first treatment, I vomited about thirty times in forty-eight hours, had tired muscles and aching joints, and was exhausted from spasmodic vomiting. Even if you didn't have cancer and just vomited that much from a flu, you'd be exhausted. And that was just the first week.

The second week, I had low blood counts, extreme fatigue, and breathlessness from the lack of sufficient hemoglobin—and consequently oxygen—in my blood. Almost exactly on the twenty-first day following the first set of three injections, my hair began to fall out. Not just on my head. I lost my pubic hair as well. But I still had my period.

After the second treatment, I had all the side effects again. And I still had my period. I thought for sure I'd beat this: I wouldn't go into menopause.

Following the third treatment, I had all the same side effects but, this time, I had a shorter period. Still, I didn't attend to it much because, by this time, my nose and anus were bleeding from chemotherapy and I grew alarmed. It seemed like I was bleeding from new places and losing the familiar bleeding from familiar places.

Three weeks later, after the fourth treatment, my period stopped. I began to get hot flashes, sometimes as frequently as one an hour. My ears glowed bright red, my face darkened, and sweat collected on the surface of my skin. I felt like a vibrating tuning fork for the next two minutes. Then my internal air conditioning took over but didn't know when to stop. I got cold; I'd quickly cover myself to avoid the chill of perspiration. I could never find the right amount of clothing because my internal thermostat was completely off. I no longer had any sense of what "room temperature," that euphemism for a sharable external reality, was. I had no reliable information from my body about the temperature of the outside world. My only information came from deep inside my body and I knew that was distorted and unreliable.

All the hair on my head fell out. Frantically, I searched for a good wig before this occurred, but nothing fit my small-size head. I found a hairdresser who worked for the opera company who used his connections to get a wig for me. The wig fit but felt foreign and made my scalp hot and itchy. I decided, like many other women who become bald from chemotherapy, not to disguise my loss.

Hats now hang off any available hook in my apartment. I have cotton hats, wool hats, berets, hats with brims, ski caps. Friends have knitted caps for me. And, even now, every time I go into the street, I am still aware that people look at me. A vital aspect of my social identity has been taken away. In the last six months, I've lost my hair twice. And, before that, three times. Practice does not make it easier.

Losing my hair has been much harder than losing my breast. No one can see underneath my clothes. But everyone can see my hair. I never thought my hair was beautiful: it was a simple brown mop that I combed and washed. It grew out of my scalp. It was a part of me. It was mine.

And as I saw it cover the pillow, as I saw gobs of it come out on the comb and gobs of it clog the shower drain, I sank powerlessly into resignation. I knew my hair would grow back when I went off the powerful chemotherapy to another combination of chemicals. It did, but thinly. And then I went off chemotherapy completely, and all my hair came back, thick and spiky. But, during that time when I didn't take chemotherapy, the cancer spread to my liver and then my lungs. I had to have chemotherapy again, the strong stuff again. Now it is clear that I will never have a full head of hair again. I now lose my hair once a month. I will always look like a Buddhist monk until the day I die.

My pubis is as smooth as a fig. Even a peach with its infantile fuzziness is too hairy to describe my pudenda. It is bald, completely smooth except for one Fu Manchu-like hair, straight and long, that resisted decimation. It is a dark sturdy branch that extends from my skin. It is my mysterious hair, this proud survivor.

Losing my pubic hair, I felt naked and embarrassed, like a prepubescent child. I was too exposed and didn't want to be touched.

My vagina was changing too. The vaginal tissue was thinning and becoming more sensitive to pressure and friction. It began to hurt when Sandy and I had sex. I then noticed that my ordinary levels of dampness seemed to be changing: I was becoming less moist. Worst of all, I stopped lubricating when I became sexually excited. That single physiological fact made me realize that the agreements and understandings I had with my body were no longer in effect. If I no longer lubricated when I got sexually aroused, then how could I know I was feeling sexy?

Until I began chemotherapy, my relationship with my body was simple, direct, and uncomplicated. I had a friendly, warm, and pleasurable relationship with my body. Sex was always fun and untroubled. The cycles of my ability to become aroused were exquisitely dependent on my hormones. Ten days before my period, like clockwork, I would begin to feel sexual. This would continue for the next ten days and, when my period came, the urge would fizzle out. In other words, I had a physiologically based definition of my own sexual excitement: if my body produced some of the sensations which, through experience, had become my standard set of signals for sexual excitement, then I knew what to do with my behavior. But when chemotherapy induced an early and rapidly onsetting menopause and my hormone levels dropped dramatically, I was no longer on a monthly hormone cycle. I could no longer tell when I felt sexy or premenstrual. I got very confused about what I was feeling and when I was feeling it.

These questions of semantic meaning were urgently preempted by the necessity of finding practical solutions. Without body clues to signal me as to when and how I was feeling sexy, I consulted my head. Sandy and I recreated situations that had a proven record of creating the right mood in me. We purposefully incorporated the old reliable environmental cues that had worked so well in the past: excellent food, candlelight, intimate conversation, music. I felt as close as could be but nothing was happening in my body. We tried romantic meals at cozy restaurants. Nothing. Massages with scented oils. Nothing. Morning hiking in the country followed by steaming coffee and good pancakes. Nothing. Everything in my head told me this should be the right moment to make love but there were no signals coming from my body. Sandy touched me in all the loving, familiar ways. It was soothing, pleasant but not sexy. Nothing. The conclusion: for me, sex does not work in the head.

We stopped making love. Instead, we found new ways of being intimate. Sandy, who is a very light sleeper and consequently sleeps far away from me so as not to be disturbed by my twists and turns, now held me through the night. Our hands found new ways to console each other. I was reminded of how animals touch, lick, and chew each other. They pick at and groom each other, making the other feel secure and loved with their paws. I would touch Sandy's throat in a spot I knew contained all her tears: she would sob. And right during the chemotherapy infusion, when the chemicals were flowing into my veins from huge syringes, Sandy helped me relax by touching my back and neck lightly.

I confess I was still nervous about not making love. Without telling Sandy, I still tried to make myself feel sexy. I believed that if I tried hard enough, I could discover a more subtle sexual language in my body. I thought maybe I could pick up these signals when alone. So, when Sandy was busy and out of the house, I tried to get in the mood to masturbate. Nothing. But our new intimacy helped ease the passage: I accepted this nonsexual period as part of my life. Ultimately the rock-bottom question remains: when facing one's own death, what happens to one's sexuality?

I suppose, for some women, sexual feelings become intensified. They become hungry for life, hungry for life through sex. Erotic energy keeps them alive. I suspect Sandy would have liked it better if I experienced the life force as erotic energy, as libido. But I don't. My life energy comes in another form, in the passion to learn everything, to feel everything, to live every moment with presence and intensity. To study new things. To master new areas of knowledge. To write: alone and with Sandy. Together, we have developed a new form that can accommodate our individual and unique voices into a dialogue. We write about things that are important to us. We make love at the typewriter, not in the bedroom.

As I write now, I see that I was learning a new language of the body but it was the language of symptoms, not of sexuality. I became sensitive to when my body was retaining water. I could glance at my various parts, my legs, arms, stomach, and chest and notice a puffiness that had not been there the day before. I learned that when I became puffy, my metabolism was off and that meant my liver wasn't functioning properly. I calculated the ebbs and flows of my energy because my activities, like taking a walk, depended on an exact calibration of that energy. I observed how I wavered, how much time I had between the waves, how it disappeared all at once, without forewarning. I discovered how close I could come to throwing up without actually having to do it. I studied the gradations of nausea and their subdivisions and how to assess when nausea would pass or when I had to take an antinausea pill. I learned how to move quickly to the curb while walking the dog, emptying the contents of my stomach there, not on the sidewalk, and how to look reasonably dignified afterward. I learned how to run fast while compressing my anal sphincter muscles, so that I wouldn't shit in my pants from the diarrhea that chemo induced. Sometimes I didn't make it.

In the last two and a half years, I peed in my pants three times. Chemotherapy irritates the bladder. That's why doctors tell you to drink half a gallon of liquid whenever you get chemotherapy. The chemicals are so strong that they can even cause cancer of the bladder. On the few occasions I couldn't control my urine, I noticed that I didn't get the usual signal that told me it was time to think about going to the bathroom. It didn't begin as a small pressure or urge, as it normally does, and then build up. No, rather, it came on with a burst of urgency, as if I'd been holding it for hours. I had to learn this new language too.

The form of my body changed too. I lost a breast. Two years ago, when I had a mastectomy, I was too worried about my life to worry about my breast. I hoped the doctors would "get" all the cancer in my breast, that postoperative radiation would control any errant cells that had not been excised by surgery. Losing a breast did alter my body image, as well as my body, but I never felt a diminishment of my femininity. My breasts were never the center of my womanness.

I knew from the responses of other women in my support group and also from my cancer counselor that losing a breast was very hard for some women. In my cancer support group, most women were concerned about reconstructive surgery. They swapped names of good plastic surgeons. They talked about aesthetic criteria for evaluating a good job, such as the surgeon's ability to make breasts match in color, tone, weight, density, shape, and identicality of nipple placement with appropriate tones of darkness. They expressed a fetishistic quality in their talk; they were desperate and afraid.

One woman in the support group told the story of someone whose husband left her from the time of the mastectomy until she got her reconstructed breast. He couldn't bear the sight of his wife, she explained matter-of-factly. And then there's the letter I got from a distant acquaintance who told me that she, too, had had breast cancer. She wrote that it wasn't so dangerous, now that they could control it with early detection. She also wrote that, since her surgery a few years before, she, herself, never got undressed in front of her husband and that, when they made love, she always wore her bra with the prosthesis tucked inside.

I couldn't even imagine how these women might feel about their partners. I would feel enraged. I cannot count the number of stories I've heard about couples, both gay and straight, breaking up. Illness places enormous strains on couples and many separate. Each person may feel guilt and abandonment simultaneously.

I'm very lucky. Sandy has been exceptionally steadfast and easy about the changes in my body. She did not compel me to pay attention to her needs, her anxieties, her worries. She never made me feel inadequate or freakish. Her face never revealed shock or terror. She was easy with my scar, touching it delicately. She always got the bucket during vomiting bouts, never cringing or complaining. She was always softly, gently there, through everything.

Sandra Butler

From Cancer in Two Voices:
Living in My Changing Body

I BEGIN WRITING THIS SITTING AT THE KITCHEN TABLE DRINKING TEA AND LISTENING to the eager clacking of her typing. Barbara has just begun to write a piece about her body, her changing relationship to it and has announced quite firmly that she wants to write alone. I sit and chafe, wishing we could work together, wondering what she will write about our sex life, our changing intimacies. Wanting to be included. Last week I spoke at the Women's Building about sexuality in the relationship of a couple dealing with life-threatening illness. It was very well received, and many of the women seemed relieved to hear me verbalize what they were experiencing in physical or emotional isolation. I was both moved and grateful for the response, and it deepened my conviction that the writing Barbara and I are doing is vital in the lives of other couples living through many of the same struggles.

I spoke to them about our sex life, how it used to be, how it is now, how we have accommodated the physical changes in her body, the emotional changes in her psyche, and the relational changes in our daily lives. I didn't talk like that, though. I talked in a daily language. One of need and dependency. Mostly mine. Of an inwardness and sometimes excruciating thoughtfulness. Mostly hers. I talked about the way I was socialized to be an appropriate heterosexual and had lived for nearly thirty-five years in response to the sexual needs of others and how hard I struggled against that early conditioning when I came out as a lesbian. I spoke of how easily I find myself slipping back into those old roles again. How I find myself feeling that Barbara's needs are the real needs and mine are not. That her feelings are the ones that matter, and mine don't. That the frequency, the form, the intensity of the sexual dimension of our lives will—no, should—be determined by her. Not by me, and rarely by us. Just like it was before, when I was in my twenties and thirties. Actually, I know it isn't like before, but I do admit to an uneasy similarity sometimes.

Now I sit here wishing she would call to me from her office down the hall and ask me what I would add to this piece. What is it like for me, as her partner? How does it feel to have lived for eight years with a woman who now has advanced cancer spreading through her body?

If she did ask, I would begin by writing about her breast. The one they excised soon after her diagnosis. The surgeon and the oncologist, both women, remarked after the surgery was over that we seemed to be "handling" the experience so well. I think what they meant was that we were not acting like some heterosexual couples. Barbara expressed no shame about "disfigurement," no embarrassment about being less of a woman, no worrying that desire would never return. I did not, like many husbands, awkwardly avert my glance from her wound but instead kissed her scar, her chest, and her body after the surgery with the same love, passion, tenderness that I had before. It was still Barbara. It was still the body of the woman I had loved all those years. It was only that the body had assumed a different shape. Quieter now. More mood swings. But she was still Barbara inside herself.

Then I would write about the loss of her pubic hair and how unusual it was for me to see her pubis exposed in that way. I had been shaved twice, in preparation for the birth of my two daughters nearly thirty years before, but had never seen another adult pubis without hair. I found myself intrigued at the odd juxtaposition of a girlish pudenda and a woman's body. I wanted to touch and stroke it, but she was uncomfortable and wouldn't allow me to. The hair on her head was gone too, which caused her more public shyness and uncertainty. But the loss of pubic hair made her feel like a child, utterly vulnerable and exposed. It was not possible for her to open further—open beyond the vulnerability of her body being so uncovered, so unprotected.

Then I would write about her edema. How her body became swollen with fluids that were not being processed properly by her liver. Barbara gained twenty-five pounds in barely a month. She described her body as being unfamiliar and alien, bloated, hairless, and always with some level of discomfort, weakness, achiness, or nausea—the endless variety of symptoms chemotherapy produces in the body.

At first I was unthinkingly delighted as her hips spread and grew wider. I reassured her that her hips (indeed hips in general) were my favorite part of a woman's body. Bigger hips meant, to me at least, better hips. I found her body very exciting and was filled with renewed desire. She however, felt trapped and alienated in this stranger's body and was unable or unwilling to respond.

She has just come down the hall carrying the pages she has written. As I read them my eyes fill with tears of recognition. I read how she experiences us making love at the typewriter. How each morning we would walk to my office laboriously, resting every few blocks, and sit beside each other, one of us at the keyboard, the other sitting closely alongside. We typed, interrupted, criticized, added, paced, drank coffee, laughed, then grew thoughtful, intense, or joyous with relief when just the right word or image emerged. It was a making of love. An honoring of our bond. Lovemaking. The work we did had the focus, the passion, the sense of completion our lovemaking once had. I often felt similarly spent when a work session ended. But so loved. So known. So deeply connected to this woman.

In rereading these thoughts about my response to Barbara's changing body, I notice that I am present only in response, in relationship to Barbara. As her body changes, as her needs, strength, focus shifts—I respond. I notice now for the first time that slowly, imperceptibly, gradually, Barbara's body became the body in our lives. I have ceased to have my body and instead have Barbara's. Her strength, her energy, her appetites delineated our day. When we awoke, if she felt strong enough for a long walk, we walked. If she felt sluggish or weak, the morning would be spent in a more sedentary way—reading, writing, visiting with friends. Or I would go to my office and spend a few hours doing my own work. When her appetite was good, and there was none of the monthly emergence of mouth sores making anything but creamy shakes impossible, we would go to eat spicy ethnic food. When she was unable to, or had lost the appetite for complex flavors, we ate very little and simply, at home.

I too have put on a lot of weight, but never noticed. I never felt full, or overly full, or stuffed, or bloated, or sated. I cannot remember thinking about whether I was hungry, what I wanted to eat, and when I had had enough. We ate. We filled our body with what we liked when we were hungry.

I exercised in relation to Barbara's body. I ate in relation to Barbara's appetite. I had somehow neglected to make a parallel assessment of my own energy, my own desires, my own need for fresh air and exercise. Just as I had been "responsive to her sexual needs," I had become an extension of her physical capacities. The mornings when I would awaken and do some yogic stretches had stopped and I didn't remember deciding to stop. The feeling of being strong and vital in my body has evaporated as well. I can't remember the last time I felt powerful, the last time my skin tingled with the rush of blood that comes from vigorous exercise.

In much the same way her sexuality had become "our" sexuality—now her body became "our" body. If she couldn't have a strong, powerful, healthy body—then I simply wouldn't have one either. At least, insofar as I could unconsciously encourage that sameness. It felt impossible for me to go out to exercise or swim, leaving Barbara weak or depleted, reading quietly on the sofa. It felt impossible to enjoy and delight in my body. It would have felt like an act of disloyalty. I can no longer take my body for granted enough to know that it will be reliable, strong, and healthy. Barbara can no longer do that, feel that, have that possibility, and it fills me with guilt. The guilt of survival. The guilt of comparison. The guilt of randomness—being selected out as the one of us who will outlast the other. The one of us who will live beyond the "us" that has been the foundation of my life. The guilt of the relief that it is not me.

And I would write further about guilt. The guilt I first felt when she was misdiagnosed. The guilt of having been impatient with what I felt was her hypochondriacal pattern of going to the doctor over "every little thing," a pattern the women in my family have all followed. It was only when her breast started to swell and the lump was clearly palpable that I began to take it as seriously as I should have. Going with her to the Kaiser clinic I saw the passivity of the patients, the waiting, the fear of taking too much time, asking too many questions, being a "nuisance." I felt guilty that I hadn't encouraged her to have her own doctor. A private doctor. That I had ignored her complaints until they were too advanced to contain.

I suppose it is always necessary to rewrite history—to replay a series of "what ifs," "if onlys," "how could I have not seen" questions that are the inevitable outgrowth of illness and accidents. I am no different in this effort to impose meaning and responsibility. The doctors were responsible. Not me. But I hadn't paid enough attention. I hadn't listened clearly enough to her words. Somehow it was my fault that this was happening to her body. And because it was my fault, I began to deny my own body and pleasure in it as well.

I have guilty feelings about my thick, heavy, rapidly growing hair. During our ceremony of commitment, now nearly ten months ago, Barbara expressed dismay over her patchy, balding, very short thin hair. "It's not as unattractive as you imagine," I assured her. "Oh?" she responded tartly. "If it's so attractive, why haven't you cut your hair to look like mine?" Hours later, I remembered her words, and even though I knew they were said in irritation and frustration at her own loss, I decided to have my hair cut as a gesture of love and support. When I look back over the photograph album of our ceremony, we both have near crew cuts, decorated with festive earrings and glowing faces.

But now she is bald and has been for many months, and my hair is growing out—luxuriant and a lovely shade of salt and pepper. I am aware of closing the bathroom door when I brush it and being very careful to take all the hair out of the drain in the shower when I shampoo.

But there is the gratitude that balances the grief. Gratitude that I can call home and hear her voice rise with eagerness at the sound of my voice. That her sculpted hairless skull contains her piercing eyes without brows, without lashes. Her unadorned face smiles at the phone when she hears my voice. She is still there inside her changing body—the body so different from the body I first touched and held. One breast, still high and firm. I have two breasts, though somewhat fallen and considerably less firm. My body too has changed, grown older, and softened. We have become clearer to each other and to ourselves, though—our bodies less opaque. We can see through, into each other. We are living in changed and changing bodies—living with full hearts and open minds and great love.

II

Audre Lorde

Uses of the Erotic: The Erotic As Power

THERE ARE MANY KINDS OF POWER, USED AND UNUSED, ACKNOWLEDGED OR OTHER-wise. The erotic is a resource within each of us that lies in a deeply fe-male and spiritual plane, firmly rooted in the power of our unexpressed or unrecognized feeling. In order to perpetuate itself, every oppression must corrupt or distort those various sources of power within the culture of the oppressed that can provide energy for change. For women, this has meant a suppression of the erotic as a considered source of power and information within our lives.

We have been taught to suspect this resource, vilified, abused, and de-valued within western society. On the one hand, the superficially erotic has been encouraged as a sign of female inferiority; on the other hand, women have been made to suffer and to feel both contemptible and sus-pect by virtue of its existence.

It is a short step from there to the false belief that only by the suppres-sion of the erotic within our lives and consciousness can women be truly strong. But that strength is illusory, for it is fashioned within the context of male models of power.

As women, we have come to distrust that power which rises from our deepest and nonrational knowledge. We have been warned against it all our lives by the male world, which values this depth of feeling enough to keep women around in order to exercise it in the service of men, but which fears this same depth too much to examine the possibilities of it within themselves. So women are maintained at a distant/inferior posi-tion to be psychically milked, much the same way ants maintain colonies of aphids to provide a life-giving substance for their masters.

But the erotic offers a well of replenishing and provocative force to the woman who does not fear its revelation nor succumb to the belief that sensation is enough.

The erotic has often been misnamed by men and used against women. It has been made into the confused, the trivial, the psychotic, the plasticized sensation. For this reason, we have often turned away from the exploration and consideration of the erotic as a source of power and information, confusing it with its opposite, the pornographic. But pornography is a direct denial of the power of the erotic, for it represents the suppression of true feeling. Pornography emphasizes sensation without feeling.

The erotic is a measure between the beginnings of our sense of self and the chaos of our strongest feelings. It is an internal sense of satisfaction to which, once we have experienced it, we know we can aspire. For having experienced the fullness of this depth of feeling and recognizing its power, in honor and self-respect we can require no less of ourselves.

It is never easy to demand the most from ourselves, from our lives, from our work. To encourage excellence is to go beyond the encouraged mediocrity of our society. But giving in to the fear of feeling and working to capacity is a luxury only the unintentional can afford, and the unintentional are those who do not wish to guide their own destinies.

This internal requirement toward excellence that we learn from the erotic must not be misconstrued as demanding the impossible from ourselves nor from others. Such a demand incapacitates everyone in the process. For the erotic is not a question only of what we do; it is a question of how acutely and fully we can feel in the doing. Once we know the extent to which we are capable of feeling that sense of satisfaction and completion, we can then observe which of our various life endeavors bring us closest to that fullness.

The aim of each thing that we do is to make our lives and the lives of our children richer and more possible. Within the celebration of the erotic in all our endeavors, my work becomes a conscious decision—a longed-for bed which I enter gratefully and from which I rise up empowered.

Of course, women so empowered are dangerous. So we are taught to separate the erotic demand from most vital areas of our lives other than sex. And the lack of concern for the erotic root and satisfactions of our work is felt in our disaffection from so much of what we do. For instance, how often do we truly love our work even at its most difficult?

The principal horror of any system that defines the good in terms of profit rather than in terms of human need, or that defines human need to the exclusion of the psychic and emotional components of that need—the principal horror of such a system is that it robs our work of its erotic value, its erotic power, and life appeal and fulfillment. Such a system reduces work to a travesty of necessities, a duty by which we earn bread or oblivion for ourselves and those we love. But this is tantamount to blinding a painter and then telling her to improve her work, and to enjoy the act of painting. It is not only next to impossible, it is also profoundly cruel.

As women, we need to examine the ways in which our world can be truly different. I am speaking here of the necessity for reassessing the quality of all the aspects of our lives and of our work, and of how we move toward and through them.

The very word *erotic* comes from the Greek word *eros*, the personification of love in all its aspects—born of Chaos, and personifying creative power and harmony. When I speak of the erotic, then, I speak of it as an assertion of the life force of women; of that creative energy empowered, the knowledge and use of which we are now reclaiming in our language, our history, our dancing, our loving, our work, our lives.

There are frequent attempts to equate pornography and eroticism, two diametrically opposed uses of the sexual. Because of these attempts, it has become fashionable to separate the spiritual (psychic and emotional) from the political, to see them as contradictory or antithetical. "What do you mean, a poetic revolutionary, a meditating gunrunner?" In the same way, we have attempted to separate the spiritual and the erotic, thereby reducing the spiritual to a world of flattened affect, a world of the ascetic who aspires to feel nothing. But nothing is further from the truth. For the ascetic position is one of the highest fear, the gravest immobility. The severe abstinence of the ascetic becomes the ruling obsession. And it is one not of self-discipline but of self-abnegation.

The dichotomy between the spiritual and the political is also false, resulting from an incomplete attention to our erotic knowledge. For the bridge which connects them is formed by the erotic—the sensual—those physical, emotional, and psychic expressions of what is deepest and strongest and richest within each of us, being shared: the passions of love, in its deepest meanings.

Beyond the superficial, the considered phrase, "It feels right to me," acknowledges the strength of the erotic into a true knowledge, for what that means is the first and most powerful guiding light toward any understanding. And understanding is a handmaiden that can only wait upon, or clarify, that knowledge, deeply born. The erotic is the nurturer or nursemaid of all our deepest knowledge.

The erotic functions for me in several ways, and the first is in providing the power that comes from sharing deeply any pursuit with another person. The sharing of joy, whether physical, emotional, psychic, or intellectual, forms a bridge between the sharers that can be the basis for understanding much of what is not shared between them, and lessens the threat of their difference.

Another important way in which the erotic connection functions is the open and fearless underlining of my capacity for joy. In the way my body stretches to music and opens into response, hearkening to its deepest rhythms, so every level upon which I sense also opens to the erotically satisfying experience, whether it is dancing, building a bookcase, writing a poem, examining an idea.

That self-connection shared is a measure of the joy that I know myself to be capable of feeling, a reminder of my capacity for feeling. And that deep and irreplaceable knowledge of my capacity for joy comes to demand from all of my life that it be lived within the knowledge that such satisfaction is possible, and does not have to be called *marriage*, nor *god*, nor *an afterlife*.

This is one reason why the erotic is so feared, and so often relegated to the bedroom alone, when it is recognized at all. For once we begin to feel deeply all the aspects of our lives, we begin to demand from ourselves and from our life-pursuits that they feel in accordance with that joy which we know ourselves to be capable of. Our erotic knowledge empowers us, becomes a lens through which we scrutinize all aspects of our existence, forcing us to evaluate those aspects honestly in terms of their relative meaning within our lives. And this is a grave responsibility, projected from within each of us, not to settle for the convenient, the shoddy, the conventionally expected, nor the merely safe.

During World War II, we bought sealed plastic packets of white, uncolored margarine with a tiny, intense pellet of yellow coloring perched like a topaz just inside the clear skin of the bag. We would leave the margarine out for a while to soften, and then we would pinch the little pellet to break it inside the bag, releasing the rich yellowness into the soft pale mass of margarine. Then taking it carefully between our fingers, we would knead it gently back and forth, over and over, until the color had spread throughout the whole pound bag of margarine, thoroughly coloring it.

I find the erotic such a kernel within myself. When released from its intense and constrained pellet, it flows through and colors my life with a kind of energy that heightens and sensitizes and strengthens all my experience.

We have been raised to fear the *yes* within ourselves, our deepest cravings. But, once recognized, those that do not enhance our future lose their power and can be altered. The fear of our desires keeps them suspect and indiscriminately powerful, for to suppress any truth is to give it strength beyond endurance. The fear that we cannot grow beyond whatever distortions we may find within ourselves keeps us docile and loyal and obedient, externally defined, and leads us to accept many facets of our oppression as women.

When we live outside ourselves, and by that I mean on external directives only, rather than from our internal knowledge and needs, when we live away from those erotic guides from within ourselves, then our lives are limited by external and alien forms, and we conform to the needs of a structure that is not based on human need, let alone on an individual's. But when we begin to live from within outward, in touch with the power of the erotic within ourselves, and allow that power to inform and illuminate our actions upon the world around us, then we begin to be responsible to ourselves in the deepest sense. For as we begin to recognize our deepest feelings, we begin to give up, of necessity, being satisfied with suffering and self-negation and the numbness that so often seems like their only alternative in our society. Our acts against oppression become integral with self, motivated and empowered from within.

In touch with the erotic, I become less willing to accept powerlessness, or those other supplied states of being which are not native to me, such as resignation, despair, self-effacement, depression, self-denial.

And yes, there is a hierarchy. There is a difference between painting a back fence and writing a poem, but only one of quantity. And there is, for me, no difference between writing a good poem and moving into sunlight against the body of a woman I love.

This brings me to the last consideration of the erotic. To share the power of each other's feelings is different from using another's feelings as we would use a kleenex. When we look the other way from our experience, erotic or otherwise, we use, rather than share, the feelings of those others who participate in the experience with us. And use without consent of the used is abuse.

In order to be utilized, our erotic feelings must be recognized. The need for sharing deep feeling is a human need. But within the european-american tradition, this need is satisfied by certain proscribed erotic comings-together. These occasions are almost always characterized by a simultaneous looking away, a pretense of calling them something else, whether a religion, a fit, mob violence, or even playing doctor. And this misnaming of the need and the deed gives rise to that distortion which results in pornography and obscenity—the abuse of feeling.

When we look away from the importance of the erotic in the development and sustenance of our power, or when we look away from ourselves as we satisfy our erotic needs in concert with others, we use each other as objects of satisfaction rather than share our joy in the satisfying, rather than make connection with our similarities and our differences. To refuse to be conscious of what we are feeling at any time, however comfortable that might seem, is to deny a large part of the experience and to allow ourselves to be reduced to the pornographic, the abused, and the absurd.

The erotic cannot be felt secondhand. As a Black lesbian feminist, I have a particular feeling, knowledge, and understanding for those sisters with whom I have danced hard, played, or even fought. This deep participation has often been the forerunner for joint concerted actions not possible before.

But this erotic charge is not easily shared by women who continue to operate under an exclusively european-american male tradition. I know it was not available to me when I was trying to adapt my consciousness to this mode of living and sensation.

Only now, I find more and more women-identified women brave enough to risk sharing the erotic's electrical charge without having to look away and without distorting the enormously powerful and creative nature of that exchange. Recognizing the power of the erotic within our lives can give us the energy to pursue genuine change within our world, rather than merely settling for a shift of characters in the same weary drama.

For not only do we touch our most profoundly creative source, but we do that which is female and self-affirming in the face of a racist, patriarchal, and anti-erotic society.

Adrienne Rich

Splittings

1.

My body opens over San Francisco like the daylight raining down   each pore crying the change of light
I am not with her   I have been waking off and on
all night to that pain   not simply absence but
the presence of the past   destructive
to living here and now   Yet if I could instruct
myself, if we could learn to learn from pain
even as it grasps us   if the mind, the mind that lives
in this body could refuse   to let itself be crushed
in that grasp   it would loosen   Pain would have to stand
off from me and listen   its dark breath still on me
but the mind could begin to speak to pain
and pain would have to answer:

                    We are older now
we have met before   these are my hands before your eyes
my figure blotting out   all that is not mine
I am the pain of division   creator of divisions
it is I who blot your lover from you
and not the time-zones nor the miles
It is not separation calls me forth   but I
who am separation   And remember
I have no existence   apart from you

2.

I believe I am choosing something new
not to suffer uselessly   yet still to feel
Does the infant memorize the body of the mother
and create her in absence?   or simply cry
primordial loneliness?   does the bed of the stream
once diverted   mourning   remember wetness?
But we, we live so much in these
configurations of the past   I choose
to separate her   from my past we have not shared
I choose not to suffer uselessly
to detect primordial pain as it stalks toward me
flashing its bleak torch in my eyes   blotting out
her particular being   the details of her love
I will not be divided   from her or from myself
by myths of separation
while her mind and body in Manhattan are more with me
than the smell of eucalyptus coolly burning   on these hills

3.

The world tells me I am its creature
I am raked by eyes   brushed by hands
I want to crawl into her for refuge   lay my head
in the space   between her breast and shoulder
abnegating power for love
as women have done   or hiding
from power in her love   like a man
I refuse these givens   the splitting
between love and action   I am choosing
not to suffer uselessly   and not to use her
I choose to love   this time   for once
with all my intelligence

1974

Sarah Schulman

The Penis Story

THE NIGHT BEFORE THEY SAT IN THEIR USUAL SPOTS. JESSE'S HAIR WAS LIKE TORRENTS of black oil plunging into the sea. Ann watched her, remembering standing in the butcher shop looking at smoked meat, smelling the grease, imagining Jesse's tongue on her labia. She was starving.

"I'm just waiting for a man to rescue me," Jesse said.

"Look, Jess," Ann answered. "Why don't we put a timeline on this thing. Let's say, forty. If no man rescues you by the time you're forty, we'll take it from a different angle. What do you say?"

"I say I'll be in a mental hospital by the time I'm forty."

Jesse was thirty-two. This was a realistic possibility.

"Jesse, if instead of being two women, you and I were a woman and a man, would we be lovers by now?"

"Yes." Jesse had to answer yes because it was so obviously true.

"So what's not there for you in us being two women? Is it something concrete about a man, or is it the idea of a man?"

"I don't think it's anything physical. I think it is the idea of a man. I want to know that my lover is a man. I need to be able to say that."

Ann started to shake and covered her legs with a blanket so it wouldn't be so obvious. She felt like a child. She put her head on Jesse's shoulder feeling weak and ridiculous. Then they kissed. It felt so familiar. They'd been doing that for months. Each knew how the other kissed. Ann felt Jesse's hand on her waist and back and chest. Jesse reached her hand to Ann's bra. She'd done this before too. First tentatively, then more directly, she brushed her hands and face against Ann's breasts. Ann kissed her skin and licked it. She sucked her fingers, knowing those nails would have to be cut if Jesse were ever to put her fingers into Ann's body. She looked at Jesse's skin, at her acne scars and blackheads. She wanted to kiss her a hundred times. Then, as always, Jesse became disturbed, agitated. "I'm nervous again," she said. "Like, *oh no—now I'm going to have to fuck.*"

Suddenly Ann remembered that their sexual life together was a piece of glass. She put on her shirt and went home. This was the middle of the night in New York City.

When Ann awoke the next morning from unsettling dreams, she saw that a new attitude had dawned with the new day. She felt accepting, not proud. She felt ready to face adjustment and compromise. She was ready for change. Even though she was fully awake her eyes had not adjusted to the morning. She reached for glasses but found them inadequate. Then she looked down and saw that she had a penis.

Surprisingly, she didn't panic. Ann's mind, even under normal circumstances, worked differently than the minds of many of those around her. She was able to think three thoughts at the same time and, as a result, often suffered from headaches, disconnected conversation, and too many ideas. However, at this moment she only had two thoughts: "What is it going to be like to have a penis?" and "I will never be the same again."

It didn't behave the way most penises do. It rather seemed to be trying to find its own way. It swayed a bit as she walked to the bathroom mirror, careful not to let her legs interfere, feeling off balance, as if she had an itch and couldn't scratch it. She tried to sit back on her hips, for she still had hips, and walk pelvis first, for she still had her pelvis. In fact, everything appeared to be the same except that she had no vagina. Except that she had a prick.

"I am a prick," she said to herself.

The first thing she needed to do was piss and that was fun, standing up seeing it hit the water, but it got all over the toilet seat and she had to clean up the yellow drops.

"I am a woman with a penis, and I am still cleaning up piss."

This gave her a sense of historical consistency. Now it was time to get dressed.

She knew immediately she didn't want to hide her penis from the world. Ann had never hidden anything else, no matter how controversial. There was nothing wrong with having a penis. Men had them, and now she did too. She wasn't going to let her penis keep her from the rest of humanity. She chose a pair of button-up Levis and stuffed her penis into her pants where it bulged pretty obviously. Then she put on a t-shirt that showed off her breasts and her muscles and headed toward the F train to Shelley's house to meet her friends for lunch.

By the time Ann finished riding on the F train she had developed a fairly integrated view of her new self. She was a lesbian with a penis. She was not a man with breasts. She was a woman. This was not androgyny, she'd never liked that word. Women had always been whole to Ann, not half of something waiting to be completed.

They sat in Shelley's living room eating lunch. These were her most attentive friends, the ones who knew best how she lived. They sat around joking until Shelley finally asked, "What's that between your legs?"

"That's my penis," Ann said.

"Oh, so now you have a penis."

"I got it this morning. I woke up and it was there."

They didn't think much of Ann's humor usually, so the conversation moved on to other topics. Judith lit a joint. They got high and said funny things, but they did keep coming back to Ann's penis.

"What are you going to do with it?" Shelley asked.

"I don't know."

"If you really have a penis, why don't you show it to us?" Roberta said. She was always provocative.

Ann remained sitting in her chair but unbuttoned her jeans and pulled her penis out of her panties. She had balls too.

"Is that real?"

Roberta came over and put her face in Ann's crotch. She held Ann's penis in her hand. It just lay there.

"Yup, Ann's got a penis alright."

"Did you eat anything strange yesterday?" Judith asked.

"Maybe it's from masturbating," Roberta suggested, but they all knew that couldn't be true.

"Well, Ann, let me know if you need anything, but I have to say I'm glad we're not lovers anymore because I don't think I could handle this." Judith bit her lip.

"I'm sure you'd do fine," Ann replied in her usual charming way.

◆ ◆ ◆

Ann put on her flaming electronic lipstick. It smudged accidentally, but she liked the effect. This was preparation for the big event. Ann was ready to have sex. Thanks to her lifelong habit of masturbating before she went to sleep, Ann had sufficiently experimented with erections and come. She'd seen enough men do it and knew how to do it for them, so she had no trouble doing it for herself. Sooner or later she would connect with another person. Now was that time. She wore her t-shirt that said, "Just visiting from another planet." Judith had given it to her and giggled, nervously.

The Central Park Ramble used to be a bird and wildlife sanctuary. Because it's hidden, and therefore foreboding, gay men use it to have sex, and that's where Ann wanted to be. Before she had a penis, Ann used to imagine sometimes while making love that she and her girlfriend were two gay men. Now that she had this penis, she felt open to different kinds of people and new ideas, too.

She saw a gay man walking through the park in his little gym suit. He had a nice tan like Ann did and a gold earring like she did too. His t-shirt also had writing on it. It said, "All-American Boy." His ass stuck out like a mating call.

"Hi," she said.

"Hi," he said.

"Do you want to smoke a joint?" She asked very sweetly. He looked around suspiciously.

"Don't worry, I'm gay too."

"Okay, honey, why not. There's nothing much happening anyway."

So, they sat down and smoked a couple of joints and laughed and told about the different boyfriends and girlfriends that they had had, and which ones had gone straight and which ones had broken their hearts. Then Ann produced two beers and they drank those and told about the hearts that they had broken. It was hot and pretty in the park.

Ann mustered up all her courage and said, "I have a cock."

"You look pretty good for a mid-op," he said.

His name was Mike.

"No, I'm not a transexual. I'm a lesbian with a penis. I know this is unusual, but would you suck my cock?"

Ann had always wanted to say "suck my cock" because it was one thing a lot of people said to her and she never said to anyone. Once she and her friends made little stickers that said, "End Violence in the Lives of Women," which they stuck up all over the subway. Many mornings when she was riding to work, Ann would see that different people had written over them, "Suck my cock." It seemed like an appropriate response, given the world in which we all live.

Mike thought this was out of the ordinary, but he prided himself on taking risks. So he decided "what the hell" and went down on her like an expert.

Well, it did feel nice. It didn't feel like floating in hot water, which is what Ann sometimes thought of when a woman made love to her well with her mouth, but it did feel good. She started thinking about other things. She tried the two-gay-men image but it had lost its magic. Then she remembered Jesse. She saw them together in Jesse's apartment. Each in their usual spots.

"What's the matter, Annie? Your face is giving you away."

"This is such a bastardized version of how I'd like to be relating to you right now."

"Well," said Jesse. "What would it be like?"

"Oh, I'd be sitting here and you'd say, 'I'm ready,' and I'd say, 'Ready for what?' and you'd say, 'I'm ready to make love to you Annie.' Then I'd say, 'Why don't we go to your bed?', and we would."

"Yes," Jesse said. "I would smell your smell, Annie. I would put my arms on your neck and down over your breasts. I would unbutton your shirt, Annie, and pull it off your shoulders. I would run my fingers down your neck and over your nipples. I would lick your breasts, Annie, I would run my tongue down your neck to your breasts."

Ann could feel Jesse's wild hair like the ocean passing over her chest. Jesse's mouth was on her nipples licking, her soft face against Ann's skin. She was licking, licking then sucking harder and faster until Jesse clung to her breasts harder and harder.

"You taste just like my wife," Mike said after she came.

"What?"

Ann's heart was beating. The ocean was crashing in her ears.

"I said, you taste just like my wife, when you come I mean. You don't come sperm, you know, you come women's cum, like pussy."

"Oh, thank God."

Ann was relieved.

♦ ♦ ♦

Another morning Ann woke up and her fingers were all sticky. It was still dark. First she thought she'd had a wet dream, but when she turned on her reading lamp she saw blood all over her hands. Instinctively she put her fingers in her mouth. It was gooey, full of membrane and salty. It was her period. She guessed it had no other place to come out, so it flowed from under her fingernails. She spent the next three and a half days wearing black plastic gloves.

The feeling of her uterine lining coming out of her hands gave Ann some hope. After living with her penis for nearly a month, she was beginning to experience it as a loss, not an acquisition. She was grieving for her former self.

One interesting item was that Ann was suddenly in enormous sexual demand. More women than had ever wanted to make love with her wanted her now. But most of them didn't want anyone to know, so she said no.

There was one woman, though, to whom she said yes. Her name was Muriel. Muriel dreamed that she made love to a woman with a penis and it was called "glancing." So she looked high and low until she found Ann, who she believed had a rare and powerful gift and should be honored.

Ann and Muriel became lovers, and Ann learned many new things from this experience. She realized that when you meet a woman, you see the parts of her body that she's going to use to make love to you. You see her mouth and teeth and tongue and fingers. You see her fingers comb her hair, play the piano, wash the dishes, write a letter. You watch her mouth eat and whistle and quiver and scream and kiss. When she makes love to you she brings all this movement and activity with her into your body.

Ann liked this. With her penis, however, it wasn't the same. She had to keep it private. She also didn't like fucking Muriel very much. She missed the old way. Putting her penis into a woman's body was so confusing. Ann knew it wasn't making love "to" Muriel, and it certainly wasn't Muriel making love "to" her. It was more like making love "from" Muriel, and that just didn't sit right.

One day Ann told Muriel about Jesse.

"I give her everything within my capacity to give, and she gives me everything within her capacity to give—only my capacity is larger than hers."

In response Muriel took her to the Museum of Modern Art and pointed to a sculpture by Louise Bourgeois. Ann spent most of the afternoon in front of the large piece, an angry ocean of black penises that rose and crashed, carrying a little box house. The piece was called *Womanhouse*. She looked at the penises, their little round heads, their black metal trunks, how they moved together to make waves, and she understood something completely new.

They got together the next day in a bar. As soon as she walked in Ann felt nauseous. She couldn't eat a thing. The smell of grease from Jesse's chicken dinner came in waves to Ann's side of the table. She kept her nose in the beer to cut the stench.

"You're dividing me against myself, Jesse."

Jesse offered her some chicken.

"No thanks, I really don't want any. Look, I can't keep making out with you on a couch because that's as far as you're willing to go before this turns into a lesbian relationship. It makes me feel like nothing."

Ann didn't mention that she had a penis.

"Annie, I can't say I don't love being physical with you because it wouldn't be true."

"I know."

"I feel something ferocious when I smell you. I love kissing you. That's why it's got to stop. I didn't realize when I started this that I was going to want it so much."

"Why is that a problem?"

"Why is that a problem? Why is that a problem?"

Jesse was licking the skin off the bone with her fingers. Slivers of meat stuck out of her long fingernails. She didn't know the answer.

"Jesse, what would happen if someone offered you a woman with a penis?"

Jesse wasn't surprised by this question because Ann often raised issues from new and interesting perspectives.

"It wouldn't surprise me."

"Why not?"

"Well, Annie, I've never told you this before, actually it's just a secret between me and my therapist, but I feel as though I do have a penis. It's a theoretical penis, in my head. I've got a penis in my head and it's all mine."

"You're right," Ann said. "You do have a penis in your head because you have been totally mind-fucked. You've got an eight-inch cock between your ears."

With that she left the restaurant and left Jesse with the bill.

Soon Ann decided she wanted her clitoris back and she started to consult with doctors who did transsexual surgery. Since Ann had seen, tasted, and touched many clitorises in her short but full life, she knew that each one had its own unique way and wanted her very own cunt back just the way it had always been. So, she called together every woman who had ever made love to her. There was her French professor from college, her brother's girlfriend, her cousin Clarisse, her best friend from high school, Judith, Claudette, Kate, and Jane and assorted others. They all came to a big party at Shelley's house where they got high and drank beer and ate lasagna and when they all felt fine, Ann put a giant piece of white paper on the wall. By committee, they reconstructed Ann's cunt from memory. Some people had been more attentive than others, but they were all willing to make the effort. After a few hours and a couple of arguments as to the exact color tone and how many wrinkles on the left side, they finished the blueprints. "Pussy prints," the figure skater from Iowa City called them.

The following Monday Ann went in for surgery, reflecting on the time she had spent with her penis. When you're different, you really have to think about things. You have a lot of information about how the mainstream lives, but they don't know much about you. They also don't know that they don't know, which they don't. Ann wanted one thing, to be a whole woman again. She never wanted to be mutilated by being cut off from herself, and she knew that would be a hard thing to overcome, but Ann was willing to try.

Sarah Lucia Hoagland

From Lesbian Ethics:
Desire and Political Perception

THE MEANING OF OUR EMOTIONS, BELIEFS, INTENTIONS, INTUITIONS, IS DEVELOPED IN a social context, and we can challenge or develop that context and so challenge or develop meaning. This is not an individual project, neither the challenge nor the development. It involves the interactions of lesbians who question and analyze and evaluate. And that means it is a political endeavor—an endeavor that involves interacting and in which reasoning and emotions are not perceived as distinct entities.

Consider, for example, patriarchal definitions of sexuality and desire. Within the dominant ideology, sex is heterosexual or male homosexual. Elements of the meaning of sex in patriarchy include the beliefs that: (1) sex is necessary to a man's health; (2) sexual desire involves a death wish (eros); (3) male sexuality is a powerful and uncontrollable urge; (4) rape is natural behavior; (5) sex is an act of male conquest; (6) sexual freedom includes total male access to females; (7) sexual feeling is a matter of being out of control; and (8) sex is a natural phenomenon such that women who resist male sexual advances are "frigid."[1]

Audre Lorde has begun challenging this dominant meaning of our desire. She argues that the erotic is power, that it is a resource within us, and a source of knowledge. She opposes the erotic to the pornographic, since the pornographic emphasizes sensations without feelings, without engagement, and hence perpetuates the fragmentation of our energy. She argues that the erotic is nonrational and suggests that "the erotic is not a question only of what we do. It is a question of how acutely and fully we can feel in the doing."[2]

Thus, Audre Lorde has begun to revalue our desire by naming it a power-from-within, and she points out that it is life-invoking. This is central to lesbian thought, and while I agree with most of her analysis, my focus is slightly different.

In the first place, I think it a mistake to characterize desire as nonrational.[3] Attraction does not exist in a vacuum; the meaning of our feelings and responses is developed in depth and complexity through the social context in which we realize them. That we desire lesbians is not incidental; our desire is focused. And that focus results from integrating and reasoning and emotions.

Secondly, I want to suggest that there are problems with calling our desire "erotic," problems with invoking the concept of 'eros'. 'Eros', as developed in the homopatriarchal greco-christian tradition, is quite the opposite of life-invoking; is it death or other-world oriented. Mary Daly has explored the necrophilic focus that defines eroticism in patriarchy.[4] 'Eros' is the will to get and possess; it is a force that strives for perfection, for immortality. It is associated with priestly desires and male sadomasochistic death wishes as well as heterosexual procreation; it involves the idea that men lose their vital fluids by engaging in sexual intercourse. (Thus, before a "big game," men are to lie alone.) In religious terms, 'eros' represents an ecstatic loss of self, a love that is directed toward a god and whose climax, in christian mysticism, is self-annihilation (perfection). (Thus christian mysticism and sadomasochism embrace the same ideology, share the same erotic roots.)

In the homopatriarchal greco-christian tradition, a tradition which permeates our thinking, in addition to 'eros' there are essentially three other kinds of love: 'agape', 'nomos', and 'philia'.[5] 'Agape' is unconditional giving, total and unevaluated—so-called christian love or motherly love—and particularly devoid of desire. It bestows grace on its object, thus implying that its object by itself has no reason to merit such love. 'Agape' is a love in spite of the person, not because of her.

'Nomos', properly meaning 'law', involves a love which subordinates reason to faith; it is a submission to a divine law and order "beyond" man's understanding. Under this concept, it is not man's place to question the will of a god; thus we gain the idea of love being acceptance of authority. And under this concept, reason is a threat because it implies independent will and possible rebellion. Reason creates doubt and insecurity; faith, on the other hand, gives confidence and peace (comfort, numbness).

And, finally, 'philia' is brotherly love, giving rise to the unity of things, a communion among men. In this case, the saving force is that which unifies, connects, and draws all together into one indiscriminate mass. It is a universal love for mankind without any attention to particular individuals, differences among individuals, or the complexity and distinctness of the conditions of their lives. That which separates, differentiates, alienates, is the destructive force.

I find *all* these concepts—'eros', 'agape', 'nomos', and 'philia'—fragmented and fragmenting. I think we can weave our own concepts of lesbian love and desire and energy and power.

I will add here some thoughts about the word 'sex'; there are problems as well with using it to talk about our desire. The word 'sex' comes from the latin *sexus*, akin to *secus*, derivative of secare, "to cut, divide," as in "section," and itself suggests fragmenting or severing. As a result, Mariel Rae suggests that 'sex' is a term which erases lesbian desire, sensuality, and orgasm.[6]

In discussing the meaning of 'sex', Claudia Card asks whether sex is a purely biological phenomenon like eating and drinking and sleeping, or whether it is something whose meaning emerges through an institutional context, as is the case with breakfasting, dining, or going to potluck dinners. She suggests that if we regard sex as a purely biological phenomenon, then "when one tries to abandon a phallocentric conception of sex, it is no longer clear what counts as sexual and what does not."[7] She suggests that the only preinstitutional sense of sex she can make out is a biological one that refers in one way or another "to reproductive capacities of members of a species that reproduce sexually rather than asexually." In this respect, of course, the clitoris is not a sexual organ:

> In short, I do not see how it is possible to give an account of what it means to call…clitoral pleasure…sexual without reference to the institution of sexuality. If there is such a thing as "plain sex," which does not mean simply "femaleness or maleness" but which is ordinarily pleasurable and had only intermittently and is independent of the institution of sexuality (logically prior to it), it seems also to be a purely androcentric phenomenon.[8]

In other words, if one refers to 'sex' as a purely biological phenomenon, such as eating, rather than an institutional phenomenon, such as potlucking, then clitoral pleasure is not part of sex.

Thus, understanding sexuality is not just understanding a "drive" but understanding the context, indeed the institutions, that gives our urges and responses depth of meaning. Now in evaluating the patriarchal institution of sex, Claudia Card notes that it sanctions hatred and domination—they are integral rather than peripheral to it. Further, the institution of sex, even imagined outside a patriarchal context, remains essentially a male phenomenon. As Marilyn Frye has pointed out, sex is a phenomenon which requires having one or more male sexual organs present; penetration of almost anything counts as having sex.[9]

In considering the Philip Blumstein, Pepper Schwartz survey on sex,[10] Marilyn Frye notes that it was brought to her attention that what 85% of long-term heterosexual married couples do more than once a month (which lesbians, according to the studies, do far less frequently) takes, on the average, eight minutes to do.[11] She goes on:

> I know from my own experience and from the reports of a few other lesbians in long-term relationships, that what we do that, on the average, we do considerably less frequently, takes on the average, considerably more than eight minutes to do. It takes about thirty minutes, at the least. Sometimes maybe an hour. And it is not uncommon that among these relatively uncommon occurrences, an entire afternoon or evening is given over to activities organized around "doing it." The suspicion arises that what 85 percent of heterosexual married couples are doing more than once a month and what 47 percent of lesbian couples are doing less than once a month is not the same thing.[12]

Marilyn Frye wonders what violence lesbians do to our experience when answering the same questions heterosexuals answer, as though they have the same meaning for us. She notes that in her experience and reading of the culture, heterosexuals count what they report in these surveys according to the man's orgasm and ejaculation. And she suggests that the attempt to encode our lustiness and lustfulness in the words 'sex' and 'sexuality' has backfired: "Instead of losing their phallocentricity, these words have imported the phallocentric meanings into and onto experience which is not in any way phallocentric."[13] For example, the joy lesbians can feel in swirling a lover's vagina and in having our vaginas swirled as a potter swirls a pot has nothing to do with banging and penetration, and the male organ is inadequate to the task.[14] I want to try to leave behind the word 'sex' and focus instead on 'desire'.

Our attraction to each other and our desire take many forms. Yet the institution of sexuality portrays all desire as leading to orgasm, and that, too, is inadequate for us. The point of desire is not necessarily orgasm. As JoAnn Loulan writes:

> Even those of us who usually have orgasms find ourselves tyrannized by this supposed goal of sex. When we constantly work toward having an orgasm, we are unable to experience each sexual encounter for the pleasure it can give us. Our preoccupation with this particular muscle spasm echoes our general approach in a consumer-oriented society: striving for a goal, while disregarding the pleasure (or lack thereof) that we experience in the process. For women who never reach that goal, there often may be little reason to have sex.[15]

The institution of sexuality portrays all sensuality as "foreplay," as simply part of the trek toward orgasm.[16] This diminishes all our sensual abilities. I mean to suggest that orgasm, along with all other aspects of our sensuality and desire, ceases to be powerful when we work to make it conform to homo- and heterosexual meaning: we will remain fragmented so long as we regard orgasm as the focus and point of all lesbian desire and sensuality while everything else remains a mere excuse.

Claudia Card reminds us that the language of what she calls eroticism is different from the language of sex. She distinguishes what she calls eroticism from sexuality, suggesting it is emotional, not a biological category. She notes that the patriarchal institution of sexuality presents the erotic as sexual "by construing erotic play...as a sexual invitation."[17] Pointing out that the "erotic" may or may not be "sexual," Claudia Card suggests that it is a way of touching, one which does not succeed unless the other is also touching. In other words, it is interactive. Further, "erotic" interchange "can work like super-glue—just a little bit can have one hooked for years. This is not true of sexual activity in general."[18]

We need new language and new meaning to develop our lesbian desire, especially as we explore and develop what draws us, where our attraction comes from, what we want to keep, what we want to change and why, how our attractions vary, how our desires change over time, and so on.[19] And this is an interactive, not an introspective, matter. We need a lot more discussion and exploration among ourselves in something like consciousness-raising groups, certainly among intimates—lovers and friends—to develop the meaning of lesbian desire, and to heal our fragmentation.

One indication of our fragmentation is that we have severed and continue to sever our lesbian desire from our work, our interactions outside the bedroom. Or we pretend our desire is not present anywhere but in the bedroom, partly out of a false belief about what commitment to a lover means. Our lesbian desire is present in our work, in our meetings, at take-back-the-night rallies, in the bars, in heated debates, as well as in the bedroom. And to separate these aspects of our lives is to fragment our power; for our desire enables us, as lesbians.

Another indication of our fragmentation is that at times we find ourselves attracted to lesbians we don't especially like. We also are attracted to difference as exotic, not as something to discover and learn from but rather as a mystery and hence something we objectify and keep at a distance. As a result, we use vulnerability or, alternatively, a stoical approach with each other, rather than developing intimacy. Perhaps we are afraid that if the other is no longer a mystery, we will find ourselves reflected back as ordinary, not special. We often opt for melodrama to create meaning.

Further, we tend to believe that to be safe we must be rational and in control, but to feel anything we must be emotional and out of control. Thus we regard desire as a matter of 'eros' (ecstatic loss of self) and success as a matter of being either in or out of control. And we often try to separate desire from feelings for a particular lesbian in order to avoid the risk of connection—being momentarily and allegedly out of control (during "orgasm") while still maintaining strict control over our feelings. This way we think we can have the "goodies" while remaining "safe."

I want to suggest that desire is neither a matter of being in or out of control, nor need it be a matter of being "safe" or "in danger." Desire is a matter of connection. It is our lesbian desire which moves us to connect with each other. And when we open deeply to another through desire, we create channels which will remain with us through this living—even when the desire changes.

Again, the depth of our feeling expands through the meaning developed in our social context. As we begin to revalue our lesbian desire, I think we will be less likely to be attracted to difference as exotic, as that which is a threat to who we are and hence a thrill, or as an arena for conquest.[20] We may also be less likely to move toward sameness just because it offers the apparent security of familiarity. Thus, we can come to embrace more fully both desire and difference as biophilic, not necrophilic.

A third indication of our fragmentation is the idea prevalent among us that making love can ruin a friendship. We are intent upon maintaining a distinction between friends and lovers. I think this is because, to varying degrees, our love and desire have been oriented toward eros in patriarchy, toward the necrophilic. Under the homopatriarchal construction of the erotic, desire becomes a threat to us, can steal (sweep) us away—we *fall* in love, we go out of control.[21] Thus we don't want to muddy or threaten our friendships with desire. We keep very strict limits on what counts as appropriate engagement with those toward whom we direct our desire, whether they be insistence on the distance of one-night stands or whether they involve moving in forever and ever with someone we've made love with. And we act to protect our friendships so when our lover relationships blow up, we have a haven, a resource, with our friends.

A fourth indication of our fragmentation is that we seldom laugh while making love (or if we do, we're keeping quiet about it). Kate Clinton connects humor to lesbian desire, suggesting those hilarious moments of laughter come from the same source as our desire:[22]

> Feminist humor…is a deeply radical analysis of the world and our being in the world because it, like the erotic, demands a commitment to joy…. The demand for our presence in the moment is another way in which our sense of humor and the erotic are entwined. For full participation in the erotic, you have to be there.[23]

As Marilyn Frye notes:

> Attention is a kind of passion. When one's attention is on something, one is present in a particular way with respect to that thing. The presence is, among other things, an element of erotic presence. The orientation of one's attention is also what fixes and directs the application of one's physical and emotional work.[24]

That is, presence is central to engaging. And Anna Lee suggests we claim our desire for the sheer lesbian joy of it.

> What does it mean to say I want a womon? I must acknowledge what I feel is real. Unclouded by attaching forevers to it. What is happening is surely powerful and is sexual. It is the smell, touch, the rhythm of the womon's body exciting my senses. All of them. Fully engaged. Full. My senses become stretched to their limits and beyond.[25]

She adds that our desire "is the underlying river often silent, frequently diverted, that connects one to another."

Thus, as Harriet Ellenberger suggests, our lesbian desire helps us move out of conditions of oppression and want to live. She notes that "we have what we need if only we look in the right places, if only we pay attention to what goes on between us," adding:

> I think that's what goes on between lesbians—that we somehow bring each other into [meaningful] existence.[26]

Our lesbian desire includes humor and joy, both of which involve presence. And being present to each other, attending each other, interacting, is part of how we bring each other into meaningful existence.

The issue of presence brings up another indication of our fragmentation—namely, the question of jealousy. When we engage with someone, we may regard anyone or anything else she focuses on as a threat. I want to challenge this. I think there are serious problems involved with how we attend each other. However, I don't think the solution lies in trying to slot our relationships into a preconceived form such that we believe we must find the one and only and that no other meaningful engagement, including work and play outside that form, must enter our lives.

When someone spends time with another, does the fact that she also spends time with a second affect the quality of time she spent with the first? Does the fact that she spends time with another by itself *change* the nature and quality of her interactions with the first? In certain respects it may. That I interact with one enhances my framework that I bring to my interactions with another. But I am present or I am not at any given moment, and that I am later present elsewhere does not change the nature of my earlier presence. At least in my experience, attention and presence are not quantitatively measured. Of course we are limited by energy, space, and time. And we cannot engage intimately with a large number of other lesbians. But, in my experience, that I am present at one time with one in no way diminishes my presence at another time with another.

The question of jealousy concerns questions of trusting our interactions. If she attends only me, then it would seem I have no worry about whether her love is "true." (This, of course, is not so.) But if she also attends another, she may be lying to me. Now there is the possibility that another may be playing us for a fool. But so what? If another plays us for a fool, it was she who wasted her time. Once we find she is lying, of course we can withdraw. But as to evaluating our time spent before that moment—well, *we* were engaged; she was, thus, the fool. So another may be dishonest. Nevertheless, that a lesbian cares deeply for someone else (a mother, a child, a lover, a friend) does not in itself diminish her care for or her presence with us.

My general point is not restricted to relationships with others. For example, one lover may be happily and intently although exhaustingly involved with her job or project. And this can as easily become a source of comparison and jealousy an can another lesbian she might be involved with. But such jealousy is unnecessary. Interacting with others and engaging in other projects enhance what we bring to a relationship. What matters is that there is quality time between us.

Some lesbians couch the issue in terms of monogamy/nonmonogamy. I think this is a mistake. As Julia Penelope argues, "Both terms name heteropatriarchal institutions within which the only important information is: *how many women can a man legitimately own?*" The terms 'monogamy' and 'nonmonogamy' presuppose that women are the property of the men who marry them.[27]

The issue is not how many lovers someone has. It may be that two lesbians want to share intimacies—physical desire as well as secrets and hopes and joys and pain—only with each other, and that this best suits their needs and wants at the time. Or it may be that lesbians want to explore intimate desire with more than one other, thereby changing the dynamics of the lover relationship. There are vehement arguments decrying the pitfalls of one choice or the other. The truth of the matter is that each focus carries its own problems and its own joys. What works is different for different lesbians as well as for the same lesbians at different times. What matters is the quality of presence.

Engaging is not all-encompassing; rather, it is a selection of focus, the result of what each of us brings to the engaging. When you and I engage, at whatever level, it is a unique engagement because it involves entwining your energy and mine. While it gains meaning from a context—patriarchal or lesbian—it is not just a matter of form. Something special happens, as a result of our attentiveness, when you and I engage. Sometimes we forget this specialness, that this energy is here now, in this living, and that it is unique. You and I need times to focus fully on each other, special time we plan together.

And no one else provides for just that. Nor should they. For when you engage with someone else, whether as lover or friend or co-worker, you focus on, attend, respond to her. That, too, is unique. What you and I have cannot be replaced by what you and she have. I think we can move away from heterosexual stereotypes.

In developing the meaning of lesbian desire, we can revalue the distinction between friend and lover together with the idea that the point of all true sensuality is orgasm and the judgment that whether one reaches orgasm with another is the significant factor in defining a relationship. Often we now act as if a lover were the only one meant for us, and we stifle desire in our relations with others and in our projects. While friends may be important, our responses to them go secondary, even with close or best friends; their wants and needs go on hold automatically. Alternatively, they become the only ones we'll be intimate with while we pursue superficial sexual engagements; we maintain 'freedom' and thrills by opting for the anonymity of objectification. Maintaining these firm distinctions means we really don't have to make choices in certain situations. We simply respond according to the dictates of the form.*

---

* One form is butch/fem. I have not talked about the categories 'butch' and 'fem' directly because, like 'monogamy' and 'nonmonogamy', I think the terms focus our attention away from deeper concerns. Certainly, we are affected by heteropatriarchy's categories of 'masculinity' and 'femininity'; we have internalized these values. Certainly, too, butch/fem are not exact replicas of masculinity/femininity. (For example, while women are expected to be responsible for the sexual satisfaction of men, it is butches who are responsible for the sexual satisfaction of fems.[28] And certainly, to simply dismiss butch/fem is to miss a great deal of our past.

However, 'butch' and 'fem' are simply conceptual boxes and not very accurate ones at that—many lesbians must strive to fit the mold. Further, both butches and fems can be fully obnoxious and arrogant; both butches and fems like to cook; both butches and fems can fix flat tires, repair plumbing, do electrical wiring, like flowers, lift weights, wear jewelry, and so on. In a particular relationship, that one lesbian likes to cook and the other likes to clean up is fine; in another relationship, the cook may retire to something else. But we don't need the labels 'butch' and 'fem'. Like any stereotypes, if we perceive the world through them, the world will come to be that way; that the world *is* that way is a result of our perceiving, agreeing, that it is that way.

In the long run, I don't focus on the issues of monogamy/nonmonogamy and butch/fem because I believe they are covers for an underlying issue. The real issue involves our urge for a code to tell us what to do, not because it yields the best possible good (since there are no guarantees), but simply because it is familiar, and uniform, and helps us fit in so we don't have to think about it, and because creating everything as we go is so arduous and takes so much energy. But then we didn't take the easy path; we're lesbians.[29]

Further, if we find our feelings change and don't fit that form, we conclude the relationship has ended, that we no longer care, no longer are able to respond. For example, many lovers will go through times when they don't take each other to orgasm; nevertheless they cuddle, give back rubs, and in general are very physical with each other. Now if one feels a lack but the other doesn't, then a problem may arise. However, more often in my experience, both are quite happy with this. If they start to feel they must regularly reach orgasm because they believe that lovers are supposed to do that, then they may decide something is wrong with their relationship when that is not the case.

When we focus on a form rather than the energy dynamics of those involved, we tend to think of relationships—whether as lovers, friends, collectives, or community—as static and not dynamic, as unchanging. As a result, when we do observe change in a relationship because someone is changing, we believe the relationship is ending, that only nothingness will follow; or if we suppress that change, we ultimately force the relationship to end because it has become stifling.* We reach for a form into which to fit ourselves to make the relationship, rather than regarding ourselves as the form, the limits, and the substance, while regarding the relationship as fluid interaction. I think if we regard orgasm not as the goal or defining factor of all encounters while, of course, continuing to delight in it, and if we overlap the concepts of "friend" and "lover," our connections in community, and community itself will become stronger, particularly through extended relationships.

Actually, we have developed far more complex relationships than the distinction between friend and lover acknowledges. I mean to suggest that we consider the energy involved in all sorts of connections. We engage in different ways with different lesbians. With some there is a chemistry that is magnetic. It may not last long, and there may not be much else in the connection, but it is engaging and fun; it becomes painful only when we try to make it something it is not. With others there is an immediate connection as if we were old friends; there is a recognition of each other and a comfort almost from the moment of meeting. And

---

* In general, fear of change inevitably leads to support of the status quo for no other reason than that it is familiar. This then becomes a conservative force: order becomes the single most important goal of the administrative mind regardless of the effects on the lives and health of those involved.

with each new meeting we can take up as if no time had passed since the last meeting, even when that time involves years. With others there is the challenge of constantly covering new ground. With still others there is the engagement of living together, of sharing space that weaves the pleasures of companionship. Besides companionship, this engagement involves each being able to find solitude without either one feeling threatened.

With some there is the pleasure of doing certain things together, working on a project or going camping, for example. Over time the connection grows. We may or may not be pursuing orgasm, but the engaging is intense. With others there is the utter joy of dancing with abandon, or wrestling, without either necessarily being a prelude to orgasm. With some we may be lovers and find thrill and joy in connecting and yet not live together because old habits would make the effort a disaster. With others, we may have been lovers and our relationship changes. Nevertheless at times we spend nights together, snuggle and hold each other, finding comfort in a deep connection that changes over time. Lesbian mothers may co-parent and be able to respond in very intimate ways with lesbians who are not their lovers. With other lesbians we have "affairs." When this occurs over time and each is "brutally honest" with the other, it can be a very stable and comforting element in our lives. Or again, some lesbians—actually many lesbians—may want to reach out and touch in a particular moment, and, without changing the main focus or our lives, share something intimate as a way of connecting, of embracing, for the sheer joy of their presence in our lives. Or a group of lesbians may make a home together and not be lovers. To live together well, whether or not as lovers, takes very special attention. This is also true of working together.

Our connections are many and varied. And I believe we can continue to vary them and stay closely connected to a number of lesbians throughout our lifetime. Our connections are a matter of our attention, our presence, and our interactions, including our lesbian desire. I think we would do well to dissolve the rigid distinction between friend and lover. What matters is our circle of intimates and their circles and so on.

Now, while we have developed more complex relationships than the distinction between friend and lover allows, nevertheless we are still deeply caught up with the models developed by men, particularly in terms of the meaning of attraction and attractiveness. Again, too often difference is pursued as erotic, whether in terms of roles or in terms of race or in other terms, because it is perceived as exotic. Or we play a numbers game either with ourselves or with others, as Kate Moran notes:

> As a fat lesbian I am so seldom seen as a possible sexual partner that I long ago stopped obsessing on how many women I would like to be involved with. It's not a relevant question for me. I don't care how many times thin, cute, small amazons sleep with each other trying to prove they are thin, cute, small amazons, or, if they meet at a softball game, buy matching running shorts, and are only seen when they run out of tofu. I am not interested in judging other lesbians on the basis of how they choose to structure (or not structure) their intimate relationships. What I do care about is how other lesbians perceive me and deal with me.[30]

She goes on:

> Proving worth through sexual conquest belongs in the stag parties of the heteropatriarchy. It certainly tells us nothing about a dyke to know how many wimmin she sleeps with or how exclusively committed she is. Looking at numbers is a game. What's important to me is talking honestly about how we deal with each other and starting to take seriously the anti-fat prejudice of many Lesbians. Quantity simply isn't an "issue" for me or for the Fat Dykes I know, but quality, and the lack of it in our relationships, certainly is.[31]

As Baba Copper notes in addressing the prejudice enacted in the community against older lesbians:

> Patriarchal standards of taste—rules of aesthetic and erotic choices—perpetuate male structures of power. If we allow male-defined standards of choice to be our default standards, then we maintain female powerlessness. We waste the opportunity that our lesbianism provides: to choose how to choose…. Unless old lesbians are re/membered as sexual attractive, useful, integral parts of the woman-loving world, then current lesbian identity is a temporary mirage, not a new social state of female empowerment.[32]

Other forms of erasure result in objectification. As Diane Hugs writes:

> Being disabled I get treated differently, not better, but often more oppressively. I have never been approached sexually by so many women than since I ended up using the wheelchair. It scares me to think others may be attracted to me because they assume that since I am disabled I will be submissive in nature. Also the physical presence thing really

gets to me. It's as though as an able-bodied lesbian I was average look-ing from the feedback I got from others, now that I'm in the chair I hear that others think I'm beautiful. It's as though I'm exceptional looking for a crip. I really get tired of it all.[33]

Our desire is connected to our attention and our choices: who we at-tend, who we ignore, and *why* and *how* we choose to ignore or attend. Our desire in a certain sense is a microcosm of the macrocosm of our op-pression: it has been erased and/or used against us to such an extent that we turn against ourselves and suppress it; and yet when we do manage to overcome what's been done with our lesbian desire and explore it in joy and discovery, it comes out all preprogrammed by the patriarchal in-stitution of sexuality and still erasing, fragmenting, destroying. Perhaps one aspect of healing our fragmentation lies in reconnecting desire with caring—real presence and attention—not the romantic haze of happily-ever-after.

> We both sat there, two disabled lesbians in our wheelchairs, each on opposite sides of the bed. Sudden feelings of fear and timidness came over us. But once we finished the transferring, lifting of legs, undress-ing and arranging of blankets, we finally touched. Softly and slowly we began to explore each other, our minds and bodies. Neither could make assumptions about the sensations or pleasures of the other. It was wonderful to sense that this woman felt that my body was worth the time it took to explore, that she was as interested in discovering my pleasure as I was in discovering hers.[34]

In revaluing our lesbian desire, Audre Lorde argues that it is essen-tially biophilic, not necrophilic:

> The erotic offers a well of replenishing and provocative force to the woman who does not fear its revelation, nor succumb to the belief that sensation is enough....
> The erotic is a measure between the beginnings of our sense of self and the chaos of our strongest feelings. It is an internal sense of satisfaction to which, once we have experienced it, we know we can aspire.[35]

And thus our desire yields a metaphor for choice:

> Within the celebration of the erotic in all our endeavors, my work be-comes a conscious decision—a longed-for bed which I enter gratefully and from which I rise up empowered.[36]

That is, the focus of our love and desire, not the pseudo-focus of discipline or self-control or the pseudo-intensity of being out of control, is the source from which we actively engage in depth of feeling and connecting in this living. Our desire informs our interactions as we choose where and how we focus and direct our attention. This is not a question of being either in or out of control.

Audre Lorde goes on to expose the impetus of traditional anglo-european duty-centered ethics which excludes desire:

> The principal horror of any system which defines the good in terms of profit rather than in terms of human need, or which defines human need to the exclusion of the psychic and emotional components of that need…is that it robs our work of its erotic value, its erotic power and life appeal and fulfillment. Such a system reduces work to a travesty of necessities, a duty by which we earn bread or oblivion for ourselves and those we love.[37]

That is, appeals to duty are necessary to motivate us to work because our desire has been severed from our work; thus when we find ourselves appealing to duty, as well as to self-sacrifice, it is an indication that we have lost the focus of our desire. We can acknowledge our lesbian desire as power, power-from-within particularly, a powerful source of connection, engagement, and focus.

From Adrienne Rich:

> Whatever happens with us, your body
> will haunt mine—tender, delicate
> your lovemaking, like the half-curled frond
> of the fiddlehead fern in forests
> just washed by sun. Your traveled, generous thighs
> between which my whole face has come and come—
> the innocence and wisdom of the place my tongue has found there—
> the live, insatiate dance of your nipples in my mouth—
> your touch on me, firm, protective, searching
> me out, your strong tongue and slender fingers
> reaching where I had been waiting years for you
> in my rose-wet-cave—whatever happens, this is.[38]

Desire involves choice, it is a judging that integrates reasoning and emotions and all our faculties. From Mary Daly:

Primarily, then, *Pure Lust* Names the high humor, hope, and cosmic accord/harmony of those women who choose to escape, to follow our hearts' deepest desire and bound out of the State of Bondage.... As [she who is moved by this desire] lurches/leaps into starlight her tears become tidal, her cackles cosmic, her laughter Lusty.[39]

When each of us came out, we invoked lesbian desire and we turned our attention to lesbian existence. It was a choice, a judgment. Now, what part was the "pure" emotion? What part the reason? (Or was there none!) What part the intuition? What part the dreams? What part the psychic? And what part was purely private? These parts were not separated. Our lesbian energy emerges from an integration of ourselves and our interactions with each other. And that integration involves both judgment of context and interaction with subjects. As such, that choice is political. Another way of putting this is to note that the whole lesbian being is greater, far greater, than the sum of the parts.

Notes

1. Note, for example, Susan Griffin, *Rape: The Power of Consciousness* (San Francisco: Harper & Row, 1979), part 1, pp. 3-22; Susan Brownmiller, *Against Our Will: Men, Women, and Rape* (New York: Simon and Schuster, 1975), pp. 257-68; and Sheila Jeffreys, *The Spinster and Her Enemies: Feminism and Sexuality, 1880-1930* (Boston: Pandora Press, 1985).

2. Audre Lorde, *Uses of the Erotic: The Erotic As Power* (Brooklyn, NY: Out and Out Books, 1978), p. 2; reprinted in *Sister Outsider* (Freedom, CA: The Crossing Press, 1984) p. 54.

3. See Naomi Scheman, "Individualism and the Objects of Psychology," in *Discovering Reality: Feminist Perspectives on Epistemology, Metaphysics, Methodology, and Philosophy of Science*, ed. Sandra Harding and Merrill Hintikka (Boston: D. Reidel Publishing Co., 1983) p. 226.

4. Mary Daly, *Gyn/Ecology: The Metaethics of Radical Feminism* (Boston: Beacon Press, 1978).

5. The thesis of the four kinds of love from the greek tradition was first proposed to me in a class by Dr. Walter Weir, University of Colorado.

6. Conversation, Mariel Rae.

7. Claudia Card, "The Symbolic Significance of Sex and the Institution of Sexuality," paper presented to the Society of Sex and Love at the Eastern Division meeting of the American Philosophical Association, New York City, December 28, 1984. A revised version of this

paper was published as *Intimacy and Responsibility: What Lesbians Do*, Series 2, Institute for Legal Studies, Working Papers, University of Wisconsin-Madison, Law School, October 1987.

8. Ibid.

9. Marilyn Frye, "To See and Be Seen: The Politics of Reality," in *The Politics of Reality: Essays in Feminist Theory* (Freedom, CA: The Crossing Press, 1983) p. 157.

10. Philip Blumstein and Pepper Schwartz, *American Couples* (New York: William Morrow and Co., 1983).

11. Marilyn Frye cites Dotty Calabrese, who presented this information in a workshop on long-term lesbian relationships at the Michigan Womyn's Music Festival, 1987.

12. Marilyn Frye, "Lesbian 'Sex'," *Sinister Wisdom* 35 (Summer/Fall 1988): 46-54.

13. Ibid.

14. Conversation, Harriet Ellenberger

15. JoAnn Loulan, *Lesbian Sex* (San Francisco: Spinsters Ink, 1984), p. 71; note also Sidney Spinster, "Orgasms and the Lesbian Touch," *Lesbian Inciter* 13 (July, 1984): 17, 18, 19.

16. JoAnn Loulan, *Lesbian Sex*, p. 73.

17. Claudia Card, "Symbolic Significance of Sex," pp. 10-11.

18. Ibid., p. 11.

19. For fun, note Tee Corinne, *Cunt Coloring Book* (San Francisco: Pearlchild Productions, 1975), subsequently published as *Labia Flowers* (Tallahassee, FL: The Naiad Press), and forthcoming as *Cunt Coloring Book* (Last Gasp, 2180 Bryant St., San Francisco, CA 94107).

20. Note Debbie Alicen's analysis of the language we often use to begin our sexual and love relationships, in particular "crush" and "infatuation": "Intertexuality: The Language of Lesbian Relationships," *Trivia* 3 (Fall 1983): 6-26. Note also Kathryn Pauly Morgan, "Romantic Love, Altruism, and Self-Respect," *Hypatia* 1, no. 1 (Spring 1986): 117-48.

21. Note, Debbie Alicen, "Intertexuality," pp. 6-26.

22. Kate Clinton, "Making Light: Another Dimension: Some Notes on Feminist Humor," *Trivia* 1 (Fall 1982): 42.

23. Ibid., pp. 39-40.

24. Marilyn Frye, "To See and Be Seen," p. 172.

25. Anna Lee, "Lust," unpublished paper.

26. Harriet Ellenberger, transcript of talk presented to the Eastern Division meeting of the Society for Women in Philosophy, Mt. Holyoke College, North Hadley, MA, April 14, 1985.

27. Julia Penelope, "The Mystery of Lesbians: II," *Lesbian Ethics* 1, no. 2 (Spring 1985): 36.

28. Conversation, Deborah Snow.

29. Conversation, Deidre McCalla.

30. Kate Moran, "When They Pick Sides, No One Asks Me to Play," *Lesbian Ethics* 1, no. 2 (Spring 1985): p. 95.

31. Ibid., p. 96.

32. Baba Copper, "The View from Over the Hill: Notes on Ageism between Lesbians," *Trivia* 7 (Summer 1985): 50-1; revised and reprinted in *Over the Hill: Reflections on Ageism between Women* (Freedom, CA: The Crossing Press, 1988).

33. Communication, diane hugs.

34. diane hugs, "Pleasures," in *With the Power of Each Breath: A Disabled Women's Anthology*, ed. Susan E. Browne, Debra Conors, and Nancy Stern (San Francisco: Cleis Press, 1985), p. 342; also in *My Story's On! Ordinary Women/Extraordinary Lives*, ed. Paula Ross

(Berkeley, CA: Common Differences Press, 1985), p. 32.

35. Audre Lorde, "Uses of the Erotic," p. 54

36. Ibid., p. 55.

37. Ibid.

38. Adrienne Rich, "(The Floating Poem, Unnumbered)," in *The Dream of a Common Language: Poems 1974-1977* (New York: W.W. Norton & Co., 1978), p. 32.

39. Mary Daly, *Pure Lust: Elemental Feminist Philosophy* (Boston: Beacon Press, 1984), p. 3.

Judith McDaniel

Politically Incorrect

On the night your lover
takes another lover   theory
takes a back seat and something
right down deep in the gut
centered between your liver
and your self-esteem shoots
bile out into your whole system
and makes you even more
unlovable than you already
have reason to feel.

As nausea clamps down and settles
in for a long stay you have
to realize she didn't get there
(you don't want to think where
just now) by herself and reluctantly
you have to admit you agreed
that too tight a relationship
could stifle individual growth
that after these many years
(how many doesn't seem to matter)
you may be relying a little
more on ritual than spontaneity
but tonight ritual—you remember—
holds many virtues.

It is probably easier if your lover
takes another lover while you
are out of town since nothing
not the anguished silence you
hold on your end of the expensive
long distance phone call
not the silence of a whole
city echoing around you on this
Saturday night when everyone else
is in love or at least in lust
nothing is quite like lying
alone in your double bed wondering
whether she will choose to come
home or stay away.

And on the morning after your lover
has taken another lover you can hold
meaningful conversations about
what this means to your relationship
and she can tell you she is taking
one day at a time and while you
are theoretically pleased she
is making sure her needs are met
you still taste the vomit
in your throat from the night before
and wonder if all of your friends
find you as unattractive
as your lover.

You have read all the theory
about nonmonogamy and how tight
dyads are politically stifling
a real drag in an anarcha-feminist
community but you still can't quite
make yourself go to the meeting
you had planned on for weeks
even if the program material falls

through a crack and your lover
tells you her sex life has nothing
to do with this meeting
but still you can't make yourself
sit down in the same room with them
as though nothing had happened
as though none of the boundaries
had shifted, no fissures had opened
and you had not fallen
through the crack.

What you want to know on this
morning is where are the stories
that tell how it feels to live
right now in your gut not your
head and how long it will be
until you can ask her how are you
and want to know the answer
and whether women die
from this or what percentage
of relationships bite the dust after
this transition from theoretical
to actual nonmonogamy.

And when you ask if she means
to still be your lover she says
she expects to have an ongoing
relationship with you and you
will have to decide whether
it matters that she has more
or better orgasms with her new
lover or if you can stop imagining
she is comparing your technique
like a clinician scoring
a novice somewhere deep down
inside that insecurity about
our sexuality so many of us

carry around and when you mumble
something about trust and being
able to let the feeling through
she tells you that you
will have to decide about that.

Still you admit she didn't
get there by herself and you want
to be able to love her and you want
to feel her love coming back at you
but the wires seem tangled
there's another voice on the line
singing   haha   haha   got you
you fool.

The Woman Who Lied

SHE MEANT TO TELL THE TRUTH, BUT SHE LIED. SHE DIDN'T MEAN TO. THE LIE WAS so minute, so unintentional, like some awkward crumb that grazes your cheek. But this was only the beginning.

It goes like this.

Hannah and Yetta are lovers. And it is new, like the smell of warm bread. They stumble and poke over each other's bodies looking for sweet spots. Yetta thinks she finds two—Hannah's nipples. Yetta squeezes Hannah's long soft nipples and whispers, "Nu? Yes?"

But Hannah feels nothing—nothing but the desire to please Yetta. So she mumbles, "Nu, yes."

Instantly her nipples grow hard and erect. Hannah eyes her nipples and laughs. This is very amusing to Hannah because she feels nothing. Yetta, on the other hand, mistakes Hannah's laugh as a sign of pleasure and begins kneading even more. Now Hannah's nipples are pulsating. They rise wildly. It's as if some she-*dybbuk* has crawled under Hannah's ear, points to her nipples, and scolds, "This will teach you, Hannah Levin, to rise above the truth."

Then the *dybbuk* giggles and moans some mysterious chant in Yiddish, which of course echoes out of Hannah's mouth. Yetta gasps joyfully and chants back. She wraps Hannah's nipples around her fingers and rocks and sucks.

Hannah's nipples rise again. They forsake their nipple shapes and ooze from her breast like coils of pastry dough. They swirl and float overhead. They circle Hannah's body and playfully touch themselves. Quickly, they swoop down and alight atop Hannah's breasts—now two perfect, warm crusty bagels.

Hannah is bewildered, but silent. Yetta does not see Hannah, only her delicious nipple-bagels.

"If only I had cream cheese," she murmurs while she chomps the firm crust.

Now the nipples leap up. They undo their circular shapes and dance and stretch and bulge into curvaceous, bulbous forms.

"*Vey is mir!*" Hannah exclaims. "My nipples they are braids of challah!"

"Not mere braids of challah, Hannahala," the *dybbuk* sneers. "Challah *bobbe meisehs*, Hannahala."

Then the *dybbuk* blows the sweet smell of challah straight into Yetta's nostrils. Yetta is *fershimmeled* by the challah smell. She squeals and wildly swings the nipple-braids overhead, like lassos.

Hannah calms Yetta down, "Shah, Yetta, the Sabbath is coming."

"Hannah, I will make good use of your challah for the Sabbath."

She delicately weaves nipple-garlands for Hannah's hair. Then with more nipple, she fashions an ornate breastplate for her chest. Next comes *tefillin* straps for Hannah's arm in case she should want to *daven*.

Hannah pleads, "Yetta, quickly, the Sabbath is coming, let's make *Shabbos*."

"We can use more of your challah for the *motzi*," Yetta announces.

Hannah nods reluctantly and drags her nipples to the table. They light the *Shabbos* candles. As Hannah's hands beckon the light of *Shabbos* into her eyes, she instantly knows she can no longer *shlep* such a burden around.

"Yetta, we must break this bread," Hannah says gravely. "These nipples are not really mine. They are *bobbe meisehs*. You do bring me pleasure, but not in those places."

They hug and chant the *motzi*: "*Hamotzi lechem min ha' aretz.*" Who bringest forth bread from the earth.

They tear soft hunks of challah off of Hannah. Instantly the braids become brittle and stale and both challah-nipples snap from her breast. Her own soft nipples reappear.

Hannah is relieved. "*Zi g'zunt.*"

Yetta is sad and hurt, but she whispers, "After dinner, Hannah, we'll just have to find those other places."

Sally Miller Gearhart

Flossie's Flashes

FLOSSIE YOROBA WOKE FOR THE THIRD TIME THAT NIGHT WITH THE TINGLING AT HER hairline skipping around to the nape of her neck. "Here she comes!" she thought, opening herself to the gathering explosion of pleasure. She grinned in the dark. "It's from the bones tonight."

Always it was one of two sources. She called the first "Volcano." In an increasingly urgent rhythm it would rise from the spot directly behind her navel, erupting in bursts upward to her arms and head, downward to her legs and feet. It moved patiently, irrevocably, relentlessly, inevitably, over muscle and bone, nerve and tendon, capturing layer after layer of forgiving flesh under its flow of molten energy. Then, in its surges toward freedom, it would strike the wall of skin and burst free of its encapsulation through welcoming pores, transforming itself always at that last second into ten thousand rivulets of pure sweat that sang and danced their way up and down her body. Or across and under it, depending on whatever position that body occupied at the moment. Her toes and fingers always got it last, just about the time the sweat on her back was beginning to cool.

The other kind, and the ones she was waking with tonight, rose from a different place, from the geometric center of each part of her body, simultaneously from thigh, elbow, backbone, phalanges, the middle of her head. This kind she called "Hot Seep," oozing as it did from the marrow of each bone outward toward the skin, not in waves but at most in small eddies, all pacing themselves according to the thickness of the flesh they sought to conquer, all carefully timing their emergence from the body to be a synchronized drench, all at once and altogether, over her whole being, top to bottom, back to front, spilling out at precisely the same instant from her big toes and her nipples, her shoulder blades and her waistline, the palms of her hands and the caverns of her ears.

This Seep was seconds short of emergence. She reached for her clitoris, carefully avoiding its tender, aggressive tip. She pressed it gently side to side, then up from under. Once. Twice. Then with a whoop of joy she flung off the quilt and arched her back into a long stretch of denouement, collapsing at last into inert flesh, drenched and dazzled in the frost-filled air.

A high wind was outflanking the protective eaves of her cabin. It drove a deluge of snow through her window and onto her naked skin. Sweat met flake in a mighty clash of elements. Flake melted. But flake won, cooling the seat in an embrace both familiar and triumphant.

Flossie whooped again. She stretched wide another time and urged more of her undaunted wetness into its stark encounter with the cold. She smiled and shuddered as she sucked a raging winter into her lungs. She felt the air transfer itself from lungs to bones, there to entrap the heat and follow its path, moving on it from behind until now her skin felt downright crisp, crisp and encased in what she knew must be a thin sheath of ice. She whooped a third time and catapulted to the window, drawing it tight against the storm.

Back under her quilt she subsided, giving thanks to Whoever Was that Daaana had decided not to stay over with her tonight. She preferred not to share a bed these days, much less Spoon, what with this waking up four and five times a night to sizzle and freeze, sizzle and freeze.

Though as for that, she thought, marveling at the completeness with which the quilt encased her, cuddled her—though as for that, Daaana was a great bedpartner for flashes. She actually envied Flossie, and advertised her in public to be better than Solar Central, hottest woman in the Grand Matrix, north-south-east-or-west.

Even from the depths of an early-dawn Spoon, Daaana could sometimes feel the moment coming before Flossie knew it herself. Then she would chuckle and cling to Flossie, holding her close in anticipation of the explosion of heat. Flossie, torn between the loving clasp of a good woman and her desire to leap to cold freedom, would throw the covers at least from her own burning flesh and lie only tokenly connected to Daaana by finger or kneecap. That, of course, threatened to deprive Daaana of one of her greatest pleasures: the slick sensuousness of their undulating sweat-bathed bodies. It led, usually, to loud laments as Daaana protected herself from the window's blast and Flossie, naked as a jay to the churlish chiding of the wintry wind, inhaled there like a card-carrying health freak. Sometimes it all led to a tussle that ended in shouts and uncontrolled laughter.

Flossie loved her nights with Daaana and sometimes missed the dreamwalking that Spooning could bring. But right now, these months, these years, she was exhilarated with her changes and often sacrificed the adventures of Spooned sleep for a night of solitary encounter with the elements. Since childhood she had loved the run from the sweat tent to the waterfall, the smell of a hard-worked body dripping in pungent clothes and the subsequent dunk into an icy mountain stream. She craved the contrasts, the sudden changes, the jig that her feet danced and the thanks that her heart sang every time she gifted them with those extremes.

Under the cover now she stroked her ample body, drawing her knees to her chest and lying Spoon with a phantom self as she cozed back into sleep. Not only did she get these wild free swings of heat and cold, but several times a night now she got to fall asleep again. Falling asleep, she thought. Sheer contentment, always, even with another Spooned body. But, she mused, there's a special balm to doing it in a wide bed all alone, with the margins of your body quite unbounded....

Alien androids were attacking the cabin, rattling the windows and whipping the roof with giant rubber hoses. They were calling her name. "Flossie! Flossie, open up!!" She clamped her legs together. She heaved her extra pillow over her head, dug deeper into the tired old foam that supported her. "Stick it where the sun don't shine," she mumbled, trying for her gentle drop back into dreamland.

"Flossie! Get the bar off this door! I gotta talk to you!" More beating on the nonoffending cabin. Flossie turned her face to the foam and smothered her breath. She willed the androids back to their planet of sterile basalt. She held her breath.

"Floss, dammit, it's me, City Lights! I'm freezing my butt off out here! Flossieeeeee!!"

Flossie breathed. No fun to wake up this way, she thought. She hauled her bare feet to the floor, feeling for her nightgown. Where had she left it? More banging. "I'm comin', I'm comin'!" she croaked. The banging stopped. Fighting her way into the warm flannel she reached the door and drew back the bar.

City Lights, No Bigger Than a Minute and Twice As Frail, stomped into the room and kicked the door back into place. She dumped a large patch of snow onto the floor with her jacket and laughed a greeting. Then she made for Flossie's stove. "You still got fire," she warbled. "How about a lamp?"

"City, I'm a gin day short of lacing you good. What you want?" Flossie cut the damper and opened her stove door. She lit a candle from a twig.

City shook possible spiders from some kindling and forced the wood under the smoldering logs. She looked over her shoulder at the flannel-clad figure, its arms akimbo, and got to the point.

"We got to Spoon, Flossie. You and me."

"You and me? City, your peanut butter's slippin' off of your bread. Last we Spooned was five years ago...."

"We can do it." The younger woman sank to a stool in front of the fire and held out her hand to Flossie. "I'm not proposin' wild abandoned sex. Only a sweet gentle little Spoon...."

"You proposin'—!"

"Not that I wouldn't love it, Floss. In fact...."

Flossie let out her breath. "Wait 'till I get my socks." She threw the quilt from her bed around City's shoulders. Then on her knees she strained to rescue one wool sock from under her bed, another from her boot. She sat on a straight chair by City. "Coldest night in a universe and you got to come knockin' your way into my sleep."

She felt a reassurance, a satisfaction, as the sock stretched itself around her leg. When nothin' else helps, she reminded herself, pull up your socks. It always worked. She cut her eyes toward City. The tiny woman was intent on moving a log to catch the center of a volunteer flame. Still pretty, Flossie thought, the girl's still pretty, else the fire's makin' a lie of her face. Flossie pulled up her second sock and resigned herself to a conversation.

"City, I'm bound to tell you I won't try that flyin' again if that's how come you want to Spoon."

City wove her hand up through folds of quilt and held it out to Flossie a second time. "No," she urged, "I just need to dreamwalk. All the demons been visitin' me lately. Like when I go to the lake where Eleeea died. You know?"

Flossie knew. She wanted to reach for her pipe, light it up and stay safe behind a cloud of smoke. Instead she took City's hand. "Umm-hmmm," she said.

"I just need you to hold me, Floss. You always been the best for walkin' together with me and findin' healin' waters. I can do a new incantation I made up for right after the master chant. It'll take us so deep, so easy." City Lights, No Bigger Than a Minute and Twice As Frail, raised the soft brown openness of her eyes to the soft brown openness of Flossie's. "Will you Spoon with me , Floss?"

There was never any brittleness to be found anywhere in Flossie Yoroba, and at this moment, she was sure, there wasn't even a trace of solid bone or cartilage. She harumphed her way toward a response. "Well, we might be ridin' a lame donkey," she growled. "It's not for certain I can stay down long enough to dreamwalk anywhere."

She was about to say more, but at that moment her forehead began to tingle, just around her hairline. Her eyes grew a millimeter bigger. She stood up and wiped her brow. "City," she said, "City, come here to me." She pulled the small woman to her feet. "How come you got on so many clothes?" She turned toward the door, heaving the quilt onto the bed as she slid the bar closed.

City Lights knew when she'd been blessed. Move, girl! she admonished herself. Don't let your coattail touch the ground! She began peeling off her clothes, struggling all the while to meet the swell of primordial earthpower that was emanating from Flossie's body. She was just working her way out of her last pant leg when Flossie flung off the flannel nightgown and stood before her, wet and shiny in the candlelight, exuding wave after wave of unquenched fire.

First it was the warmth, then it was Flossie's arms that encompassed her. As she sank onto the bed, City Lights, No Bigger Than a Minute and Twice As Frail heard the big woman say, "They's good Spoonin' tonight, girl. But first you got to let me show you what a hot woman is all about."

The candle, outdone in both heat and light, guttered, and then courteously extinguished itself.

Anna Livia

Lesbian Sexuality: Joining the Dots

POLLY AND SADIE ARE SITTING IN THE BACK GARDEN. IT IS HOT. POLLY IS TRYING TO get on with her thesis and keep an eye on Sadie. Sadie, it seems, is crazy. Sadie begins to speak, answers a question half-formulated in Polly's mind. The answer brings relief, as when a nameless fear is shared, solved by articulation. Polly looks at Sadie: her height, her wide face, her smooth skin. The sun shines persuasively. Sadie smiles and Polly no longer thinks her crazy, no longer thinks, only wants her, wants Sadie.

While striving not to close the kitchen curtains discreetly, draw a veil of lilac buddleia over the proceedings, but to go all the way and describe two women making love, I found I had written of "passionate biting and scratching, kissing so hard it bruised." Horrible stuff, also untrue, as I hate being bitten and cannot imagine it pleasant. Why was I writing about sex at all? How should I do it so it said something I could recognize? I do not believe in an essential, purely sexual experience which it sufficeth to describe accurately and in detail, but rather that the words we choose create the experience; bestow context, metaphor, image, connotation; forge parallels with other, seemingly disparate, experiences: cunt as lotus blossom, pomegranate, dried apricot half, black hole, split beaver.

Writing sex located it, the words its wedge into the world. Gone were the days of mute embarrassment when I couldn't say what I wanted because I wasn't sure which bit was my clitoris, let alone how to pronounce it. I began looking for predecessors, wondering in which contexts I had seen that word "clitoris," why violent sexual imagery came so quickly to mind.

My search led me back along my bookshelves through lesbian literature to Radclyffe Hall and coy avoidance: "for now she could find no
words anymore...and that night they were not divided,"[1] which seemed
to state my problem admirably: a) how to find the words, and b) how to
join the dots.

Believing Jane Rule when she told me that it was still unclear whether,
according to Gertrude Stein's complicated code, "cow" meant turd or orgasm,[2] I passed on to Djuna Barnes, and her mystifying imprecation:

> Look for the girls also in the toilets at night, and you will find them
> kneeling in that great secret confessional crying between tongues:
> "May you be damned to hell!...May you die standing upright! May
> this be damned, terrible and damned spot! May it wither into the grin
> of the dead, may this draw back, low riding mouth in an empty snarl
> of the groin![3]

—which you read three times in perplexity only to conclude that women
you know don't do that, or at least not kneeling in the toilet. And hell's
teeth, the "empty snarl of the groin"? I think I prefer Hall's "terrible
nerves of the invert."

But what about the sexual celebration? What about my positive self-
image? Jane Rule poses the problem as one, again, of vocabulary:

> Now that our experience is increasingly available to us as a subject of
> contemplation, we have to extend our language to express our new
> consciousness until we have as many words for sexuality as the Es-
> kimo has for snow.[4]

How is this "new consciousness" achieved, if not through language?
How do we recognize it? Is it not the words which make it available? For
the words are not lacking; we are not doing anything unheard of, lesbianism has, after all, its own history. Rather the words for it are more
common in anatomical, perhaps, or pornographic descriptions, carrying
these overtones into lyrical or emotional contexts. Hence, perhaps, our
reticence to turn our struggle to live out sexual contradictions into a possible turn-on for men, the consequent flight into floral or violent imagery, the dot dot dots, the language of the damned: the "always already,"
that time-honoured repository of guilt and desire. Given only the choice

between the wicked and the victim, evil sounds more exciting. Djuna Barnes's creatures of the night are far more memorable than those who "sew a quiet seam," whereas Stephen (*The Well of Loneliness*) Gordon's relationship with Mary is peculiarly undynamic, a petrification of desire versus guilt, as though struggles between the women must be silenced, subsumed to the greater struggle of taking on the world—like the Ladies of Llangollen, who must never admit to quarrels or coolness, lest the Irish relations think the ideal friendship hasn't worked. The girls in the toilets mouth "between tongues" alternately their damnation and the activity they are damned for.

Was it not part of the "new consciousness" to say that as our lives must be lived in open defiance of male opinion, as simply to live and breathe and be a lesbian is to express hostility, so our writing will honour only its own purpose, and if men have a little wank on the off-shoots, so the world is full of little wankers? Monique Wittig, with the excruciating precision of the scalpel, enumerates the layers of *The Lesbian Body*:

> A/I pull starting at the labia, it slides the length of the belly,...A/I pull starting at the loins, the skin uncovers the round muscles and trapezii of the back,...A/I reveal the beauty of the shining bone traversed by bloodcells....[5]

If words like "trapezii" make *The Lesbian Body* read like an anatomy textbook, doesn't an anatomy textbook now read more like *The Lesbian Body*? Oblivious of sentient reaction, it accepts only the resistance of the body.

Sexual descriptions that are without contradiction (either *vis-à-vis* a hostile world, or within the relationship itself) seemed pornographic in their unproblematic throbbing, possibly because only when a body is entirely objectified does it offer no resistance. Contrast Jane Rule's:

> Then they were lying together on the couch in a long kissing, for Kate so sweet a relief that she wanted nothing but to go on and on kissing into opening desire, the longing of body for body there was finally and answer for, brief but absolute, against all ugly and grieving loneliness.[6]

with Mountainspirit's:

> My finger finds her open. It is warm inside, inviting. I lick her and push my open mouth over her, my tongue circles the opening. She is moaning softly and pushing herself against me.[7]

We have moved on to the 1970s, the guilt and damnation have disappeared. The vocabulary of sexual desire, with its repetitions, its image of two bodies open and vulnerable to each other, is similar in both descriptions. Yet Mountainspirit offers only unity, the immediacy and eternity of sex, whereas Jane Rule counterposes the insight "brief" to her "absolute." Kate and partner lie together against a background of loneliness. The central contradiction shifts from guilt versus desire, to sex versus loneliness, violence versus vulnerability. The limits imposed are internal, the violence of desire translating sometimes into physical violence. Witness Ginny's desire (in *Brainchild*) to

> pin [Irene] up against a wall...tear her clothes off, push her down, fuck her hard and when she cried "Stop"...then to do it harder.[8]

Sometimes guilt has become embarrassment, a state of perplexity, of being caught between conflicting emotions: brazen and apologetic. Often the conflict is resolved by laughter. The sad tale of Dix and Eunice, those despicably unpoliticized gays of *Rubyfruit Jungle*, nearly caught by straight roommates in the shameful act Djuna Barnes (almost) describes, was the first thing I read that indicated other women like licking. Dix's confession: "So one night I'm over there and well, you know. I was— uh—I was going down on her," seeks only temporary refuge in dots and dashes and manages to say what she was doing, even though this is immediately followed by divine retribution. Dix gets her tooth brace caught on Eunice's pubic hair; her unenviable alternatives are "to go blind, shit, or run for her life."[9]

Finally she bolts from the closet. (Closet, eh, d'yer geddit? Eh, do yer?) The scene is funny, perfectly accepts they didn't oughter of been doing that. Joanna Russ, with similar, slightly exaggerated humour keeps the embarrassment strictly between friends. No sign of self-deprecation.

> We were both rather wary of touching each other again.... I was blind, deaf, overwhelmed. I kept wanting to put my finger through the central hole of the last bagel because it struck me as such an extraordinarily good joke.[10]

After this rather hurried leafing through half a dozen lesbian classics to find the descriptions of sex—instantly recognizable as those places where the pages were brownest—I had before me a wide variety of precedents from the soft sunset and roseate dawn, the tortured and damned, the coded and dotted, the anatomic, the pornographic, the embarrassed, funny or violent as the narrative tension revolved around outcasts and normality, male voyeurism and female experience, relations of dependence and vulnerability with a chronological increase in lesbian autonomy.

My page remained before me, calmly waiting, and I concluded that here, certainly, was "how." And "why," as for any other subject, was entirely up to me. My sex scene should take its context from the rest of my story, not leap off with a life of its own.

For barely the second time since entering the house Sadie smiled. Polly had a stream of hazy, soft, smooth, warm liquid thoughts starting with the calm of lying in the sun, stretching out, lazy. Then not so lazy, kissing wetly and the kiss spreading, the wetness spreading, the warmth growing, heat. "Sex!" thought Polly blatantly.[11]

Notes

1. Radclyffe Hall, *The Well of Loneliness* (Jonathan Cape, 1928). Known as a "lesbian classic" because it most nearly expresses the classic antilesbian position that women are better off dead than dykes.

2. Jane Rule, "Sexuality in Literature," essay in *Outlander* (Naiad, 1981). A collection of short stories and articles by Jane Rule, author of the wonderfully passionate *Desert of the Heart*.

3. Djuna Barnes, *Nightwood* (Faber and Faber, 1936). A novel to learn by heart for the beauty of its language, not its sentiment.

4. Ibid., "Sexuality in Literature."

5. Monique Wittig, *The Lesbian Body* (Peter Owen, 1973) Metaphor made flesh.

6. "Pictures," short story in *Outlander*.

7. Mountainspirit, "The Bus Ride," in *A Woman's Touch*, ed. Cedar and Nelly (Womanshare Press, 1979), a collection of lesbian who-puts-what-where.

8. Eve Croft, *Brainchild* (Onlywomen Press, 1980). Little known, brilliantly worded novel written with a scalpel blade.

9. Rita Mae Brown, *Rubyfruit Jungle* (Corgi, 1973). Alternative classic (see note 1 above). Jolly romp trivialization.

10. Joanna Russ, *On Strike Against God* (Out & Out, 1980). Woman academic comes out. Wildly funny and disarmingly unferocious.

11. Anna Livia, *Accommodation Offered* (The Women's Press, 1985).

The Erotic Life of Fictional Characters

I.

THE FIRST "SEX SCENE" I EVER CAME ACROSS WAS IN A NOVEL CALLED *GIDGET*, A novel with a turned-down page that was being passed around a small group of sixth-grade girls with many giggles and suggestive whispers. As far as sex goes, the scene was prudish by contemporary standards. I think it involved pulling up a sweater and unclasping a bra. I have a vague memory of Gidget breaking away at the crucial moment, though it's possible she didn't. What mattered to me, as an eleven-year-old in 1962 with an imperfect grasp of the method by which babies were produced but an already well-developed sense of sexual guilt, was the forbidden nature of the scene: Gidget was doing, or about to do, something bold, reckless, and nasty.

A lot of girls only read the one page; that's why it was turned-down, so you could easily find it. I remember that give-away page well, because that's how my father discovered that I was reading things that were (said with a stern, shocked expression) "too old for me."

I would be more secretive next time, would hide the book, memorize the page. These are trashy novels I'm talking about, and they didn't come my way often when I was growing up in the sixties, but when they did, I recognized their style immediately. As frequently as the plot allowed (and sometimes the plot allowed for a great deal of frequency), the sexual tension would build up, description and dialogue tending toward a dual but united purpose (female abandon, male release). The hand on the thigh, the fingers on the breast, the unzipping, unbuttoning, moaning and groaning—whether or not the narrator/main character was a man or a woman you always saw the woman through the man's eyes. Even the one book I managed to find with lesbian sex in it had the two women's lovemaking interrupted by one woman's husband. I wish I could remember some of those books better, remember their titles and whether they were really porn or just pulpy novels beginning to include more graphic sex scenes. I know I got excited reading them. I also knew, clearly, that they weren't literature.

Literary characters, in my mind, did not have naked bodies and sexual feelings that they acted out publicly, that is to say, on the pages before me. Knowing from early on that I wanted to be a writer, and a serious one, I therefore eschewed the possibility of describing in my fledgling stories anything to do with sex at all.

This changed, of course, as I grew older and sexual expression in literature, at least the sexual expression of white heterosexual males, became more socially acceptable. In the late sixties, finishing high school, starting college, I discovered authors like Mailer, Miller, Lawrence, Roth, writers who were not only respected, but revered in my classes and among my friends precisely because they wrote about sex. I *did* notice that women writers didn't seem to write about sex as much, if at all (there was Françoise Sagan and a censored Anaïs Nin), but perhaps I thought that was because they weren't such important writers.

I needn't have been alarmed: as the seventies rolled on we had increasing evidence that women could write sex scenes with the best of the boys, and I'm not just talking about romance writers but about self-proclaimed feminists like Erica Jong. Still, I'd become something of a literary snob by that time, as well as a somewhat puritanical feminist and then a lesbian-feminist (which may explain how I missed out on lesbian pulp novels). The women writers I most admired were Grace Paley, Virginia Woolf, Elizabeth Bowen, and Katherine Mansfield—and they didn't have any sex in their work, did they?

But I was also reading other women writers in the seventies, and as I think about it now, I realize that I found some of their books highly charged, even though there was often little overt sexuality and no graphic sex scenes. I'm talking about Jane Rule, Colette, de Beauvoir in *She Came to Stay*, Marge Piercy in *Small Changes* and *Woman on the Edge of Time*, Joanna Russ, as well as lesbian-feminist authors like Sandy Boucher, June Arnold, and Rita Mae Brown. Just the fact that the characters were lesbian was erotic to me; they didn't have to *do* anything. To be a lesbian was to be a fully sexualized being, I imagined, profoundly in tune with the eroticism of women. Even during the years before I came out I found writing by or about lesbians incredibly compelling.

That was then. Nowadays the mere creation of women characters, who are attracted to other women characters, admit their love for them, and drift blissfully off into happy coupledom is not enough for either lesbian writers or readers. It's not enough for me, even though I don't know what would be enough. Still, year by year, scene by scene, book by book, sexual descriptions in lesbian writing grow ever more explicit. The romantic soft-focus treatment of desire in *Curious Wine* by Katherine Forrest looks pale next to *Pleasures* by Robbie Sommers, a 1989 Naiad release, much less next to the boldly sexual writing of Artemys Oakgrove, Cappy Kotz, and Pat Califia. There are now quite a few collections of lesbian erotica with doubtless more in the works, and the question of a decade ago—Why can't lesbians write about sex?—has given way to its opposite—Why can't they write about anything else?

For some writers, sex is still a minor aspect of our characters' personalities—what they do, if at all, on their own time. For others, it's the primary focus of our characters' lives, something they think about and act on to a far greater extent than the ordinary lesbian who has to work for a living and needs eight hours of sleep a night. For some authors, sex is an activity that is lightly passed over (the "next morning" school of thought); for others, the "plot" is an excuse to insert as many sex scenes as possible (the "next night at the bar" school). In this welter of increasingly explicit description and conflicting attitudes toward the *necessary* and the *gratuitous*, how does any writer find her own way?

How do I?

II.

I've written sex scenes between my characters for a good ten years, written how they feel about their bodies and their lovers. Sometimes I've described them making love, sometimes just fantasizing.

Until recently I've almost always taken those scenes out or modified them before publication.

Timidity, uncertainty about the quality of the writing, a desire to remain private, to protect myself, a desire not to limit my audience, internalized homophobia, fear of exposure. All these reasons and one more: a serious question about standards, my own perhaps more than any real or imaginary censor. The old question, *Is literature supposed to have sex in it or not?* is not as relevant as *How can I, as a lesbian writer, write about sex in a way that is meaningful to me?* Is it enough that the sex scenes stand on their own, or should they be used in the pursuit of a larger goal: to further the reader's understanding of the characters' lives and thus the understanding of the reader's own life?

I also ask myself, what is the difference between writing a scene or a story that is meant primarily to arouse and writing a scene or a story about characters who express the erotic side of their nature with each other? Or is there no difference? Why, if I can write a description of two women making love in one of my novels or stories, do I balk at the idea of writing a five- or ten-page piece of erotica that also shows two women making love? As a writer I am interested in learning to write about sex well, interested in new ways of describing very timeworn acts, interested in seeing if I can find words for sensations I might have experienced. Why then not take to writing erotica as a form of practice, as a pleasure, as an end in itself? Readers have found my sex scenes arousing, what is the difference if they remain embedded in a novel or story and if they stand alone?

When I began to write my novel *Cows and Horses*, I knew that the sexuality of the protagonist, Bet Gallagher, would be very important to the story. Why? Because she was a woman in deep unrecognized mourning for the loss of her ten-year relationship with Norah Goldman. I didn't want her to understand her sexuality or to be able to express her grief other than through her sexuality. There was something I wanted to explore, and that is how sex is connected to loss. How, when we feel empty and abandoned, we sometimes turn to something powerful that we think will fill us. In this case Bet became involved with a woman who was a highly inappropriate partner for her, not necessarily sexually unsuitable, but inappropriate in terms of compatibility, expectations, background—all the things couples manuals tell you to watch out for. Possibly their personal incompatibility made the sexual encounters between Bet and her butch lover more highly charged. Bet was always resisting getting involved with Kelly; part of the erotic intensity came from the knowledge that this was "wrong" for her.

When I look back on this novel I see that the sexual scenes between Bet and Kelly drew on certain conventions of erotica. There was first of all the fact that the characters hardly knew each other. Second was the fact that Bet realized almost immediately that Kelly was not the right person for her but was attracted against her will, again a staple of erotic writing. Third were the sex scenes themselves, in which Bet often began by resisting Kelly, if not physically then psychologically, and ended by "giving in" to her. The basic scenario did not really depart significantly from a soft-porn or erotic model in its message that we are often attracted to the wrong people against our will and that "wrongness" and "resistance" can play a major role in heightening erotic attraction.

I'm more aware now than when I wrote the book of some of the conventions I was using; at the time, however, I was gropingly insistent that these sex scenes served another purpose in the novel than just to titillate the reader. Sex was the arena in which Bet was playing out her grief: Bet's sex with Kelly, her memories of sex with Norah, and Bet and Norah's quarrels over their past sex life were all important in trying to describe Bet's feeling of emptiness, her anger at Norah for betraying and leaving her, and her gradual move toward recognition and acceptance of her loss.

In writing the sex scenes themselves I tried hard not to objectify the characters too much (for reasons of feminism and curiosity as to whether it could be done), but to present their sexuality as an integral part of their personalities. Kelly made love the way she did because she was Kelly; Bet responded and made love only as Bet, being Bet, could. One of the methods I chose to keep objectification at a minimum was to describe the lovemaking in terms of metaphor. I wanted to get beyond mechanistic descriptions of what our limbs and organs do during sex to what sex actually feels like. In writing these descriptions I at first relied on trying to conjure up what making love feels like to me, but as I wrote and rewrote them the descriptions became closer to what I imagined sex might feel like to Bet. I knew her quite well by then, knew her childhood, her hopes and fears. Her sexuality was something I had to know about her too.

The second way I tried to minimize voyeurism is that I never, in the course of the entire novel, described Bet physically. I did describe the rest of the characters in great detail, but Bet was physically transparent. I hoped in this way to prevent the reader from looking at her as she made love and from getting an erotic charge from the sight of Bet's body. I wanted to keep the reader's eye focused on the person Bet was making love with, so that the process would be less like watching two women make love and more like making love oneself. In much erotica we already identify with at least one of the participants, but I wanted to increase identification with Bet as much as possible. Not so that the reader would get a greater thrill, though perhaps that was also an effect, but so that the reader would understand what sex meant to Bet. One of the end results of this desire not to objectify Bet was that Kelly became objectified, for she was the character who was *seen*.

There are five explicit sex scenes in *Cows and Horses*, and I worried a great deal about them. I worried about exposing myself as a sexual being (if I could write about lesbian sex I obviously must have experienced it, and now people would know for sure), I worried about the authenticity (does it feel anything like this to anyone else?), and I worried about the critical reaction (if I wrote about sex and wasn't Norman Mailer could I still be a literary writer?)

The heavens didn't fall after the book was published, even though the review in *Publishers Weekly* warned that "the graphic sex may preclude a wide audience." In fact, ironically (predictably?), the sex scenes were all that some lesbian reviewers liked about the novel. They couldn't understand that I was writing the story of a woman's grief and how she tried to mask it through sex; they said it was a pity the book was so "bewildering" in its focus on a depressed and "boring" person because I did write erotica awfully well.

For every reader who said to me, "My lover died and for two years after that all I did was have sex," or "That was a wonderful description of the grieving process," there were three readers who said, "Great sex scenes!"

I had become an erotic writer. I had become an author in danger of having her pages turned down.

III.

The issue of how to express lesbian sexuality forcefully, subtly, and honestly seems very different for lesbian poets than for us fiction writers. Adrienne Rich is able to write:

> ...we're out in a country that has no language
> no laws, we're chasing the raven and the wren
> through gorges unexplored since dawn
> whatever we do together is pure invention...*

but it's harder as a novelist or short story writer to achieve that lyric quality in our fiction. Lovers need names, narrators want to tell us what really happened, there is, as E.M. Forster noted, the problem of the plot ("Yes—oh, dear, yes—the novel tells a story.") Characters take on lives of their own, propel events forward—it's all we can do, as writers, to shape and polish the lives of these imaginary people. How then, do we understand and/or construct their sexuality? We're not satisfied with the little that has been written about the erotic lives of lesbian characters, but what do we write ourselves? Do we have any models?

Two years ago I read a great deal of gay men's fiction, novels full of sexual encounters of all sorts, usually described with extreme specificity. In spite of an occasional feminist shiver at the lack of "meaningful relationships," I liked the freedom that writers such as Edmund White and Andrew Hollinghurst seemed to feel in discussing sex and weaving it into their narrative. They were describing characters preoccupied with sex, for whom sex was so central as to be an obsession. This was true of both pre- and post-AIDS books. Andrew Hollinghurst's editors felt it necessary to describe *The Swimming Pool Library* in the jacket blurb as "an elegy for ways of life which, since AIDS, can no longer be lived," raising the question for me of the immense literary impact of the epidemic—can gay male literature now only be written, and read, elegiacally? And what does that mean for lesbians, so much less at risk, who turned to gay male writers for models of sexual writing?

For years I've found that the eroticism of most straight women writers—Joyce Carol Oates, Edna O'Brien, Marguerite Duras—all of whom trade heavily on female masochism and the exquisite delineation of pain, has had little to say to me. Toni Morrison is an exception in that her characters are profoundly and powerfully sexual; they ask for and are given what they want. For the most part when eroticism is joyfully described in straight women's writing it has been in the experience of fecundity, preg-

---

*Adrienne Rich, "XIII" from "Twenty-One Love Poems" in *The Dream of a Common Language, Poems 1974-1977*. (New York: W.W. Norton and Co., 1978).

nancy, diffuse sensuality. There is a wonderfully erotic scene in Doris Lessing's novel *A Proper Marriage*, in which heavily pregnant Martha Quest and a woman friend perform a spontaneous dance, naked, mud-spattered, in the driving rain.

Of straight male writers the author who interests me most is Milan Kundera, who, sexist though he can be, has the ability to take the erotic lives of his characters very seriously. *The Unbearable Lightness of Being* depicts how the sexual experiences of the characters inform and change their reality. Tomas's philandering has direct repercussions on his life with Teresa, which in turn affects the political choices they make first to leave and then return to Soviet-occupied Prague. Kundera uses desire as an opportunity to digress into important discussions about fate, character, history, and politics; he presents sexuality as a kind of meditation on the futility and hopefulness of passion in this life, as something with enormous consequences.

There are few recognizable sex scenes in Kundera's work as we commonly understand them—the tension, the act, the release—but there are sexual events that precipitate thought. Are they the result of a lifetime of evading the censors or of a decision to make sexuality a thinking activity as well as a sensual one?

When I look around me at the work of other lesbian fiction writers I am encouraged, not always inspired. Doors are opening, we feel new freedom, but much of what we're creating is not that new. The gender may be different, the shame is vanishing, but there are many complex questions that remain unanswered by the insertion of a description into the main narrative from time to time of what lesbians actually do in bed. Nor am I that interested in stories or novels that are one erotic scene after another, not for moral reasons but for literary ones. As everyone knows, more sex isn't necessarily better sex. I would like to see more questioning of romantic and sexual convention in fiction, more experimenting, not just with how far the writer can go with graphic description, but with the meaning of sexuality in our lives. Sex books perhaps, not just sex scenes.

IV.

A couple of years ago I had dinner with several English friends, two of whom had been invited, as I had, to contribute to an anthology of lesbian

erotica that a feminist publisher was putting together. Two of us had had
our writing rejected, the third her writing but not her erotic drawings.
We were kvetching a bit, in the time-honored way of all rejected writers,
but then tried to define in a clearer fashion what we thought had gone
on, and why.

I, for example, had had a chapter from *The Dog Collar Murders*, one
where artistic lesbian sex videos are being shown and discussed, where
any erotic tension is questioned and undermined by talk, turned down—
with the apology that it was funny and provocative, but not erotic, "the
way we're defining it."

"Couldn't you write something else, specifically for us?" the editor had
asked. "Because we'd love to include you."

I had been regretful, a little puzzled. "I don't think I can meet your
definition," I said. "I don't think I can write erotica detached from life
and questions about it."

"But you write sex scenes very well," she persevered.

"But those are my characters," I said. "The erotic is part of their personalities. Sex means something to them."

The poet had had her poetry rejected because it wasn't sexy enough;
ditto the artist-writer. She was currently debating whether she wanted to
let them have the erotic drawings they were so enthusiastic about. She
wondered how they would be used, what kinds of material they would
"illustrate." That got us debating what sorts of things the anthologists
were looking for. We had to agree that when it came to a choice between
the subtle sexuality of C.'s poems or P.'s bittersweet story of an
unrequited love for her therapist, and an explicit, though perhaps not as
well written, story of two women *actually* making love, the editors would
choose the latter. Then C., the poet, wondered aloud if the reason the editors might be interested in the drawings was that they were stylized, and
showed no one's face.

There is something anonymous about erotica, we agreed, and then we
could not agree on what that meant to us. C. said that there was something very strange about splitting off the erotic from everything else we
do in our lives. At the time I agreed; later I thought about fantasies I've
had, very erotic ones, that depend for their intensity on the "unknown"
factor—the stranger in a train, the unexpected arrival home of a lover,
the unlooked-for touch. And I thought about how I had used those

"erotica" elements in my depiction of Bet and Kelly's sexual relationship. They gave it a charge it wouldn't have had otherwise. They also may have contributed to the making of recognizable sex scenes, to pages that could be turned down on my characters' lives.

Since that evening two years ago I have thought a great deal about sex in my own and others' writing, without, as you can see, coming to any hard and fast conclusions. There are more contradictions in the subject than there are answers, which is appropriate to such an enormous subject as the erotic.

There is nothing more contradictory, in fact, than the sex scene in literature. Is it erotica or part of the character's life? Even if we, as fiction writers, insist that the erotic is not something which happens without meaning and consequence, even if we insist that the sexuality our characters express is part of their personalities and, thus, entirely unique to them, even if we insist that the sex our characters have is sex only they can have, no other character, no other person—even if we insist on all that, what is to prevent a reader from reading a sex scene as if it were separate from the story? From, in fact, turning down the page?

It may be that explicitness itself is not the question at all, but the separation of sex from "real life," real narrative, real literature. If early on we learn to see our sexuality as something distinct from the rest of our activities, we will see that in the books we read and in the books we write. That very distinction will be erotic to us. Sex then will be a partly fantasy activity, and work that is taken out of context or created especially to be "erotica" will not seem strange to us, but exciting, more exciting for being detached.

Each fiction writer must somehow find her own relationship to her characters' sexuality. Perhaps our first goal should be to question how we have learned to read and to write sex scenes, and then to ask ourselves whether we want to perpetuate the splitting off of sex from other feelings, other actions. Perhaps we do, perhaps that is a perfectly legitimate and honest way of writing about contemporary sex. Perhaps, however, we would rather learn to write about sexuality in new ways, comically, joyfully, painfully, as if sex mattered, as if the erotic lives of our characters mattered a great deal. We might decide that we need to know the sexual life of our characters as well as we know their childhoods, their fears, and their ambitions. We might decide that we want to write about a sexuality that is not isolated in the lives of our characters, or in *our* lives, as writers of fiction.

To decide that, to achieve that, might mean a very different sort of writing. And very possibly, different sorts of books in our libraries, without the pages turned down.

Marilyn Hacker

Nearly a Valediction

You happened to me. I was happened to
like an abandoned building by a bulldozer, like the van that missed my skull
happened a two-inch gash across my chin.
You went as deep down as I'd ever been.
You were inside me like my pulse. A new-
born flailing toward maternal heartbeat through
the shock of cold and glare: when you were gone,
swaddled in strange air, I was that alone
again, inventing life left after you.

I don't want to remember you as that
four-o'clock-in-the-morning eight months long
after you happened to me like a wrong
number at midnight that blew up the phone
bill to an astronomical unknown
quantity in a foreign currency.
The dollar's dived since you happened to me.
You've grown into your skin since then; you've grown
into the space you measure with someone
you can love back without a caveat.

While I love somebody I learn to live
with through the downpulled winter days' routine
wakings and sleepings, half-and-half caffeine-
assisted mornings, laundry, stock-pots, dust-

balls in the hallway, lists instead of lust
sometimes, instead of longing, trust
that what comes next comes after what came first.
She'll never be a story I make up.
You were the one I didn't know where to stop.
If I had blamed you, now I could forgive

you, but what made my cold hand, back in prox-
imity to your hair, your mouth, your mind,
want where it no way ought to be, defined
by where it was, and was and was until
the whole globed swelling liquefied and spilled
through one cheek's nap, a syllable, a tear,
wasn't blame, whatever I wished it were.
You were the weather in my neighborhood.
You were the epic in the episode.
You were the year poised on the equinox.

Tee Corinne

Notes on Writing Sex

SEX IS MAGICAL AND HEALING, AND SEX WORDS AND PICTURES ARE ESSENTIAL TO certain deeply felt rivers in literature and the visual arts. Yet until the last fifteen years, lesbians writing about and picturing sex were almost non-existent. In the heady, early days of the women's movement I found myself wanting to expand visual boundaries, to fill certain silences with erotic words.

In 1975 I was thirty-one, two years out of a supportive, comforting marriage, still new to lesbian sexing although not new to the passions that connected women. I was living in San Francisco working on the training staff of San Francisco Sex Information Switchboard. The switchboard was community based: a diverse group rather than the psych. professionals who tended to control sex education elsewhere. It was a fertile environment where we learned to talk about sex openly, to look and explore and question. It seemed like heaven to me.

In 1973 I'd told Betty Dodson I wanted to do drawings of women's genitals. She said "Aw, do it, honey." And I did, asking all my friends to model, confronting my own fears and taboos around this imagery. I could tell by the fuzziness, the muddiness of my first drawing that I wasn't looking hard enough, wasn't seeing clearly. I got a better lamp, took several deep breaths and began again. What I learned from that and subsequent drawings was that labia are like faces: unique, changeable, expressive. We probably inherit the size and coloring of our lips, the placement of glans and urethra, in the same way we inherit noses and hairlines—we would know this if only we had been looking.

In the beginning of 1975 very few published images of women's genitals or of women making love with other women could be found outside of pornographic bookstores and "girlie" magazines. By the end of that year the situation had dramatically changed.

Loving Women was created by four phys. ed. teachers who called themselves The Nomadic Sisters and who wanted to "expose the joyous, natural side of loving women and of sexual love between women."

What Lesbians Do was a creative intermingling of art and writing by Marilyn Gayle, Barbary Katherine and many of their friends. It was funny and serious, warm and accessible.

In January 1975 I was asked to take photographs for Victoria Hammond to use in illustrating *Loving Women*. Eight women gathered in my living room. Four were photographers; all were participants in what felt like a ground-breaking endeavor.

It was a radical undertaking as well: going for the root of the matter, going for that essential, physical level of lesbianism, the transgressive act. We were tense. This was not easy. It was daylight in a brightly lit room. We were doing that which, to many people, defines a lesbian.

Throughout the spring of 1975 I continued to work on drawings of labia, imagining them as a coloring book, dreaming of changing the world by changing how women looked at and talked about their genitals.

Loving Women was in print by the summer of 1975. *What Lesbians Do* was available by fall. My coloring book, with its confrontive name and pretty pictures, was in San Francisco Bay Area bookstores by the end of November.

It felt like we were riding a wave that was cresting.

In 1976 Effie's Press in Oakland, California, published a letterpress edition of Adrienne Rich's *Twenty-One Love Poems*, with its erotic twenty-second poem "(The Floating Poem, Unnumbered)." This exquisite poem and book gave validation by a major poet to an aesthetic interest in sex, as did Audre Lorde's "Uses of the Erotic: The Erotic As Power," delivered as a paper at the 1978 Berkshire Conference on the History of Women, followed by publication as a very popular and influential pamphlet.

Late in 1979 Nelly (coauthor of *Country Lesbians*) published a collection of erotic writing and graphics called *A Woman's Touch*. The contents ranged from graphic descriptions to science fiction. Several of my pictures were used in the book, including an image of a woman in a wheelchair kissing her able-bodied lover, and a couple of generously volumetric women embracing. I wanted to push out the expected boundaries of erotic imagery.

My first cover image for *A Woman's Touch* shows a close-up of three women entwined. The central figure has a distinctive—though muted—scar running down her nose.

On the first cover all three women were light skinned. For the second edition I used a photograph of a Black and a white woman together. The white woman's nipple is pressed fervently against one arm. Their hands, those indefatigable lesbian sex organs, cling with intensity. Each of the cover images confronted a taboo or addressed something which was missing from our collective construction of lesbian sexual imagery. Each was, however, designed so that the focus was on the eroticism, the sensual contact. I wanted the scar or the racial diversity to be the subtext, for the lovingness of the image to predominate.

In the fall of 1979 I moved from San Francisco to Brooklyn and found that the sexual discourse on the East Coast was more polysyllabic. Women did not want to take off their clothes for my camera. I illustrated Pat Califia's *Sapphistry* using research I had been doing on forgotten women artists who had pictured lezsex in the past, and I continued work on a book of complex sexual imagery, the exact shape of which kept eluding me.

I had begun work on these images a few years before. I knew I wanted something mythic, graphics which felt true to the feeling of making love rather than the static delineation of it. I also wanted words to go with the pictures, words that were transcendent rather than merely descriptive.

I moved to Oregon in 1981, where a group of us produced *The Blatant Image: A Magazine of Feminist Photography*. I had been cofacilitating Feminist Photographers' Ovulars summers there since 1979. Part of my teaching included "How to Photograph Lovemaking": How do you ask people to model for you? How directive should you be? Is it okay to ask women to wash their genitals before sitting down in front of the camera? (Sure, and to comb their hair, too).

In the early eighties I finished *Yantras of Womanlove*, an elaborate, intricate book of sexual imagery wrapped around a poem by Jacqueline Lapidus. It was published in 1982. The solarized photos were assembled into kaleidoscopic groupings as a way to show "the spirituality of sexuality, the transcendence that can take place when making love to ourselves and others, the repetition of action through which pleasure is sustained and release is possible."

In 1983 I began writing sexy stories for the anthologies *Pleasures: Women Write Erotica* and *Erotic Interludes,* edited by Lonnie Barbach. I kept writing until I had enough for a book of my own. *Dreams of the Woman Who Loved Sex* was followed by *Lovers* and then an anthology, *Intricate Passions.*

Sometimes the hardest thing for me to do is to write about sex. Sometimes I don't want the emotions, and I avoid, I run. At other times I dive into it like a warm ocean, dive and swim.

Honest stories are the ones most interesting to my mind, stories filled with details and, perhaps, a wry humor. Sometimes my body responds with enthusiasm to stories that my mind is repelled by. I explore these stories, sorting the elements of the turn-on to see which ones are essential, which can be metamorphosed, which discarded. My aim is to feel good about myself rather than to censor my responses. I look for ways to expand, rather than limit, my options.

Although there has always been great excitement in working with sexual words and imagery, I don't want to make it appear easy. It is only in retrospect that any progression seems orderly. There has also been fear and confusion, a floundering around looking for the next step, the right direction, guideposts, wise counsel. Almost daily I struggle against fear of retaliation by repressive forces in the larger society.

I am writing this at the beginning of the 1990s. There is a great deal more that I can imagine about lesbian sexuality now, because of the wealth of lesbian-created words and pictures available to me. There is an expanded awareness into which I can dream. The void that existed fifteen years ago has been illuminated with hundreds, thousands of words and pictures.

And I still want more.

I want a more memorable, meaningful portrayal of sexuality between and among women, a ripening, enriching art and literature. I long for words and images that can carry us into a larger construction of sexual experience, without leaving the world of sensual pleasure behind.

I want writing and visual art that encompasses the physical, the emotional, and the psychic connections which inform the words *bonding* and *loving.*

Gillian Hanscombe

In Among the Market Forces?

IT'S PASSION, NOT MERE SEX, THAT IS THE SURE FOUNDATION OF LESBIAN IDENTITY. And it's passion, in my opinion, that drives a truly lesbian woman all the days of her life. Yes, I know, we've had it all explained, how falling in love is a patriarchal ploy to keep women enslaved; how freedom involves divesting sex of its signifiers, its imagery, so that we can all see it for what it is: just plain sex. Then, the explanation continues, we can throw off the traps of our sentimental gushings and have sex that is "fun," or "friendly," or invigorating (like cold showers?), or positively alienating, having had its human significance demythologised.

This originally feminist argument had just cause: it was founded in a critique of heterosexual propaganda whose tradition set women up, through a dazzle of fripperies and social image pressure, to fall prey to the myth of romantic courtship and marriage. Scrupulously feminists first analysed, and then denounced, the hidden agenda of such romance: enforced dependence, enforced inequality, and enforced servitude. Romance was out, they advised: autonomy, liberated sex, self-determination were in.

For lesbians this—like all heterosexual feminist commentary—carried oblique ironies. Lesbians never had been enjoined (let alone permitted) to marry each other; nor had lesbian romance been conceived as a relationship between unequals. Nevertheless, many lesbian women took heart from this kind of feminist analysis and began to explore, both in life and in theory, what demythologised sex might mean. Some soon became aware of an obvious truth: that no human action can be divested of myth, of symbolism, of significance. What happens when a myth is successfully challenged is simply that another myth takes its place. And the myth currently being implanted in what some lesbians call lesbian erotica is a far more degrading one than anything the myth of lesbian passion might have invented.

Other lesbians, despite the feminist call for autonomous sex, have persisted in searching for "the real thing" or, having found it, have persisted in throwing everything else aside in order to keep and protect it. The real thing is lesbian passion: a fully expressed and reciprocated celebration of our femaleness, its flesh, words, perceptions, judgments, feelings, hopes; its past and its future, everything that has been ours and will remain ours.

"The sure foundation of lesbian identity," I said. But should I rather say—given the current lesbian sex industry hype—the sure foundation of lesbian-feminist identity? Simple-minded sex: monocular-visioned, alienated from feminist aims, tediously described, packaged in cheap writing and tawdry images, is now sold for profit into a mostly young, mostly undiscerning and deliberately created market. This market is often described as postfeminist, but is actually antifeminist, since its stated values do not attempt to challenge patriarchy and do not promote egalitarianism between women. Lesbian antifeminists who make and consume what they call lesbian erotica variously present themselves as happy and well-adjusted appreciators of "soft" porn (can any porn actually be "soft"?); or as converts to the liberating delights of sadomasochism (liberated to what ends and purposes?); or as intelligent opponents of censorship, supporters of free speech (but have we ever supported free speech when it came to expressions of racial hatred or incitements against lesbians?) And in any case, material defended as lesbian erotica, as "being open about sex," is not demythologised at all: on the contrary, it promotes a new and vicious fantasy in which a woman may excuse anything she does by asserting that it has "liberated" her.

The imaging of so-called erotica created from such decadent lesbian imaginations finds itself comfortably placed within the culture arising from the corruption of Anglo-American social values instanced by unbridled market forces and their accompanying ideology. This means that some lesbian media makers have responded to the new fantasy by saying, in effect, "If this is what lesbians want, then they should have it"; and "If this is what lesbians want, then it must be right." It isn't a long leap, then, to say, "If this isn't what lesbians want, then they ought to want it, or they're not real lesbians." More sinister is the implicit argument from market forces: "If lesbians want this, then we should sell it to them and make a lot of money."

Some of us who have been watching all this rather silently, now need to stand up and be counted and to say clearly what we think decent lesbian sex is really about: decent meaning satisfying; and decent also meaning ethically defensible. Decent lesbian sex, first of all, can't be traded; and decent lesbian relationships can't be successfully commercially packaged.

Sex as outlined by enthusiasts for sadomasochism (empty-headed, wrong-headed, disreputable, disrespectful, decadent), or as recommended by exponents of half-baked therapies, is not what most of us ever went to the barricades for; is not why we came out; is not the source of our strength in resistance to the patriarchy; is not the hope for development and renewal we offer to all women everywhere. Sex in its degraded modes as defiance, titillation, cruelty, blackmail, dishonesty, or childish indiscipline is not what tempts a mature woman to leave an established relationship, to suffer estrangement from family, friends, and neighbourhood, to change jobs, or to cross oceans. And sex as an expression of boredom, discontent, or petty frustration is insufficient to deceive a woman who knows she's more than the sum of her parts.

It's when two women fall in love with each other that lives are transformed, mountains moved, dormant strengths discovered, enhanced and magnified. And falling in love can't be manipulated, either by one's own will, or by a culture of erotica. Falling in love has little to do with what is outside us. Nothing falls on me from above. I do the falling; and so does she. We fall towards one another, trusting in trust, believing that the nakedness of the body indeed images the nakedness of the dreams and theories, the tempests and the narratives, that we are prepared to reveal. And the mystery of the continuity of passion lies in the capacity of the other, the partner, and in oneself, to be endless, to be never completely claimed, to be never utterly known. That capacity for endlessness, for change, is what is energised by passion. Truly shared sexuality changes us, over and over, more powerfully than almost anything else.

None of this is really new. These are things lesbians have always known and they are the things that have always sustained us, whether or not we had books and theories, bars and discos, friends or enemies. We didn't build a movement on the shallowness of one-night stands or on the poverty of sex for fun. We didn't make our arts and literature out of alienated sleeping around. We've built on richer things and they're things that can't be bought, sold, bribed, or bartered.

I don't think I mind if women cavort, or write a lot of rubbish, or swan around bars, or boast about their affairs, or flirt with each other, or invent bravados, or take up odd fashions, or give in to various unworthinesses. I've done it all myself, anyway. And the world is big enough. And none of it kills anyone. But when I see two women in love, then I'm moved. And now that I'm forty-six, I can see more of them than I used to.

I'm aware, as I write this, that my views can be brushed aside as old-fashioned, staid, boringly vanilla, even puritanical; that in my forty-seventh year I can be dismissed as a kill-joy by the vibrant, energetic young as easily as I can remember dismissing views held by my mother and her contemporaries. I'm at a vulnerable age, after all. There is the body's perceptible, inexorable giving-way to the signs of female ageing we've been taught to hate. There is the patriarchal pressure oozing from magazines and television screens that insinuates—cunningly, quietly—how undesirable we are, how tasteless and embarrassing we shall become if we attempt a presence in the world of the erotic. There are the personal dreads: to be an elderly lesbian (how to live? on what?); to be a displaced dyke, depressed or diseased or distressed, without the comfort of community on marches or demos, the heat of debate at conferences, even the seedy glamour of discos.

So mine may be merely the feeble chronic cry of the middle-aged railing against the generation gap. Much in the lesbian social scene reinforces such a view. Sexuality is for the young, it's everywhere asserted: dress codes, haircuts, genre fiction, bar scenes—the burgeoning commercial pull of designer lesbianism that says sex is easy, sex is simple, sex is liberating, sex is fun, and sex is for the young. But in middle age we know for sure—even if we didn't when we were younger—that what blows the mind, and what threatens the patriarchy, isn't two women in bed together, but two women in love together. Two women in love can do anything: make contracts, or break them; leave children, or have them; buy houses, or sell them; start careers, or give them up; provoke all manner of mayhem for those around them and yet release an intensely creative energy in the ordering of their lives. Two women in love can invent a new reality, making and remaking a world where lesbian lives are central.

My age makes it possible, of course, to mistake some important revolution or other for a wearisome minor debate. But I don't think so, in this instance. I don't think those now writing and photographing what they call lesbian erotica have discovered anything new or that they are presenting anything artistically authentic. Lesbian eroticism has always been perfectly safe and genuinely accessible to any of us who truly wanted it: in the work of writers we've searched out, in the diaries, letters, and journals we've excavated, in the stories we've told about the great and famous, or about the women we've known personally. But always what excited us was the discovery that so-and-so loved so-and-so, rather than whether they used sex aids or wore leather or rubber in bed.

Now what remains, among our other tasks and pleasures, is the continuing and renewal of the tradition we've inherited: a faithful reporting and recording of how we've loved and why, giving due attention to the contexts we've inhabited and invented; and to the signifiers and metaphors for the emotional, existential, and metaphysical dimensions from which our sexual modes—feelings and practices—acquire meaning and resonance. That can't be done through menacing rhetoric or lazy art, through following male pornographers down well-trodden paths of explicit descriptions of sexual acts. Pornography, irrespective of who produces it, leaves predictable after-images of brutalised flesh; in the mind of the consumer, objectified women become just that: objects. On the contrary, a true rendering of lesbian sexuality as it is experienced and lived is a very complex activity. It demands lesbian-feminist reciprocity: two-way interaction, comment, discussion, and evaluation between artists and audiences, utterers and listeners. It demands ethical clarity, shared between a lesbian spokeswoman and her community, about what is to be valued in lesbian experience and what is to be modified or rejected. It demands integrity of insight and accuracy in presentation. It demands willingness to accept the hardships of genuine innovation and experiment: misinterpretation, unpopularity, even rejection; not to mention negligible financial rewards for work done. But above all it demands fidelity to those in the past, and those in lives to come, for whom lesbian passion is the cornerstone of a decent life.

Judy Grahn

From Another Mother Tongue:
Modern Lesbian Sex Domains: Flaming without Burning

FOR THE PURPOSE OF DESCRIBING MODERN LESBIAN SEX AS A SOCIALLY VITAL FUNC-tion, I have imagined that there are four domains, or levels, or spheres of power involved in the sexual dynamic between and among women. The four domains are the physical, the mental, the psychic, and the transfor-mational. Each domain represents another level of the emergence of his-torical Lesbian sexual connection from its suppression over the centuries.

From Deep Within

Nature tests those she would call hers;
Slips us, naked and blank down dark paths.
Skeletons of the sea, this we would become
to suck a ray of sight from the fire.

A woman's body must be taught to speak—
Bearing a lifetime of keys, a patient soul
moves through a maze of fear and bolts
clothed in soft hues and many candles.

The seasons' tongues must be heard & taken,
And many paths built for the travelers.
A woman's flesh learns slow by fire and pestle,
Like succulent meats, it must be sucked and eaten.

—Pat Parker[1]

The First Domain: Vulva to Vulva

The first domain is the physical, the basic flesh-to-flesh contact of sexual relationship. It is based in touch, sensation, smell, intense feelings, intimacy, sharing. In the first domain a Lesbian learns to receive sexual love from another woman, to trust her vulva to a stranger's hands and lips and tongue, to be able to let go and come in her presence, in her very face. And in the first domain a Lesbian learns to give love to another woman, to develop a sensitive and sustaining tongue and knowledgeable fingers, the physical confidence and competence necessary to be the lover, the ability to read another woman's responses and be able to respond to her body on its own terms.

(The Floating Poem, Unnumbered)

Whatever happens with us, your body
will haunt mine—tender, delicate
your lovemaking, like the half-curled frond
of the fiddlehead fern in forests
just washed by sun. Your traveled, generous thighs
between which my whole face has come and come—
the innocence and wisdom of the place my tongue has found there—
the live, insatiate dance of your nipples in my mouth—
your touch on me, firm, protective, searching
me out, your strong tongue and slender fingers
reaching where I had been waiting years for you
in my rose-wet cave—whatever happens, this is.

—Adrienne Rich[2]

Sometimes a Lesbian couple will spend time learning how to come simultaneously, an exercise in controlling physical impulses that is also particularly valued in heterosexual lovemaking. Or a couple may be so close that they feel each other's sensations.

For women from families in which women's sexual expression has been denied or forcibly suppressed by church, state, and/or patriarchal ideas of ownership, the first sexual steps of Lesbianism may be very difficult to take and fraught with terror and excitement. As a teenager, I had rather cleverly learned to masturbate from reading the Kinsey Report while baby-sitting for a progressive family. However, I could not relax enough to come in front of my lovers until I was twenty years old. I literally ordered myself to relax with someone so I could do it. The lover I chose for the occasion was a woman I barely knew, older than myself. We were fully dressed and sitting in daylight in a parked car. She had her hand in my pants. She was patient and persistent and gentle and knew what she was doing. In that instant, she was a witch. After I came in her arms, with my face pressed against her cheek, I was released from my prohibition and could come with other women. I did not have any further sex with my teacher, though I suffered guilt pangs at having used her for such a thoroughly physical purpose. But it was the lack of emotional entanglement that gave me the freedom to let go and not worry so much about my partner's reactions so I could have complete feelings of my own.

At that time, 1960, for most of the women I knew, who were mostly white and lower middle class, sex was a source of embarrassment and various degrees of dissatisfaction, if not outright pain and rape by boyfriends and husbands. Some of my high school friends seemed to be enjoying sex, but since straight women were told to fake orgasm it was difficult to know for certain what women were really experiencing. Sex with your clothes on and in the dark was still a prevalent mode.

We Lesbians, despised and negated though we were, had the advantage of not being watched, and we were sexually daring. Some of us had orgasms and taught others about it. Some made love in the daylight, were "promiscuous," and did other lascivious things. But I don't think we looked at each other's vulvas openly—or our own. It would remain for the sexual revolution of the sixties and the development of independent women's groups taking gynecological childbirth and abortion functions into their own hands and developing self-help groups and clinics before Lesbian poet Olga Broumas could begin a poem, in 1976, with these lines:

> With the clear
> plastic speculum, transparent
> and when inserted, pink like the convex
> carapace of a prawn, flashlight in hand, I
> guide you

inside the small
cathedral of my cunt....

—Olga Broumas[3]

But if in the late 1950s my experience among lower-middle-class, white Lesbians in a small western town was about how to crawl out of the pit of frigidity (into the Well of Loneliness—infinitely preferable), less sexually suppressed, more sophisticated, urban and urbane Lesbians had quite another story to tell as this fruity and passionate passage, set in New York City, from Black poet, writer, and professor Audre Lorde's *Zami* shows.

> There were green plantains which we half peeled and then planted, fruit-deep, in each other's bodies until the petals of skin lay like tendrils of broad green fire upon the curly darkness between our upspread thighs. There were ripe red finger bananas, stubby and sweet, with which I parted your lips gently to insert the peeled fruit into your grape-purple flower.
>
> After I held you, I lay between your brown legs slowly playing my tongue through your familiar forests, slowly licking and swallowing as the deep undulations and tidal motions of your strong body slowly mashed the ripe banana into a beige cream that mixed with the juices of your electric flesh. Then our bodies met again, each surface touched with each other's flame from the tips of our curled toes to our tongues, and locked into our own wild rhythms we rode each other across the thundering space.[4]

Lovers who explore the infinite sensual possibilities in the first domain may experiment by using acrobatic positions, making love in all kinds of beds and places, in the outdoors, in public, on a bus or plane or car, in water, sand, dark, light, hot, cold, in a rainstorm—trying for every variety and complexity of sensation. Some Lesbians add additional numbers of people to the lovemaking or add other elements, such as sensual oils and fruits. A small number mix eroticism with other but highly charged body functions such as pissing and menstruating; a few Lesbians mix sexual sensation together with deliberate forcefulness and stylized "pain," vaginal stretching, pinching, slapping, vigorous frigging, and the like.

Sex in the first domain has become lightly industrialized and mechanized with the marketing of how-to-do-it sex manuals and electric vibrators. The purpose of sex in the physical domain is sensual contact and sensation, usually mutual, and bonding with other women in a network of lovers, ex-lovers, and potential lovers. Additionally it releases sexual sparks of a particular nature into the universe, and it helps to magnetize and direct the attention of women toward each other.

The Mental Domain: Fantasy and Control

I have on occasion been awakened by an orgasm in my sleep, accompanied by an erotic dream. And when I reached down to my vulva to continue the pleasant sensations and possibly encourage a second helping, I have found that my clitoris is quietly tucked into her vulval bed, not hot, not swollen, not sensitive, not even awake. The orgasm had not happened in my clitoris, or anywhere in my body. It had taken place in my "mind," or rather in the feeling-state of the dream imagery. I have known other women to whom this has happened.

Only some sexual experiences are physical and use the medium of the body's erotic organs and erogenous zones. Other sexual experiences take place in other domains, for instance, from seeing pictures or reading descriptions of sexual scenes. This is mental sex, sexual feeling created by mental images. Most of the sex we have operates in more than one domain at once, and they enhance each other. Fantasy amplifies our physical erotic sensations and gives our sexual being much more scope and a second dimension, breadth.

The purpose of fantasy, the manipulation of images to construct possibilities other than what is actually happening, appears to be control. So someone who is having sex in the city may fantasize that she and her lover are in a woodsy setting far away with rain softly falling on their cabin or tent or blanket, and that the siren that blares as she is coming is the howl of a wild, wild she-wolf. This seems like simple wish fulfillment.

Fantasies let us "experience" what we have chosen not to experience, so someone who is having heterosexual sex may fantasize that her male lover is a woman and that his penis is a tongue. Conversely, a Lesbian may fantasize a man, or three or four, fucking her while she is experiencing cunnilingus. Some fantasies center on bondage, punishment, being on stage, illicit relationships, strange combinations of people and animals, or even rape.

By analyzing fantasies as though they are dreams, we can learn about ourselves and what we desire to control in ourselves. Forbidden levels of assertion surface in me as a particular kidnap-rape fantasy. A captive small woman is being slowly, rather patiently, fucked by a man with a penis "too large" for her. He is a sincere, determined, sometimes angry, huge man; other kidnappers who are medium-size men and Lesbians perform other and multiple sex actions on her while the large one is telling her she can take him all the way in if she'll just concentrate on stretching. A little ashamed of this fantasy even to my private self, I decided to try analyzing it as though it were a dream. Since the fantasy occurs in my mind, not in real life, aspects of myself are each of the characters, including some that I do not like, some I respect or find amusing, some I fear or pity. All are "me" in dialogue and confrontation with myself, with something happening to me in my own life. I decided the fantasy says that I am trying to take on things that I believe are "too big" or too much for me. My little "female" energy pot is being abused by my enormous "masculine" ambition; or perhaps my svelte, slender ambition and success is being assaulted by my great hulking masculine workforce. It happens the situation in my life is that I have taken on projects requiring decades of effort, and I am trying to do them all in a short time. My fantasy precisely describes my anxiety over pressure I have put on myself and helps me understand it. Moreover, the kidnap victim's little tight vagina has stretched considerably since the first of these episodes, and she is beginning to have massive orgasms along with the kidnappers.

My fantasy sex usually uses modern settings, a pizza parlor (?), a motorboat crowded with revelers, a fertility rite of old women frigging an essential central figure (myself), one woman fucking three or four men, people both straight and Gay having sex in public or in a great hurry. The fantasy is a pressure chamber for intensifying sexual feelings and for directing orgasm. If I am particularly tense and frustrated with my life, I notice that more of the fantasies include bondage or forced circumstances; for instance, my favorite under duress in my life is the fantasy of a line of nude, horny men tied to an overhead pole who are anxious to have sex and are not allowed and cannot touch each other, while a naked woman dances a sex dance directly in front of them, sometimes with a chosen male partner. It is a fantasy of thwarted desire and pretend revenge on forces I perceive as ranged against me. But all the characters in my fantasy *are* me.

My lover, Paula, who spent years being afraid to come out as a Lesbian, tells me she sometimes fantasizes being forced to have sex with women. The deliberate illusion of "no choice" and therefore "no fault" releases her from internal social controls and allows her sexual feelings to build intensely.

While control is the main feature of fantasy sex, arousal and coming are its goals. The control helps us be specific and focused, directed and assertive, and trusting. We need rely less on the vagaries of the body and its emotions, and can demand of ourselves and our partners more specific feelings, roles, activities as we become more open about our fantasies. Some people take their fantasies into the realm of theater, acting them out with each other in carefully proscribed, even costumed, ways. This is the exertion of the will in trying to gain control in the external world by gaining control of the internal world. Blind acting out seems to me a dead-end street, however. I don't want to make a cult of my inner workings. By acknowledging all the parts of my fantasy as pieces of myself, I do have a tool for understanding my own limitations, ambitions, and fears, as well as my will to control myself or the parts of myself I see in others.

The Psychic Domain: Stroking the Rose

Journal entry, August 1981, Los Angeles: "There was a rose garden," I said, "and I became one of them, the flower, the stem and thorn and even the roots." I was speaking into Paula's mouth as her fingers relaxed trying to leave my vagina as I held her.

"The rose was pink," I said. "I didn't expect that, I have never cared for pink."

"Oh," she said, "I know that rose. When you made love to me, there was a pink rose. And Guadalupe was there. She was holding it," she said. "She was showing me how to stroke the rose. She was using her first two fingers inside the petals and holding the flower in her other hand, her left hand, saying, 'This is how to stroke the rose.'" She laughed.

"You learned very well," I said.

In the third domain the form of lovemaking between women is one that goes into a world beyond physical sensation, intimacy, fantasy, shared orgasm, mental control, and feelings of love. Beyond all these riches lies another domain, the psychic levels of consciousness, creativity, and insight. If the physical domain represents length and the mental domain breadth, then the psychic domain represents the depth of field of the cube, the third dimension in space.

To produce the psychic state, the beloved does not attempt to control what the lover is doing. She gives her body to the lover. Nor does the lover try to force something to happen. She lets herself know what to do. If the heightened state is working, they do not need to control it. If they can control it, it is not happening. The lover lets her own spontaneous sensibilities, as she tunes herself to the beloved, tell her what to do, her fingers and tongue, eyes and ears, and all her body and mind, and she will find she can "see" what to do with her fingers and tongue and become so sensitive as to experience a kind of orgasm—just from stroking the beloved's neck or head or breasts or cervix—through her fingers, the firesticks. And by entering the beloved and paying attention to the feelings, she can guide or allow her to "leave herself" and go to a different world or state of being. And she, the lover, will also leave, although she may not go so far as the beloved goes.

No fantasy is involved in this journey to the source of power. Within the altered state there is an absence of fantasy as there is an absence of pain or anxiety, violence, fear, distance, hiding from or acting out on each other in any way. There is no acting. There is rubbing. There is extreme feeling. There is receiving. There is sucking and tonguing. There is not much moving. There is staying real. There is frigging. There are highly dilated pupils. There is an altered state. There is a spinning out. There is a journey, and a return. There are visions and an understanding of the word "aesthetic." There is no attempt or necessity by either lover to deliberately control and construct mental images in the psychic domain, for control only interrupts what is happening—as do pain, anxiety, force, struggle, or anger between the two lovers. The journey goes where it goes and the imagery constructs itself. This is what creative power *is*. As happens also to artists of all kinds when they are in a creative state, or trance, images—like feelings, dreams, thoughts, melodies, understandings, and patterns—appear of themselves. In the sexual creative trance, metaphors, scenes, personages speaking and moving, one's ancestors, mentors, spirit-guides of every description from earth and sky and parts unknown arrive with messages and meanings as the lovers pass through level upon level of sexual and psychic feeling in a state that may go on for hours, at or near the level of intensity immediately preceding orgasm.

The experience is that of taking a journey to sources of power and creativity, of "making" something, and of being made. Of going somewhere and coming back different. Intimacy and pleasure and intense feelings, though present, are not the goals; orgasm is present but is not the goal. In fact, the construction of goals destroys the state of feeling, turns it aside, lowers it into the realm of fantasy and the necessity for control. When the creative sexual state proceeds on its own, the feeling or experience is prolonged, ecstatic, emotional, journeylike and with intensity barely short of orgasm over a long period of time; and though the orgasm, when it finally and brilliantly happens, may culminate in an image or a sequence of images, its purpose seems more to be to bring the dreamer back, to return the beloved to the material plane. She is not only coming, *she is coming back into herself.* And she has been away, in the sexual/psychic domain. The orgasm is the way back from the trance.

One Lesbian who has also experienced what I am calling "psychic sex" is Nancy, a Los Angeles video filmmaker. She told me that she and her lover Julie would take turns being lover and beloved and would go "out," that is, enter an entranced state. Nancy said they had a term for what the lover was doing as the guide. They described it as "spotting." So, for instance, when Julie was being the lover and Nancy, as the beloved, had gone into a psychic state, Nancy said that Julie would "spot" for her to make certain she could come back to the present world. "The 'spotter' keeps you from getting lost or dying," Nancy said. They had taken the term from the "spotter" on a trampoline, the one who stands on the bouncing canvas with the athlete, holding the strap of the safety belt and guiding her through the somersaults and other balancing maneuvers high in the air.

During their lovemaking Nancy would sometimes stay out a long time, until Julie would get tired and even worried. Julie would yell at her, "Come back! Come back!"

"Because I wouldn't always want to," Nancy says, grinning wistfully. "The other world is so harmonious and beautiful. I love it over there."

Harmony and beauty. I know just what she means. When I am at one with myself and with Paula and we enter the psychic domain, I prefer it over anything I've ever felt—it's so rich and full and deep, like *being* a painting or film or story, like *being* a wolf or storm cloud or fire. The feelings are varied, unpredictable, and not goal-oriented. Many natural elements are present and may predominate. The aesthetics are exquisite, to the point that I am willing to believe aesthetics and psychic sex and the creative trance are all the same feeling: truly the Golden Mean.

Often after psychic sex I remain in an altered state, the room and everything in it being very vibratory. The walls are three-dimensional and in motion, not still, flat surfaces. I can see into them to some extent, could possibly reach into them. I can feel into her body and see her aura. I see "spirit lights" as they are called, flickering whitely in the air, and I sometimes come to understandings during that time that seem profound and help me in my work and Paula in hers. And she does the same.

The poet Hilda Doolittle (H.D.) apparently practiced psychic sex, describing it as having access to the "love mind," or the "womb mind," the mind of vision. In men, she said, the "womb mind" corresponded to their sexual center. She advocated that like-minded people try to gain access to the love mind, and her examples indicate she also meant "like-gender."[5]

It is not Lesbians or Gay people alone who have access to the sexual psychic domains, of course. Heterosexual culture has a well-developed tradition of sexual yoga (Tantric yoga) for the purpose of psychic vision. The *Kama Sutra* is an erotic text for this practice, which requires intense physical discipline. Perhaps this helps prolong the male's orgasm, for if the orgasm comes too quickly he cannot stay "out" long enough to enter the psychic world.

The psychic sexual experiences I have described between modern Lesbians do not require any physical discipline; they do require emotional discipline. This includes openness, trust, honesty, and a willingness to display both vulnerability and strength with each other. This means each person needs to have a well-developed femme side and a well-developed butch side. Needless to say, alcohol and drugs interfere, while the study of therapeutic methods helps by clearing emotional tangles.

Entering the Fourth Domain

In the first three sexual domains Lesbians have the potential to attain sensation and female bonding through emotion and through the sexual organs of the body; to gain control and the specific ordering of forceful images and personal authority through the will of the mind and its fantasies; and to gain creative vision through the aesthetics and harmonies of the psychic world. From these uses of sexual power there is only one more step into the fourth domain, the plane of transformation. The powers released in this dimension can influence not only the participants but also the world around them and its future.

The fourth domain involves more than one person, for it is an exchange between at least two mind/bodies who share an image between or among them, greatly intensified by their close sexual and emotional connection. If they choose to pour their mutual energies into a mutual image, they greatly strengthen it and bring it closer to becoming a real thing, a material being. A "tribe" (in Shinell's sense) of hundreds of thousands of women concentrating on images of women's returning powers by using all three of the Lesbian sex domains will be using the fourth domain; they will alter consciousness, establish psychic, physical, and mental communications of all kinds, and will literally be able to bring back the power of any "goddess" force they desire, to strengthen any elements of nature and human society they wish to, and to unite with, bring forward in themselves, or bring to the attention of others outside their modern psychic "tribe" any ideas or altered understandings they want to see happen. They will be, once again, ceremonial Lesbians and ceremonial Dykes.

Transferring an Image During Sex

Transferring images during sex is a first step toward this domain, requiring a lot of effort and with a lot of reward. With us, it happened with a Diamond Light.

Journal entry, August 10, 1981, Los Angeles: I went out to the very tip of her clitoris with my tongue, staying soft and slow without pushing her into coming, and stayed there with a very soft and sensitive part of my tongue for about five to seven minutes, a long time for that much intensity. This was about midway in her total journey, which was about thirty minutes or less. Cunnilingus alone seems to create a slightly shorter trip than frigging; and the longest is some combination of the two.

While I was out on that tip, which felt very special to me, her flesh became so smooth, and the organ feeling so shapely and full; I was moaning with excitement and "seeing" an exceptional fleshy rose around my tongue. Meantime she experienced being *very* far away out of herself, deep in the night sky, and she saw a goddess whose entire being was a deep intense shiny bluish black, who spread her legs, and then spread her vulvular lips, and from her cunt came a stunning, brilliant diamond light—which Paula entered, so she was sitting in it, a pure light more like a laser than other more reflective lights. It was piercing, not diffuse. Exact. She said she had read descriptions of the Diamond Light but had not previously known what was meant until that moment. She said the goddess sent blessings and love to me. (We since began calling her the Midnight Lady.) Then a voice said she could send a message to me. She concentrated on sending a yellow light to me, and I received it as a golden glow spreading in a warm ball over my eyes and face while I was tonguing the outmost tip of her clitoris. She says she entered the Diamond Light after concentrating on pulling the sexual energy up to her third eye and above, rather than leaving it down around her cunt. She said this was very difficult, and she had to keep both places in her concentration to do it, and that the goddess with the Diamond Light between her legs appeared very suddenly and intensely. Since then we have transferred dozens of images during sex and intensified our ability to transfer images at other times, too.

Entering the Spirit World

I, too, entered the Diamond Light one night, to my surprise, and met an old friend.

Journal entry, October 29, 1981, Los Angeles: Last night we made love (after trip to New Mexico and recovery from road exhaustion).

A completely hooded, very skinny, and tall woman dressed in shiny black from head to foot insisted that I look into her crystal, which was like an eye—a white eye. She held it in both hands near the crotch of her blue-black dress. I didn't want to, but the Midnight Lady demanded it, several times. I looked closer and closer, then saw rainbow lights emanating and flowing over me from the crystal in a flashing manner, waves of rainbows sweeping out and over me, directly into my eyes.

Then I entered the crystal and was immediately standing on a riverbank. A ship with white sails—a little barque—came and turned out to be smaller—a boat with sails—maybe thirty feet long or less. It took me across to a place I knew to be the land of the dead—very pleasant, light shore, sandy like any other shore. And there I had an ordinary-seeming conversation with Vonnie—the first since her death, the first contact. Though I have often felt her presence. And its absence. She said she is often with me and looks out for me. She told me funny stories and talked in the joking way she always had. I laughed out loud as I listened to her. I could hear the cadence of her voice clearly, though I couldn't always make out the exact words. She was very reassuring. She said, "You have made a wonderful choice," I assume meaning my renewed life—and she said not to worry about X. That I also would do fine in the future, that she was happy for me and would stay in touch with me. Then the boat reappeared and brought me back exactly the way I had come, across the river and through the crystal, past the lady in black, and back to the bed with Paula making love. I then proceeded to fantasize a sex scene in order to "come" back, and Paula helped by talking, saying how much she loves to touch me, how sweet it feels to her, how swollen I was, and this helped. The orgasm was mild, but my mood and good feelings were ecstatic. A great rift in me felt filled in, and I was reunited with Yvonne in some way.

"To Suck a Ray of Sight from the Fire" (Pat Parker)

We speak of "carrying the torch" for someone and also of the "torch of knowledge," the "flame of hope," the "light of intelligence," of "civilization" and "at the end of the tunnel," of the "spark of life," the "fire of passion," "burning desire," the "cauldron of feeling," the "candles of the soul."

Perhaps these expressions are descriptions of the rainbow envelope of energies that move our material fleshy beings, the spirit that "goes" when our bodies, like the flowers they are, die back when their season is done. Or perhaps this electrifying force field can also be perceived as an entire matrix, one that connects to others, a psychic network overlying everything we know, a psychic net. It is a form of thought-being. And as the thought goes, so goes the being, for we are active participants in our own lives. A psychic net can be thought of as a shared mind, a third state of consciousness shared by two or more people who exchange thoughts on a nonphysical plane and who mutually create images. Close sexual and emotional bonds amplify the amount of energy poured into these images, giving them tremendous power to alter our consciousness and to influence the course of our lives. If enough energy is poured into an image, it will become actual in the material world. Perhaps "tribadic mind" is an apt term for this net as it applies to Lesbians.

Whoever enters this net in a directed and directing manner, singly and in groups, will alter future time, will "make" patterns for structures that will then proceed to manifest themselves as we act them out in accordance with our beliefs. The ideological battles of the cold war and all the hot wars in between are battles for the minds and attention of human beings on a mass scale. Psychic battles too, or at least competitions, are going on and will be increasingly waged. However, this does not mean that I feel that Lesbians and Gay men should rush defensively into the psychic domains in order to remake the future into a safer place for ourselves and our particular ideology. The shaman/priest/artist/teacher/leader does not operate for the sole benefit of herself and her kind but for the benefit of the people at large and of the universe and its patterns, as becomes what she perceives as fitting into place, into her sense of natural justice.

Perhaps the ancient priestesses and fire guardians stroked each other's roses and entered the Diamond Light together; perhaps they became the rain cloud and called in rain when it was needed; perhaps they called in peace when it was needed. Perhaps we modern Lesbians will learn once again to gather around our fires and locate our god-powers. Whatever the equivalent of these acts of ceremonial Lesbianism is for modern times, I feel we shall ultimately learn to do them and to direct them consciously toward purposeful and just ends.

my first beloved
present friend
if I could die like the next rain
I'd call you by your mountain name

and rain on you...

want of my want, i am your lust
wave of my wave, i am your crest
earth of my earth, i am your crust
may of my may, i am your must
kind of my kind, i am your best

tallest mountain least mouse
least mountain tallest mouse

you have put your very breath upon mine
i shall wrap my entire fist around you
i can touch any woman's lip to remember

we are together in my motion
you have wished us a bonded life

—"Funeral poem: For Yvonne Mary Robinson"
(October 20, 1939 - November 22, 1974)

Notes

1. Pat Parker, "From Deep Within," in *Movement in Black* (Trumansburg: Crossing Press, 1983).

2. Adrienne Rich, "(The Floating Poem, Unnumbered)," from "Twenty-One Love Poems," in *The Dream of a Common Language* (New York: Norton, 1978).

3. Olga Broumas, from "with the clear/plastic speculum," in *Lesbian Poetry*, ed. Elly Bulkin and Joan Larkin (Watertown, MA: Persephone Press, 1981).

4. Audre Lorde, *Zami: A New Spelling of My Name* (Watertown, MA: Persephone Press, 1982), p. 249. Zami is a Carriacou name for women who work together as friends and lovers, p. 255.

5. H.D., *Notes on Thought and Vision* (San Francisco: City Lights Books, 1982).

Carter Heyward

The Erotic As Sacred Power:
A Lesbian Feminist Theological Perspective

OPENLY LESBIAN WOMEN ARE DANGEROUS TO HETEROSEXIST PATRIARCHY BECAUSE, whether or not it is our intention, our visibility signals an erotic energy that has gotten out of control—out of men's control. Historically, we have learned that this erotic power is not good—for us, for others, for the world or for God. Operating on the basis of an interpretive principle of suspicion in relation to heterosexist patriarchal religious and social teachings, feminist liberation theologians in Christianity and Judaism have begun to suspect that our erotic power—this object of such massive fear among ruling class men, from generation to generation—is, in fact, our most creative, liberating power—that is to say, our sacred power, that which many of us call our God or Goddess. And she is indeed dangerous to a culture of alienation and abuse because she signals a better way. She sparks our vision, stirs our imagination, and evokes our yearning for liberation. In the image of old wise women, dark and sensual, she calls us forth and invites us to share her life, which is our own, in right, mutual relation. From a theological perspective, coming out as lesbians—icons of erotic power—is not only a significant psychological process. It is also a spiritual journey, a movement of profoundly moral meaning and value in which we struggle, more and more publicly, to embrace our sisters, our friends, and ourselves as bearers of sacred power. Let me say a bit more about eros as sacred power.

Christian theology, which has shaped the prevailing relational norms of European and American cultures, traditionally has held that *eros* (sexual love) and *philia* ("brotherly" love, or friendship) are, at best, merely derivative from *agape* (God's love for us, and ours for God and our neighbor—"neighbor" being interpreted usually as those who are hardest to love: humankind in general, our enemies, those who aren't like us...). The moral distinctions among the three forms of love have been fastened in the classical Christian dualisms between spiritual and material reality and between self and other and, moreover, in the assumption that it is more difficult—therefore, better—to express God's (spiritual) love of enemies and strangers than to love our friends and sexual partners.

These distinctions represent a radical misapprehension of love. They fail to reflect, as godly and sacred, the embodied human experience of love among friends and sexual partners because they are steeped in the assumption that erotic power—or, in patriarchal, androcentric culture, women's power—is dangerous and bad and therefore always in need of spiritual justification.

To this, many feminist liberation theologians say, "*No.*" The erotic is our most fully embodied experience of the love of God. It is the source of our capacity for transcendence, or the "crossing over" among ourselves, making connections between and among ourselves. The erotic is the divine Spirit's yearning, through us, toward mutually empowering relation, which becomes our most fully embodied experience of God as love.

And how do we know this? We know this by living life, by experiencing the power in mutuality. We know this by having learned to trust our own voices, not in isolation, but in relation to the voices of those whose lives we have learned to trust—prophets, poets, people in our past and present, known personally to us or only by reputation, those whose ways of being in the world, and in history, draw us more fully into mutual connection with one another.

Mutuality is not a matter simply of give and take. It is not, Margaret Huff notes, mere reciprocity.[1] Nor is it equality. Mutuality is not a static place to be. It is movement into a way of being in a relation in which both or all parties are empowered *with* one another to be more fully themselves: mutually, we come to life.

In the context of mutually empowering relationship, we come to realize that our shared experience of our power in mutual relation is sacred: that by which we are called forth more fully into becoming who we are—whole persons, whose integrity is formed in our connection with one another. And our shared power, this sacred resource of creation and liberation, is powerfully erotic.

Audre Lorde speaks of erotic power as

> an assertion of the life force of woman; of that creative energy empowered, the knowledge and use of which we are now reclaiming in our language, our history, our dancing, our loving, our work, our lives.[2]

She associates the erotic with wisdom—"the nurturer or nursemaid of all our deepest knowledge,"[3] and, again, with creativity—"There is, for me, no difference between writing a good poem and moving into sunlight against the body of a woman I love."[4]

Recognizing the fear-laden conditions of our lives in a culture of alienation and isolation, Lorde warns that

> We have been raised to fear the yes within ourselves, our deepest cravings....The fear of our desires keeps them suspect and indiscriminately powerful, for to suppress any truth is to give it strength beyond endurance. The fear that we cannot grow beyond whatever distortions we may find within ourselves keeps us docile and loyal and obedient, externally defined....[5]

Even our inner voices, which we may call "conscience" or "God" or "ethics" or "intuition," are trained to speak to us in the spirit of homage to a force invisible to us because it is our fear of our YES to our own life force. We fear this life force, our erotic power because, if celebrated rather than denied, it would "force us to evaluate [all aspects of our existence] in terms of their relative meaning within our lives."[6] Nothing would remain the same. For, as Lorde affirms,

> Once we begin to feel deeply all the aspects of our lives, we begin to demand from ourselves and from our life pursuits that they feel in accordance with that joy which we know ourselves to be capable of.[7]

The capacity to begin moving through fear toward this joy is the beginning of healing. It is erotic power at work among us. It is the spiritual context in which lesbians are coming out, rearranging ourselves in relation to friends, families, lovers, work, and the world itself.

Notes

1. Margaret Huff, "The Interdependent Self: An Integrated Concept from Feminist Theology and Feminist Psychology," *Philosophy and Theology*, Vol. 2, Number 2, pp. 160-172.

2. Audre Lorde, "Uses of the Erotic: The Erotic As Power," *Sister Outsider* (Freedom CA: The Crossing Press, 1984) p. 55.

3. Ibid., p. 56.

4. Ibid., p. 58.

5. Ibid., pp. 57-58.

6. Ibid., p. 57.

7. Ibid., p. 57.

Lise Weil

Lowering the Case:
An After-Reading of Sex and Other Sacred Games

> "With us, it seems to me that everything is accomplished through desire. With us, to desire proves that we are doubly alive. Desire is a grand, irrational invasion which liberates more and more joy. In desire, we know we are united, that through us courses the memory of our grandmothers, the hearts of our mothers. It is nourishing beyond belief, beyond all logic."
>
> Jovette Marchessault, *Lesbian Tryptich*

> "I just want to say: I think lesbians have a chance here to keep a flame alive...we can keep writing, writing poems and dreaming, about the power of the erotic. It's like keeping the sacred texts alive."
>
> Joan Nestle, *The American Voice*

When I came out in the late seventies in the USA I came out into a land that was all on fire. Lesbian Desire was the pulsing center of an entire way of life, a culture, a movement. Our singers echoed our poets, our philosophers quoted our singers. The air throbbed with erotic possibility. There was wild fire burning in our country,[1] amaryllis blooming in our thighs, "sheer / linen billowing / on the wind...."[2]

With one daring gesture, it seemed, we had burst out of romance, out of family, out of the same old story, out of history itself. Lesbian Desire catapulted us far far from our origins, out of our separate selves, into a world of women come together in a common refusal of male values, a common longing for the feel of a woman's skin, the soft soft touch of her lips. Lesbian Desire, at that time and in that place, was Pure Lust.

Sex and Other Sacred Games by Kim Chernin and Renate Stendhal (New York: Times Books, 1989). After-readings are a special feature of *Trivia: A Journal of Ideas*.

Out of Lesbian Desire all other desires flowed: the desire for creation, the urge to make the world anew. In it all other desires were contained: our desire for a world in which women would be not marginal but central, originary. A world wholly other than this grim and murderous patriarchal world we all inhabit now. Therefore: our desire for subversion!

There was not much room for specifics, for qualifications. We had no time for them! Nobody asked, *"How* do you desire? Under what circumstances? What keeps it alive?" Those were petty questions, distractions. Nobody asked, "Why Lesbian Desire? Why not Female Desire?" If they had, we would have said, "How to separate a man from the territory that goes with him? Pure Lust for a man: a contradiction in terms!"

Then in the 1980s Lesbian Desire as an upper-case phenomenon began to break down. For one thing, many of us who had been born aloft by the euphoria of the seventies had begun to come down for a landing. For another thing, lesbians who for very good reasons had not participated in that euphoria began to make their voices heard. Listening to them, some of us began to realize we ourselves had not been represented in our entirety—that parts of ourselves had retreated before the vast and breathless sweep of our vision. And much of what we thought we'd left behind—class, skin color, place of origin, childhood wounds—had really only been in hiding all along. We had to admit that, as Joan Nestle put it, "we do not yet know enough at all about what women—any women—desire...."[3] Clearly, then, it was time for more specific descriptions, time to lower the case: to speak of lesbian desires.

Sex and Other Sacred Games by Kim Chernin and Renate Stendhal explores that territory where Lesbian Desire tends to come most violently undone—in the very heart and bowels of a love relationship. Essentially, the book is an extended conversation between two women on the subject of sex. In the course of the conversation, which is laced with echoes of Platonic dialogue, the two women fall in love. What makes this dialogue both highly charged and evocative of a whole chapter of feminist history is that one of the women, Alma Runau, is a lesbian feminist and the other, Claire Heller, is a self-declared (heterosexual) *femme fatale.*[4]

Alma and Claire are writers living in Europe. They meet in a café in Paris, part after a long afternoon of conversation, then write long and furiously to and about each other in the three years following the meeting—letters that alternately mask and reveal them, their deepest desires, their deepest fears. Such is the force of their encounter that it sends each woman on a journey back through her own personal history and, in the case of Claire, back to antiquity, to Greek myth and legend where our Western notions about sex and love were born.

Chernin and Stendhal collaborated in writing the book, with Chernin writing Claire Heller's parts and Stendhal Alma Runau's—so a note at the beginning informs us. But I was a hundred and fifty pages into the book before I saw this note and by that time had already decided Kim Chernin, whose writings I knew, was behind the German Alma, and that her counterpart was the mysterious, elusive Claire. For the American Claire, with her body consciousness, her charm, her belief in social ritual and role-playing, has the feel of a European woman. Alma, like her creator, is German, but her transparency, her plodding honesty, her wholesome feminist values make her familiar in a very American kind of way.

In other words, though conceived as opposites, Claire and Alma partake of each other's substance, and their identities have a way of shifting throughout the book. Surely this has something to do with the fact that not only have Chernin and Stendhal written much of themselves and their own stories into their characters, but also, being lovers, they have in significant ways already been written into each other's stories.

We see their first meeting through Alma's eyes, which are full of criticism, silent judgment—the fairly predictable judgments of a self-righteous feminist. "How can anybody make love with such nails?...But she doesn't make love, of course, she's made love to. *Voilà la différence.*" "What if you recognized your frustration with men? What if the clown stopped playing the game? What would appear under your shining mask?"

And Claire? From the beginning, with Alma, she is all swagger, positioning, bravado. She claims to have devoted her life to the quest for her own female power. She accuses Alma and her brand of feminism of naïveté, of retreating into victimhood. "You think men are powerful? You're all worried about their uses and abuses of power? I tell you, the most powerful thing walking this earth is a sexual woman. She's out there, I tell you, for the body."

Claire, we learn, has spent a good portion of her life seducing men, teaching them everything she knows about the body, embracing the ancient role of the courtesan, the hetaera. In a series of long letters to Alma, Claire puts herself inside the myths of the goddess and her hero, imagines the sacred magic and reciprocity that once existed in sexual acts between man and woman, arguing that it was not feminists who "invented the link between eros and the sacred.... The idea was more than two thousand years old."

But at this point the question arises: Why? Why this defensiveness, this urge to convince Alma? Why these urgent letters addressed to a lesbian feminist?? Why, in short, is Claire pursuing Alma?

On the other hand, what is it Alma sees in Claire? This dolled-up woman with bright red lips and nails?

One thing is clear: in the context of Lesbian Desire, there is no way to answer these questions. In the context of Lesbian Desire, Lesbian is itself an upper-case phenomenon: She Who *embodies* Otherness. In her very way of being in the world she is a challenge to the patriarchal order, a refusal of their categories, their oppositions: masculine/feminine and all derivatives thereof—active/passive, dominant/submissive, taker/giver. Nowhere is this more true than in her sexual life, where none of these categories apply.

In the context of Lesbian Desire there is no way to explain the unmistakable fact that we are all of us drawn to otherness: boyish to womanly, lean to round, light to dark, WASP to Jew. Or the less visible dynamics: she who needs to control to she who won't be controlled; she who rushes to she who takes her own sweet time; she who indulges herself to she who denies herself; she who's always doubted her looks to she who's always liked hers; she who likes being taken care of to she who likes to "make things right." (And who are we kidding to say this doesn't show up in bed? She who takes/is taken, she who initiates/is seduced, she who tends to end up on top/bottom?) In short, there is no way to talk about power in our relationships with each other. And, as Amber Hollibaugh says, "the question of power affects who and how you eroticize sexual need. It's absolutely at the bottom of sexual inquiry."[5]

Alma, at the point when Claire's letters come into her hands, is in the south of France recovering from a bad breakup. It's the kind of breakup that wreaks havoc with one's lesbian-feminist identity, that forces you to sit back and rethink everything you thought you knew about love between women, about yourself. There are questions, you are shocked to discover, that feminism can't begin to answer. *She brings out the worst in me, but I can't live without her. I've lost all respect for her, but I'd give anything to be in bed with her.* There is a shattering of ideals, most of all, an ideal of self. *Why can't I stop thinking about her? Why am I identifying with all the lyrics on FM 95?*

In her writer's solitude in the French countryside, Alma begins to ask such questions of herself. Among other things, she is beginning to realize how little she has known, or acknowledged, about her own desires, how little these desires have entered her own idea of herself. And this realization has everything to do with the appearance of Claire Heller in her life. "The irony of my preaching equality while I was already hopelessly hooked by Solveig's difference. I didn't want to admit the attraction her otherness held for me. Just as I didn't want to admit how Claire Heller in her feminine attire fascinated me. How I was shocked by my sudden longing to be a man and ravish this femininity that she offered and withheld." Suddenly coming to understand: "I desired like a woman, like one who doesn't know how to take."

Claire is a cure for her lesbian smugness, a virginity that insists it knows all that needs to be known about sex, that refuses to acknowledge the presence of power in relationships between women. What Alma calls "the dogma of tenderness." As she puts it, "in the sweet nest of our bodies the longing to recognize the stranger, be the stranger, to conquer, seduce, surrender, had gone to sleep…" "Sex, I suppose, in such a cradle, can come to be felt as part of the danger of life.…Shielding ourselves from the conventional notions of sex (domination, passive surrender, giving up self), we came close to eliminating sex altogether."

Feminism itself, Alma sees, held her virginity in place. "Feminism taught me to suspect any power that would drive others to their knees. It taught me to keep my own knees straight. No more submission! Beware domination!"

You saw me as an icon. Artemis, you said. Virginal in my independence. Uncompromising in my choices. Embodying otherness: "the necessity of an impulse whose goal or origin / still lie beyond me."[6] *Besides, I had the weight of a whole movement behind me.*

No wonder you couldn't believe me when I said I didn't mind at all, in fact, it was a point in your favor, I was fascinated, really wanted to know…never having been in love with a man, myself. Being unable to imagine it.

You thought I was being polite. Or was it just condescending.

What if I'd told you: My best friends were always boy-crazy. I was always listening to them, hanging on to the little sops thrown my way—"no one's ever listened to me like this." "I wish he could talk to me like you do." Who knows, maybe I wanted to be able to remember the pain of loving women who loved men, my whole life long (beginning of course with the mother).

Maybe I wanted to remember how it was to be queer. Unaggrandized, demythologized. Not a proud deviant. An outcast. Kinky hair and buck teeth and clothes that were always wrong.

What if I'd told you: I was a freak for not needing what they needed. Differently abled. I believed in their needs, their desires. I made them mine by listening. Could listen to D. for hours, days, when she talked about Billy. The summer of "lo–ove" when they moved into the attic room in Ann Arbor, the one that got so hot that summer some days they only went out for ice cream. The weekend trip to Chicago when "we were really getting into fucking" and they shared a twin bed with creaky springs.

How she followed him to Berkeley after he left her. Longing so bad she would spy his tall figure down the street, run to catch up, follow several lengths behind, her arms aching to circle his waist. Near her apartment was a famous French bakery, she brought home pastries in cartons, Napoleons, eclairs, cream puffs. She lined them up along the rim of the bathtub, popped them in her mouth as she took her bath, one after another. Over the weeks her body began to change. It bulged, it pushed out against her skin. Soon she was fat. Then the longing wasn't as bad, she said.

Like a fairy tale it all was to me, the body taking over, assuming a new shape. Metamorphosis. That one could let one's body go that way, allow love to shape one's life.

I imitated her, I found myself a boy who talked like Billy, wore cowboy shirts, baggy pants, like Billy. His name was Jules and I said it with a soft "l" the way she did when she said "Billy." Jules started coming by, sometimes he'd spend the night.

I admit I wanted her approval, I looked for it. One day she gave it. "You know, I think I'm a little jealous." My heart pumping out of control. Not wanting to want it to mean what I wanted it to mean. "Jealous! But why?" "Well, I just think Jules is really cute, that's all."

I got hold of myself right away. It never showed. I never did let anything show, not then, in those days. You couldn't afford to when you'd been ugly, been queer.

Later all this worked in my favor. It made me the perfect lesbian. The only one at camp with no picture of a boyfriend in her wallet. The one who always knew better. Never cared what people thought, never wore makeup. Independent. Admired by the needy ones, the ones I listened to. The ones I loved.

Funny how things got turned around. Now you're the one who has to hide. Make up stories or say nothing. The one who can't let anything show. Did it have to come to this? Me smugger than ever, you more vulnerable.

Gulfs of silence that couldn't be crossed. Secrets kept out of fear of judgment. Desires never acknowledged. The price we paid for insisting on Lesbian Desire, at the expense of lesbian desires, was in many cases the possibility of an honest relationship with another woman.

Gradually, Alma and Claire begin to force each other to greater honesty, toward self-knowledge. Claire, who has insisted on sex as a sacred game, requiring roles, who has defied feminism to teach her a thing she hasn't figured out for herself—Claire arrives at Alma's door, naked in her need. In the end, she admits that the myths of the goddess and her hero are just that: myths, reflections of another time. They can't be lived out between men and women today: "what, before writing to you, I had not seen."

Alma, too, is humbled, as she realizes this woman she dismissed as a spineless floozy has much to teach her about claiming her own desires: "She pains me because she simply, naturally has what I don't have. What I've longed for my whole life and have to struggle to work and sweat for inch by inch. This feminine version of sexual boldness, self-assurance, pride. This power..."

When I say "an honest relationship with another woman" I mean just this: one that does not attempt to hide or play down how we *impress* each other, threaten each other, disturb each other, terrify each other. Change each other forever. One that does not pretend away our differences.

As I write this in the early nineties, the testimonies and the explorations of the last decade have brought us all closer to the possibility of such a relationship, closer to being able to "talk realistically about what people *are* sexually."[7] If nothing else, I think, we have become more honest with ourselves. Lesbian Desire, to the extent it functioned as a moral standard, marking some forms of sexual behavior as acceptable and others as unacceptable, has in the past decade effectively been overthrown, and this is surely a good thing.

Yet in the process of documenting our infinite divergences as sexual beings, in the rush to deconstruct Lesbian Desire, the terms of our struggle have also been redefined. Too often, it seems to me, the cataloging of our differences has served to reduce our status to that of a sexual minority and our struggle to a civil rights agenda.[8] And yes, I understand that desire can sometimes be about no more than just a body, or a body part, I understand it's obnoxious to be told lesbian desire should be utterly *other*, I understand we haven't had our turn at *this* world yet, and we need to be free to explore all possibilities. I also understand that U.S. feminism, with its middle-class, sexually conservative bias, has been a major obstacle to this exploration—that Pure Lust, in practice, has had a tendency to translate into puritanical lust. But having said all this, I am not ready to concede that what we're here for, along with Queer Nation, is to make the world safe for our raunchiness.

As lesbians we constitute the greatest threat ever known to a male order that wants us all to feel wrong in our bones, to feel split from each other and from ourselves. When lesbian desires are articulated, recorded, inscribed, utterly outside such a vision of creation and subversion, I feel as if our most unique and precious gift had been squandered.

Every time I touch a woman for the first time—with a touch that says "I want"—it could be her lips, it could be just her arm, I see a space open up where everything is possible again, there are stunning shifts of meaning, the walls begin to fall. Lesbian Desire comes rushing back in, all of it. And when she looks at me, when I feel her saying "I want," all of history reverses itself in one vertiginous moment, I am lifted out of my own history, and there is not a trace of teenage ugliness, I am not queer.

I'm not ready to let go of this: the great upheaval of history in our embrace—not felt all the time, not every time, but always there as possibility: "two women, eye to eye / measuring each other's spirit, each other's / limitless desire, / a whole new poetry beginning here."[9]

As Alma sifts through the pieces of herself laid bare by Claire's presence in her life, and through what she has pieced together about Claire's life, she makes the discovery that the two of them, for all their differences, have something very deep in common: both of them have been "dreaming ourselves out of patriarchy....We have the same longing for body wholeness."

Nothing is more threatening to this patriarchy than our desire for each other, especially when this desire begins truly to encompass our differences. Probably because it is when desire embraces the particulars of our experience—our own and others'—that we begin to hit the surest common ground. To see that truly we are all in this together—and that we need all our dreams to survive.

But none of this is easy. Sometimes it can mean giving up dreams we thought we couldn't live without; always it means—I'm thinking here of Claire and Alma, of Chernin and Stendhal—having to stretch very, very far to take each other in.

"You mean, we've changed each other?" says Alma at their last meeting, having just crossed an ocean to be with Claire.

For Chernin and Stendhal this point marks the end of one collaboration and the beginning of another.

"What else matters!" says Claire.

Notes

1. Some of these words are taken from song lyrics by Cris Williamson, *The Changer and the Changed*, Olivia, 1975.

2. Olga Broumas, "Leda and Her Swan," *Beginning with O* (New Haven: Yale University Press, 1977).

3. Joan Nestle, "The Fem Question," in Carole S. Vance, ed., *Pleasure and Danger: Exploring Female Sexuality*, (London: Pandora Press, 1989) p. 234. Nestle's *Restricted Country* (Ithaca, NY: Firebrand, 1987) was one of the most important texts to emerge in the eighties in terms of exploring lesbian desires.

4. Other brave and revealing conversations on this subject have been Cherríe Moraga and Amber Hollibaugh's "What We're Rolling Around in Bed With," in *Powers of Desire*, eds. Ann Snitow, Christine Stansell, Sharon Thompson (New York: Monthly Review Press, 1983), pp. 394-405; Esther Newton and Shirley Walton's "The Misunderstanding: Toward a More Precise Sexual Vocabulary" in *Pleasure and Danger*, and a hilarious lovers' dialogue (recorded in bed) in Melanie Kaye/Kantrowitz's "Sexual Power," *Sinister Wisdom* 15, Fall 1980.

5. Amber Hollibaugh and Cherríe Moraga, "What We're Rolling Around in Bed With," p. 397

6. Broumas, "Artemis" *Beginning with O.*

7. Hollibaugh and Moraga, p. 396.

8. I am thinking, for example, of anthologies like *Powers of Desire* and *Pleasure and Danger*, where differences between women are recognized in a context of liberal pluralism whose net effect is to subvert the revolutionary implications of sexual difference: that is, of lesbians as distinct from gay men—and even of women as distinct from men. This is not to take away from the often radical and groundbreaking writing to be found in these books.

9. Adrienne Rich, "Transcendental Etude" in *The Dream of a Common Language* (New York: W.W. Norton, 1978).

Gale Jackson

From the precision of the embrace:
translations

"salud"
"health"
"and money"   she's feeling herself tonight but she's watching
him weary, too hard to be close like this and not close.   you
know, cool.
"everybody's serving time, one way or another" he said, picking up
our conversation just where we had left off when the waiter came.
"nay" i says to keep the conversation flowing.
"hey that's good, how long you said she's been here?" he's asking
her, that's a concession to her territory and you know how men
are, but she's not using it so he answers himself: "two days,
wonderful.   keep that up and you'll be talking like a native in
no time."
"nay" i says
he roars.   rearing back in his chair with laughter.   he tips
but he don't fall which would be funny though cause he's a big
guy.

the taverna meglau in hellenica.   the menu is in greek.   the
waiters.   the liquor list and the prices.   no
translations.   no touristas.   no people, 'cept us, from the
base.

"logarisis mou paracalo" he says and the waiter begins to tally it
up.   the meal has been a feast.   his treat.   greek
style.   the big black man with the very white smile has known

more greek women than i have known women, has seen the sun rise
over mount ida every day for the past eight years. wc will
take over his house. he gleefully orients us.
"how do you say girlfriend?"
"boyfriend is felos."
"no, oshe. thelo 'girlfriend.'"
again, the festive lion, he roars; his mouth like a pink tunnel
lined with piano keys and strung with chords. he's laughing
and laughing while she and i sit patiently waiting, the perfect
dinner couple. who do you think thinks i'm really her
cousin. but uncle sam is dumb. from the inside "the war"
could scare you to death.
"and how do you say happy?"
he won't tell.
"curses?"
oh yes. his lips burst open with a gay perversity.
"but this gesture" he shows us "says everything...thou who commits
adultery with your mother's mother, thou who sucks a mule's dick,
thou with breath like scum..." he can not stop laughing.
she smiles.
the waiter brings more wine.

the taverna meglau in hellenica. it buzzes in my ears like
sing song and bazookie music. i am speaking without
connectors; knowing only nouns and verbs. the black man,
ordering, fluent, is also an american despite the sculpted
markings that identify us as africans once and always. he's
fun loving and only vaguely, ritually commercial (like he
probably brush with pepsodent). the taverna is a streetside
roped off from the limitless speed of cars rushing by. across
the street is a temple; curvaceous, doomed, womanish. i meet
her eyes across the table and catch a look to set the night on
fire. i fold my hands in my lap. look down. even across
this table she is too sensual. the loose clothing, the
secrets, this new place excites me, and her sex, but we
keep a wall of silence for these others.

looking up from my drink i catch his eye catching mine catching
hers. i don't give a damn. he's giddy with freedom drunk
with wine drinking to the end of his personal war with the
american government. back to the world now. he leaves
whatever life that has accumulated here for him as though it be only a
matter of lost or borrowed time. back to the world, going home
after a ten-year duty tour. "here is to the world."
our glasses click over the room filled with food and talk and
probably lots of lovers waiting for a more auspicious hour; for
the night to stop throbbing.
"salud" she says.
we drink, swallowing to the sounds of knife and fork against
plates & against themselves. and then in a teeny tiny voice i
ask:
"how do you say pussy?"
she holds her glass mid motion.
"what?" he shouts above the din.
and so a
little louder but still teeny tiny i say "pussy."
he now cannot help himself from falling from the chair. say
big say little say deep say wide say wet. he is laughing from
the floor. anyway you want to say it. say it. even the
waiter chuckles shoulders and throat. other diners give
friendly nods then turn back to their business at hand. our
friend is their friend and there are no strangers here where the
language is its own. our friend is a fountain of laughter; a
magnificent geyser from the taverna floor. i throw my arms
around her high on his exhilaration. fearing no evil, feeling
no pain. first night out in our new home and when she touches
me back smiling i feel every muscle in my body sigh.

Nicole Brossard

Marlene Wildeman, Translator

Lesbians of Lore

IN THE FIRST PLACE, NOT EVERYONE IS A WRITER AND NOT ALL WOMEN ARE LESBIANS. We are dealing here with two modes of existence which inscribe themselves in the margins of the normal-normative course of language and the imaginary and, consequently, in the margins of reality and fiction.

Before going any further, I would like to propose that we study this question: what is necessary in order to write? Of course, I could ask: what does it mean, to write? But it seems to me more pertinent—given our subject—to try to answer the first question, which to a certain extent has bearing on the identity of lesbian writers.

Generally speaking, I would say that in order to write one must a) know that one exists, b) have a captivating and positive self-image, and c) respond to the inner necessity—if only in self-defense—to inscribe one's perception and one's vision of the world in language. In other words, one must have the desire, be it conscious or not, to make one's presence known, to declare one's existence in the world. Finally, one must d) feel a profound dissatisfaction with the prevailing and mainstream discourse, which denies differences and obstructs thought.

In sum, then, to write is to be a subject in process: moving, changing, a being in pursuit of. To write, you must first belong to yourself.

We could, at this point, conclude that writing, its practice, is a subject that concerns the individual first and foremost. But as Jean Piaget so aptly remarks, "One who has not had a sense of a potential plurality has absolutely no awareness of his or her own individuality."[1] This means that in order to be conscious of oneself as an individual, as someone unique in the world, what must come first is an acknowledgement of one's belonging to a group or a collectivity. Whatever our ethnic or religious origins, we all belong quite visibly to the category "women." What characterizes women as a group is our colonized status. To be colonized is not to think for oneself, to think on behalf of "the other," to put one's emotions to work in the service of "the other." In short, not to exist. Above all, one is unable to find in one's own group those sources of inspiration and motivation essential to all artistic production. It is crucial that we find in our own group captivating images which can nourish us spiritually, intellectually, and emotionally. What and who inspire women? What and who then inspire lesbians? Integrally, in a nonfragmented manner. In fact, perhaps we should distinguish between what motivates us and what inspires us. Thus, I could say that women motivate me because as a woman and feminist among women, I have a profound motivation to change the world, to change language, and to change society. I could also say that lesbians inspire me in the sense that we are a challenge for the imagination and, in a certain way, a challenge for ourselves, to the extent that we give birth to ourselves in the world. Only through literally creating ourselves in the world do we declare our existence and from there make our presence known in the order of the real and the symbolic.

When I say literally give birth to ourselves in the world, I really do mean that literally. *Literal* means "that which is represented by letters." Taken literally. Taken to the letter. For we do take our bodies, our skin, our sweat, pleasure, sensuality, sexual bliss to the letter. From the letters forming these words emerge the beginnings of our texts. We also take our energy and our cleverness to the letter, and we make of our desire a spiral which delivers us into the movement toward sense. Sense which originates with us. Not a counter-sense, a misinterpretation, which would have us trailed in tow throughout the patriarchal universe, like so many tiny stars. Symbolically, and realistically, I think only women and lesbians will be able to legitimize a trajectory toward the origin and future of sense, a sense that we are bringing about in language.

To be at the origin of sense means that we project to the world something resembling what we are and what we dis/cover about ourselves, unlike the patented version of women which patriarchal marketing has made of us, on posters and in person.

To write, for a lesbian, is to learn how to take down the patriarchal posters in her room. It means learning how to live with bare walls for a while. It means learning how not to be afraid of the ghosts which assume the colour of the bare wall. In more literary terms, it means renewing comparisons, establishing new analogies, braving certain tautologies, certain paradoxes. It means starting one's first sentence a thousand times over: "a rose is a rose,"[2] or to think with Djuna Barnes that "an image is a stop the mind makes between uncertainties."[3] To take the risk of having too much to say or not enough. To take the chance of not finding the right words to say with precision what only we can imagine. To risk everything for the universe that takes shape between the words, a universe which, without this passion we have for the other woman, would remain a dead letter.

I think that wild love between two women is so totally inconceivable that, to talk or write *that* in all its dimensions, one almost has to rethink the world, to understand what it is that happens to us. And we can rethink the world only through words. Lesbian love therefore seems to me intrinsically a love that largely goes beyond the framework of love. Something inside us and yet beyond us—now there's an enigma for writing and fiction, but especially for poetry.

That being said, it seems to me that for lesbians to come abreast of who they are, what they need is a bed, a worktable to write on, and a book. A book we must read and write at the same time. This book is unpublished, but we are already quite familiar with its substantial preface. In it, we find the names Sappho, Gertrude Stein, Djuna Barnes, Adrienne Rich, Mary Daly, Monique Wittig, and others. This preface contains, as well, a certain number of biographical annotations recounting guilt, humiliation, contempt, despair, joy, courage, revolt, and the eroticism of lesbians throughout time.

The book is blank; the preface sets us dreaming.

I know that lesbians don't look up at the ceiling when they're making love, but one day I looked up and saw revealed to me the most beautiful fresco ever seen by women—on my lesbian word of honour. It was perfectly real, this fresco, and at the bottom of it was written: a lesbian who does not reinvent the world is a lesbian in the process of disappearing.

◆ ◆ ◆

...
the poem if tournament tempts me
absent line
abstracts me even closer to you
in order to bring itself
about
at the outer edge of lips, the poem be/
comes inseparable from everyday reality
from the moment there is decision
to make a sign with the hand lights the temples

an image is a state of the soul
between women
a state of the soul is an image

<u>lesbian</u>

Excerpt from the poem "Tempes" in
Dont j'oublie le titre.

Notes

1. Quoted by Edgar Morin in *L'Homme et la mort*, Collection Point, No. 77 (Paris: Seuil, 1976), p. 112.
2. Gertrude Stein.
3. Djuna Barnes, *Nightwood* (1936; rpt. New York: New Directions Paperbook No. 98, 1961), p. 111.

Daphne Marlatt

musing with mothertongue

THE BEGINNING: LANGUAGE, A LIVING BODY WE ENTER AT BIRTH, SUSTAINS AND CON-
tains us. it does not stand in place of anything else, it does not replace the
bodies around us. placental, our flat land, our sea, it is both place (where
we are situated) and body (that contains us), that body of language we
speak, our mothertongue. it bears us as we are born in it, into cognition.

language is first of all for us a body of sound. leaving the water of the
mother's womb with its one dominant sound, we are born into this other
body whose multiple sounds bathe our ears from the moment of our arrival. we learn the sounds before we learn what they say: a child will
speak baby-talk in pitch patterns that accurately imitate the sentence patterns of her mothertongue. an adult who cannot read or write will speak
his mothertongue without being able to say what a particular morpheme
or even word in a phrase means. we learn nursery rhymes without understanding what they refer to. we repeat skipping songs significant for
their rhythms. gradually we learn how the sounds of our language are
active as meaning and then we go on learning for the rest of our lives
what the words are actually saying.

in poetry, which has evolved out of chant and song, in riming and tone-
leading, whether they occur in prose or poetry, sound will initiate
thought by a process of association. words call each other up, evoke each
other, provoke each other, nudge each other into utterance. we know
from dreams and schizophrenic speech how deeply association works in
our psyches, a form of thought that is not rational but erotic because it

works by attraction. a drawing, a pulling toward. a "liking." Germanic *lik-*, body, form; like, same.

like the atomic particles of our bodies, phonemes and syllables gravitate toward each other. they attract each other in movements we call assonance, euphony, alliteration, rhyme. they are drawn together and echo each other in rhythms we identify as feet—lines run on, phrases patter like speaking feet. on a macroscopic level, words evoke each other in movements we know as puns and figures of speech (these endless similes, this continuing fascination with making one out of two, a new one, a simultitude.) meaning moves us deepest the more of the whole field it puts together, and so we get sense where it borders on nonsense ("what is the sense of it all?") as what we sense our way into. the sentence. ("life.") making our multiplicity whole and even intelligible by the end-point. intelligible: logos there in the gathering hand, the reading eye.

hidden in the etymology and usage of so much of our vocabulary for verbal communication (contact, sharing) is a link with the body's physicality: matter (the import of what you say) and matter and by extension mother; language and tongue; to utter and outer (give birth again); a part of speech and a part of the body; pregnant with meaning; to mouth (speak) and the mouth with which we also eat and make love; sense (meaning) and that with which we sense the world; to relate (a story) and to relate to somebody, related (carried back) with its connection with bearing (a child); intimate and to intimate; vulva and voluble; even sentence which comes from a verb meaning to feel.

like the mother's body, language is larger than us and carries us along with it. it bears us, it births us, insofar as we bear with it. if we are poets we spend our lives discovering not just what we have to say but what language is saying as it carries us with it. in etymology we discover a history of verbal relations (a family tree, if you will) that has preceded us and given us the world we live in. the given, the immediately presented, as at birth—a given name a given world. we know language structures our world and in a crucial sense we cannot see what we cannot verbalize, as the work of Whorf and ethnolinguistics has pointed out to us. here we are truly contained within the body of our mothertongue. and even the physicists, chafing at these limits, say that the glimpse physics now gives us of the nature of the universe cannot be conveyed in a language based on the absolute difference between a noun and a verb. poetry has been demonstrating this for some time.

if we are women poets, writers, speakers, we also take issue with the given, hearing the discrepancy between what our patriarchally-loaded language bears (can bear) of our experience and the difference from it our experience bears out—how it misrepresents, even miscarries, and so leaves unsaid what we actually experience. can a pregnant woman be said to be "master" of the gestation process she finds herself within—is that her relationship to it? (see Julia Kristeva, *Desire in Language*, p. 238.) are women included in the statement "God appearing as man" (has God ever appeared as a woman?) can a woman ever say she is "lady of all she surveys" or could others ever say of her she "ladies it over them"?

so many terms for dominance in English are tied up with male experiencing, masculine hierarchies and differences (exclusion), patriarchal holdings with their legalities. where are the poems that celebrate the soft letting-go the flow of menstrual blood is as it leaves her body? how can the standard sentence structure of English with its linear authority, subject through verb to object, convey the wisdom of endlessly repeating and not exactly repeated cycles her body knows? or the mutuality her body shares embracing other bodies, children, friends, animals, all those she customarily holds and is held by? how can the separate nouns mother and child convey the fusion, bleeding womb-infant mouth, she experiences in those first days of feeding? what syntax can carry the turning herself inside out in love when she is both sucking mouth and hot gush on her lover's tongue?

Julia Kristeva says: "If it is true every national language has its own dream language and unconscious, then each of the sexes—a division so much more archaic and fundamental than the one into languages— would have its own unconscious wherein the biological and social program of the species would be ciphered in confrontation with language, exposed to its influence, but independent from it" (*Desire in Language*, p. 241). i link this with the call so many feminist writers in Quebec have issued for a language that returns us to the body, a woman's body and the largely unverbalized, presyntactic, postlexical field it knows. postlexical in that, as Mary Daly shows, with intelligence (that gathering hand) certain words (dandelion sparks) seed themselves back to original and originally-related meaning. this is a field where words mutually attract each other, fused by connection, enthused (inspired) into variation (puns, word play, rime at all levels) fertile in proliferation (offspring, rooting back to *al*, seed syllable to grow, and leafing forward into *alma*, nourishing, a woman's given name, soul, inhabitant.)

inhabitant of language, not master, not even mistress, this new woman writer (Alma, say) in having is had, is held by it, what she is given to say. in giving it away is given herself, on that double edge where she has always lived, between the already spoken and the unspeakable, sense and non-sense. only now she writes it, risking nonsense, chaotic language leafings, unspeakable breaches of usage, intuitive leaps. inside language she leaps for joy, shoving out the walls of taboo and propriety, kicking syntax, discovering life in old roots.

language thus speaking (i.e., inhabited) relates us, "takes us back" to where we are, as it relates us to the world in a living body of verbal relations. articulation: seeing the connections (and the thighbone, and the hipbone, etc.). putting the living body of language together means putting the world together, the world we live in: an act of composition, an act of birthing, us, uttered and outered there in it.

Judith Barrington

For a Friend Whose Lover Has Left

They say memory resides in the head
but I say it lives in the tips of fingers
the insides of thighs and forearms:
yes, the concave belly remembers
what it once embraced sleeping.

Your limbs remember skin; in sleep you reach
for someone whose name you have almost forgotten.
It is not your brain that recalls
the hollow above her collarbone
and the shoulder blade like a wing.

They say the brain's cells die with age.
You will forget the number you dialed
over and over, but one day your finger
will remember (as mine once did) leaping deftly
from the six to the four to the one.

You will not pay attention to the voice
that says "hello" because memories lurk
among whorls and scrolls of fingerprints.
"Sorry" you'll say and hang up, but still
your palm will hold the exact curve of her cheek.

Betsy Warland

untying the tongue

WHAT PROMPTED ME TO WRITE *OPEN IS BROKEN* WAS THE REALIZATION THAT THE English language tongue-ties me. this "restricted mobility" was most apparent in my attempts to speak of my erotic life. such speechlessness is not peculiar to me. few erotic texts exist is north american women's writing. is it taboo? TABOO: "ta, mark + bu, exceedingly." are women afraid to "mark" the paper? or as Hélène Cixous writes, "inscribe" ourselves? it is difficult. women already feel (are) far too vulnerable in this society. "To write: I am a woman is heavy with consequences."
(Nicole Brossard, *These Our Mothers*)

"Patriarchal development of consciousness has an indisputable inner need to 'murder the mother,' that is, as far as possible to negate, exclude, devalue, and repress the 'maternal-feminine' world which represents the unconscious."
(Erich Neumann, "Narcissism, Normal Self-Formation and the Primary Relation to the Mother")

immediately surfaces the second intimidation: fear of narcissism. though few mirrors stand in which we can see our eroticism reflected, we are terrorized by the thought of this accusation. safer to have no "marks." no marks? pornography is ignorance. and romance? we have been persuaded to believe eroticism is romance. ROMANCE: "made in Rome." so much for romance! the word itself connotes fabricating an image *outside* ourselves compared to discovery of the erotic wellspring *within*.

TABOO   **ROMANCE**

"Where the god is male and father only, and…is associated with law, order, civilization, *logos* and super-ego, religion—and the pattern of life which it encourages—tends to become a matter of these only, to the neglect of nature, instinct,…feeling, *eros*, and what Freud called the 'id.' Such a religion, so far from 'binding together' and integrating, may all too easily become an instrument of repression, and so of individual and social disintegration."
(Victor White, *Soul and Psyche: An Enquiry into the Relationship of Psychotherapy and Religion*)

the language itself does not reflect women's sensual experience. for most of us, however, it is our native tongue. the only language we have. *open is broken* is about the words i abandoned. ABANDON: "(to put) in one's power; a, to, at, from Latin ad, to + bandon, power." so, when we abandon words, it isn't a simple matter of leaving them behind but rather a turning over of our power *to* those who keep them: speechlessness the consequence.

the word is the act. when i abandon a word i relinquish the experience it calls up. yet, how can i use the word "intercourse" as a lesbian? and what do i say as a feminist, when in my deepest erotic moments words like "surrender" pulse in my head? a dictionary defines surrender as: "to relinquish possession or control of to another because of demand or compulsion." still, my body insisted, my instincts persisted/pulled me toward this word. it seemed full of life, and indeed, in IX, i find it is. truth is in the roots.

contemporary *usage* of our words is what tongue-tied me. the repressed is the absent. women have been DISMEMBERED: "dis-, (removal) + membrum, member" from the word. in tracing words back, i have found that etymology nearly always re-members the feminine sensibility of our inner landscapes.

ABANDON   DISMEMBERED

263

usage is selective. Cixous writes: "I maintain unequivocally that there is such a thing as *marked* writing; that, until now, far more extensively and repressively than is ever suspected or admitted, writing has been run by a libidinal and cultural—hence political, typically masculine—economy; that this is a locus where the repression of women has been perpetuated... that this locus has grossly exaggerated all signs of sexual opposition (and not sexual difference), where woman has never her *turn* to speak."
("Laugh of the Medusa")

Mary Daly describes the dominance of male culture as the "presence of absence." this presence of absence in our language has resulted in the abandonment of our most significant words. tongue-tied. no marks. no rituals. RITUAL: "rite." RITE: "retornare, to return." RETURN: "turn, threshold, thread." the thread knotted around our tongues—untied, spirals us to the edge. MARK: "merg-, boundary, border, marking out the boundary by walking around it (ceremonially 'beating the bounds')."

mark of the spirit. painted bodies. marked objects. sacred openings. threshold to altered states. TABOO: "exceedingly marked, marked as sacred." invisible made visible.

abandoned words spring up from deep places. claiming our eroticism reclaims the dismembered.

"homesickness without memory
yet tongues are not fooled
tissue 'clairvoyant'
memorizes, re-members 'chiaroscuro' history"

(XI)

RITUAL   RITE   RETURN   MARK   TABOO

Audre Lorde, in her essay "Uses of the Erotic: The Erotic as Power" names the erotic "the nurturer or nursemaid of all our deepest knowledge." tracing the etymology of abandoned words has that same reconstructive power. reclaims what we subconsciously know, passionately BELIEVE: "leubh-, livelong, love, libido,"

intact. the texts woven in/are the very fibers of our tissue. TISSUE: "teks-, text." the body of language whole again.

Daphne Marlatt, in her poetic statement "musing with mothertongue," characterizes this phenomenon: "inhabitant of language, not master, not even mistress, this new woman writer...in having is had, is held by it, what she is given to say. in giving it away is given herself, on that double edge where she has always lived, between the already spoken and the unspeakable, sense and non-sense. only now she writes it, risking nonsense, chaotic language leafings, unspeakable breaches of usage, intuitive leaps. inside language she leaps for joy, shoving out the walls of taboo and propriety, kicking syntax, discovering life in old roots."

writing comes out of chaos much as Eros was born out of Chaos. in trusting the relationship between eroticism/etymology and tissue/text, the language—my language—broke open. my tongue freed. to mark exceedingly.

BELIEVE   TISSUE

open is broken

Prologue

the talisman for their love
a tornado in her hand.
she had found the old woman on the stone
the surrounding maze had not confounded her.
she asked her questions in the flash of time allowed
"should i pursue this love?"
                                        "yes."
"will it be painful?"
                            "yes."
"are we archetypes?"
                            "yes."
then it was time for the talisman.
                                        "open your right hand.
a tornado emerged as the fingers unfolded.
she shook
yet felt the calm of its eye within/re-membered
the egg
origin of all
                    "open is broken."
pecking her way out
she heard a voice tranquilly say
"consider me dangerous."
recognized it
as her own

I

it is morning
the animals are out early
sniffing and switching their tails
sense something in the garden not present before

i move carefully
and egg without shell, yolk and white shimmering
an eye alone trembling
an image among
images without meaning except in relation

you opened me
whispered "come back" was it
some other life between us before?

an eye with no mind i stood skinless before you
a flower unbolted, quivering in its moment

the animals are out early
sniffing and switching their tails
sense surrender

as you left
you called "come see the moon!"
its full eye stared at me
it knows about breaking

II

the roses rise up
stretch into morning
each bush a brothel of red and pink orgy of opening
petals provoke
the do of desire

come womb-wooing
tongues bloom blooming

III

the leaves witness you unsheathing me
my bud my bud quivering in your
mouth you *leaf* me (leaf: "peel off")
in front of a window full of green eyes we climb
the green *ladder:* "clitoris, incline, climax"
on the tip of your tongue you flick
me leaf: "lift" up
to tip tree top
point of all i am to the sky
"roof of the world"
leaves
sink slow into darkening
with my resin on your swollen lips
leaves us in our
betrothal: "truth, tree"

IV

the tree tides out of itself
ring: "search, circle, crest"
spirals its truth
going around in circles
we ex-change rings
"Latin ex-, from ex, out, out of"
out of change we wear the sign of search shared
H.D.'s trees, "concentric circles"
Virginia "The being grows rings, like a tree"
Nicole's spiralling lines
and your rings of consciousness in '69
you, my lover of endless eyes, of "rings within rings"

V

"small hill" becomes sun
"incline(s)" in my mouth
smooth burning on my tongue
south in the mouth of north
star radiant
centre of our system
heartbeats a heart hungry
comes come spilling everywhere
leaving no darkness in me no corner of refusal
the light the light words ignite that have nursed their nightmares
fondled fears inherited
we do not fall off
perspective is a line given us
with your sun
rising is setting
centrifugal : centripetal
we enter our horizons and do not vanish

VI

bodies joined north and south
we are each other's entrance

kissing vulva lips
tongues torque way into vortex
leave syllables behind

sound we are sound
original vocabulary
language: "lingua, tongue"
not separate but same
this is how we came

we have been here before
we are here before
other times other tongues
uterus the *universe:*
"universus, whole, entire, turned into one"

VII

the k(no)wing is the telling
is the leaving some things out

root up the word trees
in the manure the manuscript

the sows have come home

VIII

when she began she used words like moon, egg
words that did not startle
then she was pulled into a whirlpool
claim, surrender, sow, manure flying out
words her tongue never trusted
words from another place, old place, vaguely remembered

each time they slid between the sheets to open each other
they slid between the pages of an ancient text
                    turns of a hidden scroll
the bed the *map:* "napkin, sheet, cloth"

the route her tongue took
the root of the word

IX

you claim me with your tongue
speak my skin's syntax
know my desire's etymologies, *idiom:*
"idios, own, personal, separate"
indigenous imagery
no longer indecipherable i *surrender:*

                    "sur - over + rendr - to deliver"

      render: "to give back"

             deliver: "dē - completely + līberāre - to set free"

the code broken by your fluency
fluent: "soft, wet, naked, exposed"
you part the covers
              to set free

urged by your *fluency:* "to swell, well up, overflow"
our fluids spout out hot gold
                   rivulets punctuating ecstasy

X

egg broken
mouth open
tongues *bloom:* "blow"
tornados cresting our *mounds:*
"manure, manuscript, command"
text of our bodies (tongue come)
under the *tornado's:* "moan"
surrendering ground hungry for home

XI

the *claim?*
between your legs home soil
homesickness without memory
yet tongues are not fooled
tissue "clairvoyant"
memorizes, re-members "chiaroscuro" history
at your taste i "cry out"
"reclaim(ed)" by the "Paraclete"

XII

soil: (verb) "to make dirty, defile, pollute with sin"
from "pig, hyena, sow"
soil: (verb) "to siege"
dirty sows...
this soil's noun "filth, stain"
this soil's noun "manure"
its noun
its name

XIII

soil: (noun) "top layer of the earth's surface, land, country"
from "sit, seat"

seat: "a place in which one may sit
        the buttocks
        residence
        a center of authority"

between your legs
home soil, native soil
land things grow, flourish, thrive in

you re-turn me to the noun
the "found/ation"

   XIV

wer - wel - kwel:
"to turn; to turn; to revolve"

wer: "verse, version" the k(no)wing is the telling
"invert, universe, vortex, vertigo"
the palimpsest your body

wer - wel - kwel

wel: "helix, volume, involve, revolve, evolve, vulva" ear
hearing all

wer - wel - kwel

kwel: "cycle, wheel, talisman"
the talisman for their love
a tornado in her hand

wer - wel - kwel:
"to turn; to turn; to revolve, dwell"

   XV

helix: "a volute on a Corinthian or Ionic capital"
is this when the helix was changed
this when tornado tongues became
"scroll-like ornament"
on virile columns?

helix: "wellspring" of our hearts

"three-dimensional curve that lies on a cylinder or cone
and cuts the elements at a constant angle"

helix: "volume(s)" of our obliterated stories
secreted in our bodies
helix: "the folded rim of skin around the outer ear"
helix: "involve, revolve, evolve, vulva" ear
hearing all
forgetting nothing

XVI

this is a place we touch and taste each other to
where the *person:* "persona, mask" falls away

faces forget disguise
when no longer set against uncertainty
re-turn

in your mirrors is the face of one just dead
fear re-formed into lyric

clarity, it is a kind of death
we are claimed
surrender, resist nothing

i kiss you after we pass through
i kiss a cloud

XVII

]
[
]
[
]
[
no words
]
listen
[
wind: of our
]
being
[
"air"
]
"aura"
[
"wing"/each
]
a wing
[
riding
]
our own wind
[
"weather, storm"
]
"wē, wing, to blow"
[
wing/each
]
a wing
[
the body invisible between us

]
"vāti, (s)he blows, Nirvana"
[

the body
]
Nirvana between us
[
]
[

XVIII

as you hold this/these pages throb
a radiant throat in your hands
each line a wave/blood/pulse
beware
words alter *change:*
"to curve, bend"

you expected to be uneasy
(wave/blood/pulse)
but not afraid
lungs fisting the air amulet against...
you could stop reading
but the pulse in your hands has led you here

Suniti Namjoshi

Homage to Circe

This frame wee looke upon hath beene upon
our trenchers; In briefe, we have devoured ourselves.
　　　　　—Religio Medici 1, 37

She rewards her lovers at random
　　like Circe feeding tit-bits to mice,
　　almonds to bears,
　　　　　　　　and whatever's handy
to miscellaneous swine.

The snake curled about Circe's shoulder
　　tracing the whorl of her perfect ear
　　　　　　　　with an agile tongue.

The little dog barked,
was a good little dog,
　　　　　　　burrowed
its nose in her warm thighs.
The dog, who barked
　　　　　　　and laughed,
had bright eyes.

I am all animals to you?
I could sit cat-like and gaze
　　　　　　　sisterly.

I am all animals to you,
　　　　　　could offer myself
　　　　　　　　on a wide lily-pad,

drink from your cup and eat from your lip,
turn bird for your purpose, feed
from your hand — disarm the wary.
She draws the birds from the trees,
they would say, she tames the hungry.

                                    Circe,
all animals adore you,
you are all things to each
in the tutelary garden, at the continuous feast.

Jeffner Allen

Passion in the Gardens of Delight

BLUE BUTTERFLY MORNING GLORY HEART NO LONGER DEAD OF HEART NOW I LIVE multiples of you wandering you divining. Blue butterfly morning glory heart no longer dead of heart leapfrog somersault until you I vanish.

Flying breathing we touch the roundness of being.

Butterflies light on my hair when books are closed and I forget my lessons. Then you I race to the rivers of life and we dive in.

The dance of the marvelous and the believable jumping jumping jumping still bouncing bouncing jumping jumping you I desiring melting jumping jumping meadows forest clouds jumping you I breezes sun jumping still looking desiring melting feet leave ground ground feet smiling smiling twinkling dissolving twinkling melting meadows forest clouds sun lift whirl turbulence freeflow twinkling is there a touch overturns everything jumping jumping surprisingly surprised.

By the sunflowers you I pick the petals. She loves me.

Two eyes looking at two eyes two hands holding two hands hold eyes in palms eyes bring to see alchemical equations life lines of earth blood red of fire ocean.

The intensity of living things awakens us when skin to skin on a clear night you I glide with the stars and moon feeling how what might be is.

The most perfect of spiderwebs may catch a butterfly flying into another dimension. The web breaks. The butterfly flies on.

Moving through time is sorcery magic simple anticipation. Horizons turn cartwheels the present whirls by you I skip along.

You sail to islands luminous in the mist and silver dawn. I sail to islands pink at sunset and sunrise. The space between is not empty to be feared but waves in which you I swim and sometimes embrace.

Delight runs free delights in running free

The North 40 *Lavender Jane Loves Wimmin* a pond wimmin sunning dipping lesbian concentrate ripples of excitement energy mid-afternoon drifts away from the continent.

The delights of touch and tongue abound when paradise is lost. Delight is not found in paradise: *pairidaēza* an old Persian word from which the Hebrew and Greek terms are derived a walled garden the hunting park of the king. Delight is celebrated and written apart from hedges fences fortresses which would discipline freedom.

A small tree shrine to she of the wild appears between two arms of one stream flowing in opposite directions. The shrine at Ephesus is on marshy grounds to move with the earth when the earth shakes.

Dancing a round dance a shield dance quivers rattling amazons are with hawks ibex bulls axes   sphinx wings rising tail arched   boar mane rising eye in the shape of a flower petal   horse rising from the waves. A winged goddess grasps two lions at the root of their tails and holds the lions downward forepaws touching the ground heads turned upward with open jaws snarling.

The marsh is drained by king Croesus in the sixth century b.c. The Artemision monumental edifice one of the wonders of the world is erected over tree shrine hawks double-axes amazons.

A morning glory winds along disappears reappears sometimes takes life on the way and blossoms each morning.

Sky rock water you I leap from ledge to ledge around the fire that brightens cliffs night skies. At dawn you I slip into the sea.

NO NUDISM NO CAMPING read orange plastic signs in French German English Greek posted on Lesbos by Sun Med Holidays. At Scala Eressos rugged hills red poppies blue water the beach is bulldozed by tractors. Wimmin no longer gather outside and knit fishing boats no longer land on the shore olive trees are cut down property is bound by barbed wire.

When in the mist the land floats above the sea you I curl around each other at the end of the beach.

Composting weeds worms the connection of the elements lets the earth grow   leaves the soil richer than it was before.

Ethics slips into aesthetics feeling flourishes without the command when slowly so slowly you I meet with ecologies of the emotions.

In intimacy how to cultivate wilderness? How to live in the wilds with the wilds emotions which escape the name? How to feel the futures which inhabit the blue glacial lakes?

Bare-skinned you I soar with the wind tumble to earth in the warm rain.

Not enough theory? The end of discipline? What if a field were to burst into bloom mountains become deserts washed by ocean?

Snap fingers cluck tongue flutter lips touch lips flutter tongues harmonic glissando tambourine rainbows water songs

We dance

If you have rushed to this point burn incense rest visit friends.

Clitoris tongue rolls over and over you I now alive vibrations all over clitoris tongue rolls over to kiss blue butterfly morning glory heart.

Adrienne Rich

XVII from "Twenty-One Love Poems"

No one's fated or doomed to love anyone.
The accidents happen, we're not heroines,
they happen in our lives like car crashes,
books that change us, neighborhoods
we move into and come to love.
Tristan und Isolde is scarcely the story,
women at least should know the difference
between love and death. No poison cup,
no penance. Merely a notion that the tape-recorder
should have caught some ghost of us: that tape-recorder
not merely played but should have listened to us,
and could instruct those after us:
this we were, this is how we tried to love,
and these are the forces they had ranged against us,
and these are the forces we had ranged within us,
within us and against us, against us and within us.

Jeffner Allen is the author of *Lesbian Philosophy: Explorations,* editor of *Lesbian Philosophies and Cultures,* and coeditor of *The Thinking Muse: Feminism and Recent French Thought.* She is Associate Professor of Philosophy at SUNY Binghampton and is currently completing a book of lesbian experimental writing.

Gloria Anzaldúa is a tejana now living in the Bay Area. She is the author of *Borderlands/La Frontera: The New Mestiza,* the editor of *Making Face, Making Soul: Haciendo Caras,* and coeditor of *This Bridge Called My Back.*

June Arnold is the author of *Sister Gin, The Cook and the Carpenter, Baby Houston,* and *Applesauce.* She cofounded one of the first feminist publishing houses, Daughters, Inc., with Parke Bowman. She died in 1982.

Judith Barrington grew up in England and moved to Oregon in 1976. She is the author of two collections of poetry, *Trying to Be an Honest Woman* and *History and Geography,* and the founder of *The Flight of the Mind,* a residential writing workshop for women. She recently wrote the libretto for an oratorio, *Mother of Us All,* music by David York, which was performed by the Concord Choir in 1991.

Robin Becker is the author of a recent collection of poems, *Giacometti's Dog.* She continues to teach poetry and fiction writing courses at M.I.T., where she has taught for over a decade. She serves as Poetry Editor for *The Women's Review of Books.*

Becky Birtha is the author of two collections of short stories, *For Nights Like This One: Stories of Loving Women* and *Lovers' Choice.* Her most recent book is a collection of poems, *The Forbidden Poems,* published in 1991.

Beth Brant is a Bay of Quinte Mohawk from Tyendinaga Mohawk Territory in Ontario, Canada. She is the editor of *A Gathering of Spirit,* a collection of writing and art by Native American women, and author of *Mohawk Trail* and *Food & Spirits.* She currently lives in Michigan and is a lesbian mother and grandmother.

Nicole Brossard was born in Montreal in 1943. Poet, novelist, and essayist, she has published more than twenty books since 1965. Seven have been translated into English, among them *The Aerial Letter, A Book, Daydream Mechanics, French Kiss, Lovhers,* and *These Our Mothers.* She is cofounder of La Barre du Jour and codirector of the film *Some American Feminists.*

Olga Broumas was born in Syros, Greece, and published her first book there in 1967. Her books in English include *Beginning with O, Soie Sauvage, Pastoral Jazz,* and a collaboration with Jane Miller, *Black Holes, Black Stockings.* She resides in Provincetown, Massachusetts and teaches at Boston University.

Sandra Butler is a writer and community organizer who works in the field of violence against women. She has recently recovered from thyroid cancer and is propelled by the urgencies of time, the solidity of community and the grace of women's language.

Chrystos is a Native American, born in 1946 and raised in San Francisco. She has made her home on Bainbridge Island in the Pacific Northwest for the past ten years. She is the author of two collections of poetry, *Not Vanishing* and *Dream On*.

Tee Corinne is the author of *Cunt Coloring Book*, *Dreams of the Woman Who Loved Sex*, and *Lovers*. She is the editor of *Intricate Passions* and *Riding Desire*. Her first novel, *The Sparkling Lavender Dust of Lust* will be published in the fall of 1991.

Marilyn Frye is a philosopher and the author of *The Politics of Reality: Essays in Feminist Theory*. She is in the sixteenth year of lesbian relating with Carolyn Shafer (who is an artist now, a painter). She has been doing it more since she wrote this paper.

Sally Miller Gearhart lives on a mountain of contradictions in Northern California. She is the author of *The Wanderground: Stories of the Hill Women* and *A Feminist Tarot* (with Susan Rennie). She has appeared in the documentary films *Word Is Out* and *The Times of Harvey Milk* and teaches speech at San Francisco State University. She is active in the movements for lesbian/gay rights, animal rights, and Central American solidarity.

Janice Gould is a mixed-blood Native American enrolled in the Maidu tribe of Northern California, now living in New Mexico. Her first book of poetry, *Beneath My Heart*, was published in 1990.

Judy Grahn is the author of the groundbreaking Gay and Lesbian cultural history, *Another Mother Tongue: Gay Words, Gay Worlds*. Her poetry includes a mythic drama, *The Queen of Swords*, set in a Lesbian bar. Other books are *The Queen of Wands* and *The Work of a Common Woman*; a novel, *Mundane's World* and essays on and selections from Gertrude Stein. She has recently released a cassette tape of poetry written for the ear: *March to the Mother Sea*. She is working on *Blood, Bread and Roses*, how menstruation created the world.

Marilyn Hacker is the author of seven books of poetry, most recently *Going Back to the River* and *Love, Death, and the Changing of the Seasons*. *The Hang-Glider's Daughter*, a collection of selected and new poems, will be available in the U.S. in 1991. She received the National Book Award in poetry in 1975 for her first book, *Presentation Piece*. From 1982 through 1986 she was editor of *13th Moon*, a feminist literary magazine. She is currently editor of the *Kenyon Review*.

Gillian Hanscombe was born and educated in Melbourne, Australia but has lived in Britain since 1969. She is the author of seven books, including *Between Friends*, *Flesh and Paper* (with Suniti Namjoshi), *Hecate's Charms*, *Writing for Their Lives: The Modernist Women 1910-1940*, and *The Art of Life: Dorothy Richardson and the Development of Feminist Consciousness*. She now lives in rural Devon with poet and writer Suniti Namjoshi.

Carter Heyward is Professor of Theology at the Episcopal Divinity School in Cambridge, Massachusetts. She is the author or editor or seven books including her most recent: *Touching Our Strength: The Erotic As Power and the Love of God.*

Sarah Lucia Hoagland is the author of *Lesbian Ethics* and coeditor of *For Lesbians Only: A Separatist Anthology.*

Gale Jackson works in the book arts. She is a poet, a writer, a storyteller, a librarian, and an organizer in cultural education. Her work has been published in a number of journals and in the collaborative volume *We Stand Our Ground* with Kimiko Hahn and Susan Sherman. She coedited *Art Against Apartheid: Works for Freedom.* Among her current works are the novel of short stories *the precision of the embrace* from which "translations" and "clove and challdice" are taken. Gale lives and works in Brooklyn, New York.

Jano is a writer and union organizer living in Oakland, California with her son. She likes to write about *dybbuks* who meddle in lesbians' lives, lesbian mothers who face the whole *schmear*, and workers who work for *bupkes.*

Melanie Kaye/Kantrowitz is former editor of *Sinister Wisdom*, one of the oldest lesbian/feminist journals, coeditor of *The Tribe of Dina: A Jewish Women's Anthology* and author of *My Jewish Face & Other Stories.* Her writing appears in a wide range of feminist, lesbian, progressive, and Jewish publications and anthologies. She teaches in the independent study Graduate Program of Vermont College and works on the National Steering Committee of New Jewish Agenda.

Irena Klepfisz is a poet, essayist, and political activist in the lesbian and Jewish communities. She is the author of *A Few Words in the Mother Tongue: Poems Selected and New* and *Dreams of an Insomniac: Jewish Feminist Essays, Speeches, and Diatribes.*

Anna Livia was born in Dublin, Ireland, grew up in Africa and has just moved to the Bay Area from London. She is working on a Ph.D. in French linguistics at U.C. Berkeley. Previous books include *Relatively Norma, Accommodation Offered, Incidents Involving Warmth* and *Bulldozer Rising.* Her most recent book, *Incidents Involving Mirth*, is the source for "Lust and the Other Half." *Minimax*, a novel, will be published in the fall of 1991.

Audre Lorde was born in 1934 in Harlem, New York. Among her many books are *From a Land Where Other People Live; Coal; The Black Unicorn; Our Dead Behind Us; The Cancer Journals; Zami: A New Spelling of My Name;* and *Sister Outsider.*

Daphne Marlatt is the author of a number of books of poetry and/or prose, including *Steveston, Touch to My Tongue,* and *How Hug a Stone.* Her most recent publications are a novel, *Ana Historic*, and a poetic collaboration with Betsy Warland, *Double Negative.* She has coedited several little magazines and is a founding member of the feminist editorial collective that publishes *Tessera*, a journal of new Québecoise and English-Canadian feminist theory and writing. She lives on Salt Spring Island off the coast of British Columbia with Betsy Warland.

Judith McDaniel is a writer, teacher, and political activist with a rich fantasy life. She has just published her first lesbian romance, *Just Say Yes*. She is also the author of *Metamorphosis: Reflections on Recovery* and *Sanctuary: A Journey*.

Cherríe Moraga is a native of Los Angeles and now lives in the Bay Area, where she teaches at the University of California, Berkeley. She is the coeditor of *This Bridge Called My Back* and the author of *Loving in the War Years*. Her plays, *Giving Up the Ghost* and *Shadow of a Man*, have been performed around the country. Her latest work, *Heroes and Saints*, will be produced by Brava! for Women in the Arts in 1992.

Suniti Namjoshi was born in India in 1941. She is the author of eight books of poetry, including *The Authentic Lie, From the Bedside Book of Nightmares, Flesh and Paper* (with Gillian Hanscombe) and *Because of India: Selected Poems*. She's the author of five books of fiction: *Feminist Fables, The Conversations of Cow, The Blue Donkey Fables, The Mothers of Maya Diip* and *Aditi and the One-eyed Monkey*, written for children. She has worked as an Officer in the Indian Administrative Service and in academic posts in India and Canada and now lives and writes in Devon, England.

Joan Nestle, fifty-one years old and born in the Bronx, New York, is cofounder of the Lesbian Herstory Archives, author of *A Restricted Country*, and coeditor of *Women on Women*. She is currently working on an anthology of writings born of the butch-femme lesbian experience to be called *The Persistent Desire: A Femme-Butch Reader*. She still thinks that the gift of the caring human touch is one of our most precious and endangered resources.

Lesléa Newman's books include *Love Me Like You Mean It, Secrets, A Letter to Harvey Milk* and *Heather Has Two Mommies*. Her newest collection of poetry is entitled *Sweet Dark Places*, and her latest novel, *God's Waiting Room*, will be published in 1992.

Pat Parker is the author of five books of poetry: *Child of Myself, Pit Stop, Womanslaughter, Movement in Black* and *Jonestown & Other Madness*. She was the director of the Oakland Feminist Women's Health Center until her death from cancer in 1989.

Emma Pérez, a tejana, is an Assistant Professor of history at the University of Texas, El Paso. Her publications include "A la Mujer: A Critique of the Partido Liberal Mexicano's Gender Ideology" in *Between Borders* and "Speaking from the

Margin: Uninvited Discourse on Sexuality and Power" in *Building with Our Hands*. Along with completing her novel, *Gulf Dreams*, she is writing a social history of Mexican American women in Houston from 1900 to 1940. She also continues to theorize Chicana lesbian feminisms.

Minnie Bruce Pratt is a poet, essayist, and teacher, born in Selma, Alabama, in 1946. She has published three books of poetry, *The Sound of One Fork, We Say We Love Each Other*, and *Crime Against Nature*, which was the 1989 Lamont Poetry Selection by the Academy of American Poets. Together with Elly Bulkin and Barbara Smith, she coauthored *Yours in Struggle: Three Feminist Perspectives on Anti-Semitism and Racism*. She lives in Washington D.C., and teaches Women's Studies part-time at the University of Maryland at College Park. She is completing a volume of collected essays, tentatively titled *Rebellion*, and a fourth book of poetry, *Walking Back Up Depot Street*.

Adrienne Rich was born in 1929 in Baltimore, Maryland. She has published thirteen volumes of poetry, and her new collection, *An Atlas of the Difficult World*, will appear in the fall of 1991. Among her prose works are *Of Woman Born; On Lies, Secrets, and Silence;* and *Blood, Bread, and Poetry*. She is a founding editor of *Bridges: A Journal for Jewish Feminists and Our Friends*. Since 1984 she has lived and taught in California.

Barbara Rosenblum died of breast cancer on February 14, 1988. *Cancer in Two Voices*, from which this excerpt has been taken, will be published in the fall of 1991. It is a document of the psychological, relational, political, and social dimensions of her life with cancer.

Joanna Russ is a science fiction novelist and short story writer. Her most recent book is a collection of short stories, *The Hidden Side of the Moon*. Other books include *Magic Mommas, Trembling Sisters, Puritans and Perverts; The Zanzibar Cat; The Adventures of Alyx; How to Suppress Women's Writing; On Strike Against God; The Two of Them; We Who Are About To; The Female Man; And Chaos Died;* and *Picnic on Paradise*. She has won both of science fiction's most prestigious awards, the Nebula and the Hugo.

Sarah Schulman is the author of five novels: *The Sophie Horowitz Story; Girls, Visions and Everything; After Delores,* winner of the American Library Association Gay Book Award in 1989; *People in Trouble,* winner of the Words Project AIDS/Gregory Kolovakos Memorial Prize; and *Empathy,* which will be published in 1992.

Maureen Seaton lives with her spouse, the sculptor Lori Anderson, in Chicago. "The Bed" is taken from *Fear of Subways*, her second book of poetry and the 1990 winner of The Eighth Mountain Poetry Prize. Her first book, *The Sea Among the Cupboards*, won the 1990 Capricorn Award.

Dorothea Smartt is the daughter of Bajan migrants, born in 1963 in London, England, a Capricorn Zami. She is working in London, completing her M.A. in Anthropology for Hunter College (CUNY). Her poems have appeared in *Black Women Talk Poetry* and in various journals in the U.S. and U.K.

Betsy Warland, Canadian West Coast writer and editor, has published four books of poetry. *Proper Deafinitions,* a collection of essays and prose, was published in 1990. She is currently editing an anthology of U. S., Canadian and Quebec lesbian writers writing on their own work.

Lise Weil is editor of *Trivia, A Journal of Ideas* and translator of *Vagabonding: Feminist Thinking Cut Loose,* by Christina Thurmer-Rohr. She is currently editing an anthology of writings responding to the question, "What Is a Lesbian?"

Barbara Wilson is the author of *Miss Venezuela,* a collection of short stories, and six novels, including *Cows and Horses* and the recent mystery, *Gaudi Afternoon.* She is the cofounder and copublisher of Seal Press, which celebrates its fifteenth anniversary this year.

Louise Wisechild is a writer, musician, and bodyworker who lectures and teaches workshops on creative healing for survivors and professionals working with childhood trauma. She is the author of *The Obsidian Mirror: An Adult Healing from Incest* and the editor of *She Who Was Lost Is Remembered: Healing from Incest Through Creativity.* She lives on Vashon Island with her partner and three cats and is currently writing a book about her childhood relationship with her mother.

Continuation of Copyright Page: